THE MORAL ORDER OF THE WORLD

The Gifford Lectures

DELIVERED BEFORE THE UNIVERSITY

OF GLASGOW IN 1898

SECOND SERIES

THE MORAL ORDER
OF THE WORLD

IN ANCIENT AND MODERN THOUGHT

BY

ALEXANDER BALMAIN BRUCE, D.D.

PROFESSOR OF APOLOGETICS AND NEW TESTAMENT
EXEGESIS IN THE FREE CHURCH COLLEGE,
GLASGOW

Eugene, Oregon

Wipf and Stock Publishers
199 West 8th Avenue, Suite 3
Eugene, Oregon 97401

The Moral Order of the World
in Ancient and Modern Thought (the Gifford Lectures, 1898)
By Bruce, A.B.
ISBN: 1-59244-567-5
Publication date 2/24/2004
Previously published by Hodder and Stoughton, 1899

PREFACE

OUR theme is still the Providential Order. The new title, however, is used not merely to make a nominal distinction between the two courses of Lectures, but because there is a real, though slight, difference in meaning which makes the title the more appropriate to this course. A Providential Order implies a God who provides. One who speaks of a Providence is a Theist, who believes in a God caring for, and governing, all. The Moral Order, on the other hand, is impersonal, and one may use the phrase and believe in the thing it denotes, who is no Theist, no believer in a living personal God in the ordinary theistic sense of the words. Buddha, the theme of our first Lecture, is an instance.

Of course this historical survey is not exhaustive. It is, however, fairly representative, and brings the whole subject, by samples, sufficiently under view to answer the question, What have the wisest thought on the great theme of the Moral Order of the universe in its reality and essential nature?

Publication of these Lectures has been delayed for a twelvemonth by the state of my health.

A. B. BRUCE.

GLASGOW, *April* 1899.

CONTENTS

LECTURE I

BUDDHA AND THE MORAL ORDER, ... 1

LECTURE II

ZOROASTER: DUALISM, ... 34

LECTURE III

THE GREEK TRAGEDIANS: NEMESIS, ... 66

LECTURE IV

THE STOICS: PROVIDENCE, ... 103

LECTURE V

DIVINATION, ... 140

LECTURE VI

THE HEBREW PROPHET 174

LECTURE VII
THE BOOK OF JOB, ... 207

LECTURE VIII
CHRIST'S TEACHING CONCERNING DIVINE PROVIDENCE, . 243

LECTURE IX
MODERN OPTIMISM: BROWNING, ... 279

LECTURE X
MODERN DUALISM: SCIENTIFIC AND PHILOSOPHIC ASPECTS, 312

LECTURE XI
MODERN DUALISM: RELIGIOUS AND SOCIAL ASPECTS, . . 346

LECTURE XII
RETROSPECT AND PROSPECT, ... 380

INDEX, ... 417

LECTURE I

BUDDHA AND THE MORAL ORDER

THE Providential Order is still our theme. Now, however, it is not to my own thoughts that I solicit attention. I ask you to engage with me in a sympathetic while critical study of the thoughts of other men in ancient and modern times. The subject is sufficiently large, attractive, and difficult to justify a second course. It cannot be said to be exhausted till we have made ourselves acquainted in some degree with the more important contributions towards its elucidation. Earnest thought on Divine Providence, however ancient, cannot but be interesting, and it may be instructive, not only by the abiding truth it contains, but even by its doubts, its denials, its crudities, its errors. It is obvious, however, that selection will be necessary. Attention must be confined to outstanding types of thought, in which an exceptionally intense moral consciousness is revealed, and deep, sincere protracted brooding, as of men wrestling with a great hard problem.

On this principle preference must be given in the

first place to representative thinkers in India, Persia, and Greece, the countries in which, in far-past times, human reflection on the august topic of the moral order may be said to have reached the high-water mark. In India, the centre of attraction is Buddha, with his peculiar way of viewing life and destiny; in Persia, Zoroaster. To each of these great characters a lecture will be devoted, and in these two lectures my representation, through lack of first-hand knowledge, must rest on the authority of experts. On the contributions of Greece we shall have to tarry longer. The Tragic Poets and the Stoics have both strong claims on our regard, the former as conspicuous assertors of the moral order, the latter as not less prominent champions of a universal Providence. With these representatives of Greek wisdom two lectures will be occupied. Our next topic will be one having no exclusive connection with Greek thought or with the Greek people, but with which the name of the Stoics is closely associated. I mean Divination. The oracles have long been dumb, and it requires an effort to revive interest in the subject. But we cannot understand the views of the ancient world without taking the belief in Divination into account. This, therefore, will form the subject of the concluding lecture on Pagan thought.

Hebrew thought, on its own intrinsic merits, claims serious attention. The Prophets of Israel, as we all know, had much to say concerning the moral government of God. The Book of Job also is a unique contribution to the discussion of the problems of Providence which cannot be overlooked. Prophetic teaching, therefore, having been disposed of, all too inadequately, in a single lecture, that book will receive the consideration it claims in another. A reverent study of the teaching of Jesus on the Providence of the Divine Father in a third will close the discussion of Hebrew wisdom.

The foregoing part of our programme will take up eight lectures. Three of the remaining four will be devoted to modern thought on topics bearing on our theme, while the final lecture will assume the form of a retrospect and a forecast.

Modern thought is a wide word, and a point of view will be needed to guide selection. Let it be the question, What tendencies characterise those who have been anxious to abide as far as possible by the Christian idea of God? Two broadly contrasted tendencies may be discriminated, one optimistic, the other dualistic. The one accepts without abatement Christ's idea of a Divine Father and says: All is well with the world, or is on the way to be well. The other also accepts the Christian idea of God, but, unable to take an optimistic view of the past, present, or future of the world, introduces in some form a rival to the beneficent Deity of Christian faith. Two types of modern dualism may be distinguished, one of which discovers in the world of nature traces of a personal rival to the Good Being, counter-working His beneficent purpose, while the other finds a foe of the Divine even in the reason of man. Each of these types of dualism will engage our attention in a separate lecture.

The subject of the present lecture is *Buddha*[1] and his view of the moral order of the world.

Buddha was the originator of a type of religion called Buddhism, which to-day is professed in the East by one-third of the human race. He was born in India, of a royal family, in the sixth century before the Christian era. The religion of India had run through a long course of development before he arrived on the scene. There was first the religion of the Vedic Indians, a comparatively simple nature-worship, poetic in feeling, and cheerful in spirit, setting a high value on the good things of this life and making these the chief objects of prayer. Then there came ancient Brahmanism, with its pantheistic conception of the universe as an emanation out of Brahma, its view of the world as an unreality, its elaborate ritual, its asceticism, and its caste distinctions. This system Buddha found in vogue, and to a large extent accepted. But in some respects his attitude was protestant and reforming. He discarded the sacred books—the Vedic hymns, he set

[1] Buddha is an epithet rather than a name. Buddha's name was Gotama Sakya.

BUDDHA AND THE MORAL ORDER 5

no value on sacrifice, he treated the Brahmanical gods with scant respect, and he disregarded caste, at least in the religious sphere.

In his religious temper Buddha differed widely both from the Vedic Indian and from the Brahman. In the cheerfulness and the frank worldliness of the former he had no part, and in contrast to the latter he set morality above ritual. He was a pessimist in his view of life, and he assigned to the ethical supreme value. From the moment he arrived at the years of reflection, he had an acute sense of the misery of man. At length, so we learn from biographical notices, a crisis arrived. One day various aspects of human suffering—old age, disease, death —fell under his observation, and thereafter a hermit came in view with a cheerful, peaceful aspect which greatly struck him. He was now resolved what to do. He would forsake the world and seek in solitude the peace he had hitherto failed to find. He withdrew into the wilderness, and lived a severely ascetic life, alone—Sakya-muni, *i.e.* Sakya the lonely. Still he was not happy, nor did he attain peace till he discovered that the seat of evil was in the soul, and that the secret of tranquillity was to get rid of *desire*. This seen, Sakya-muni had become Sakya-Buddha— Sakya the enlightened. Having found the way of salvation for himself, he felt impelled by sympathy with suffering humanity to make it known to others. He commenced to preach his gospel; in technical phrase, to turn the wheel of the law. The essence of his doctrine was summed up in four propositions: (1) Pain exists—pain, the great fact of all sentient life ; (2) pain is the result of existence ; (3) the annihilation of pain is possible ; (4) the way to the desired end is self-mortification, renunciation of the world both outwardly and inwardly. All who were willing to receive this message, of whatever caste or character, were welcome to the ranks of discipleship. Discipleship in the strict sense meant not merely a pure life, but an ascetic habit in the solitude of the forest or in the still retreat of the monastery. From being a few, disciples grew to be many through the missionary ardour of converts, till at length the sombre faith of the Buddha became one of the great religions of the world.

On that account alone, if for no other, Buddhism would be entitled to some notice in even a short study of the thoughts of men on the moral order of the world, unless indeed it should turn out that so widely diffused a religion had nothing to say on the subject. That, however, is so far from being the case that few religions have anything more remarkable to say. For Buddhism, true to the spirit of the founder, is an ethical religion. It finds in moral good the cure of physical evil, and in moral evil the cause of physical evil. It asserts with unique emphasis a *moral* order as distinct from a *providential* order, the difference being that a moral order is an

BUDDHA AND THE MORAL ORDER

impersonal conception, while a providential order implies a Divine Being who exercises a providential oversight over the world. Even an atheist, like Strauss, can believe in a moral order, but only a theist can believe in a Providence. Buddha taught no doctrine either of creation or of providence, or even of God. He was not an atheist. He did not deny the being of God, or of the gods of ancient India, poetically praised in the hymns of Vedic bards and elaborately worshipped in Brahmanical ritual. He treated these gods somewhat as the Hebrew worshippers of Jehovah treated the deities of other peoples, allowing them to remain as part of the universe of being, while refusing to acknowledge them as exceptional or unique in nature, dignity, or destiny. It is characteristic of the Buddhist system to treat the gods in this cavalier fashion and to regard them as inferior to Buddha. When Buddha summons them into his presence they come; they listen reverently to his words, and humbly obey his behests. Yet Buddha is but a man, though more than divine in honour. Buddhism, it has been remarked, is the only religion in which the superiority of man over the gods is proclaimed as a fundamental article of faith.[1] That the destinies of the world should be in the hands of such degraded and dishonoured beings is of course out of the question.

Equally out of the question is it that one who

[1] Koeppen, *Die Religion des Buddha und ihre Entstehung*, p. 123.

viewed human life as Buddha viewed it could possibly believe in a benignant Providence. Buddha's idea of life, according to all reliable accounts, was purely pessimistic. For him the great fact of life was pain, misery, and the four chief lessons to be learnt about life were that pain exists and why, that it can be put an end to and how. Birth, growth, disease, decay, death—behold the sorrowful series of events which make life a mere vanity and vexation of spirit. Such is it as we see it, such it has ever been, such it ever shall be. The process of the whole universe is an eternal, monotonous, wearisome succession of changes, an everlasting *becoming*. Nothing abides, for all is composite, and all that is composite is impermanent. And the best thing that can happen to a man is to be dissolved body and soul, and so find rest among the things that are not.

While knowing nothing of a Divine Providence in our sense of the word, the religion of Buddha is honourably distinguished by its emphatic assertion of a moral order of the world. The moral order is the great fact for the Buddhist. It is the source of the physical order. Moral facts explain the facts of human experience. Wrong action is the cause of sorrow, *not only in general and on the whole, but in detail and exhaustively*. What a man does or has done sometime or other, explains completely what he suffers. I say 'has done, sometime or other,'

BUDDHA AND THE MORAL ORDER 9

because perfect correspondence between conduct and lot is not held to be verifiable within the bounds of this present life. Buddha was fully aware of the lack of correspondence as exhibited in many startling contrasts of good men suffering and bad men prospering. But he did not thence conclude that life was a moral chaos, or that there was no law connecting lot with conduct. He simply inferred that to find the key to life's puzzles you must go beyond the bounds of the present life and postulate past lives, not one or two, but myriads, an eternal succession of lives if necessary, each life in the series being determined in its complex experience by all that went before ; the very fact that there is such a life at all—that we are born once more, being due to evil done in former lives.

This conception of successive lives is so foreign to our modes of thought that it may be well to dwell on it a little.

Buddha did not invent the doctrine of *transmigration*; he inherited it from the pre-existing Brahmanical religion. How it came to be there, seeing there is no trace of it in the Vedic hymns, is a question which very naturally suggests itself. Students of Indian religions have found the explanation, both of this theory and of the pessimistic conception of human life associated with it, in the Brahmanical view of God's relation to the world, according to which all being flows out of Brahma

10 THE MORAL ORDER OF THE WORLD

by way of emanation.[1] Anthropologists prefer to see in the Indian idea a special form of a more general primitive belief having its fact-basis in observed resemblances between ancestors and descendants, and between men and beasts, naïvely accounted for by primitive men as due to the souls of ancestors passing into children, and of men into beasts. In higher levels of culture, as in India, they see this crude physical theory invested with ethical significance, so that 'successive births or existences are believed to carry on the consequences of past and prepare the antecedents of future life.'[2]

What amount of truth may be in these hypotheses it is not necessary here to inquire. What we are concerned with is the relation of Buddha to the doctrine in question. Now at first it may seem strange that one who discarded the traditional theory of the emanation of the world out of Brahma did not also part with the kindred theory of transmigration. But on reflection we see that, while the latter theory might have no attraction for Buddha, as forming part of a merely speculative conception of the universe, it might be very welcome to him on *moral* grounds. This is indeed so much the case that, had he not found the theory ready to his hand, he would have had to invent it as a postulate of his ethical creed, which maintained without qualification

---

[1] So *e.g.* Koeppen, p. 33.
[2] *Vide* Tylor, *Primitive Culture*, ii. pp. 3 and 9.

that men reap as they sow. That thesis is not verifiable within the bounds of the present life, at least not in a sense that would have seemed satisfactory to Buddha. You must go beyond, either forward or backward. Christians go forward, and seek in a future life a solution of the mysteries of the present. Buddha went both forward and backward, and more especially backward; and with characteristic thoroughness he gave to the hypothesis of transmigration, in an ethical interest, a very comprehensive sweep, making the range of migration stretch downwards 'from gods and saints, through holy ascetics, Brahmans, nymphs, kings, counsellors, to actors, drunkards, birds, dancers, cheats, elephants, horses, Sudras, barbarians, wild beasts, snakes, worms, insects, and inert things.'[1]

The application of the doctrine, in the Buddhistic system, is as minute as it is wide. For everything that happens to a man in this life an explanation is sought in some deed done in a former life. Character and lot are not viewed, each, as a whole, but every single deed and experience is taken by itself, and the law of recompense applied to it.

The Buddhist *Birth Stories*, the oldest collection of folk-lore, contain curious illustrations of this habit of thought. One story tells how once upon a time a Brahman was about to kill a goat for a feast, how the intended victim had once itself been a

[1] Tylor, ii. p. 9.

Brahman and for killing a goat for a feast had had its head cut off in five hundred births, and how it warned the Brahman that if he killed it he in turn would incur the misery of having his head cut off five hundred times. The moral is given in this homely stanza:—

> 'If people would but understand
> That this would cause a birth in woe,
> The living would not slay the living;
> For he who taketh life shall surely grieve.'[1]

A less grotesque instance is supplied in the pathetic history of Kunala, a son of the famous King Asoka, the Constantine of Buddhism, related at length by Burnouf in his admirable *Introduction to the History of Indian Buddhism*. Kunala had beautiful eyes, which awakened sinful desire in a woman who, like his mother, was one of Asoka's wives. Repulsed, she conceived the wicked design of destroying his beauty by putting out his eyes, and carried out her purpose on the first opportunity. From our point of view this was a case of innocence suffering at the hands of the unrighteous, an Indian Joseph victimised by an Indian Potiphar's wife. But this did not content the Buddhist. He asked what had Kunala done in a previous life to deserve such a fate, and he received from his teacher the reply: Once upon a time, in a previous life, Kunala was a huntsman. Coming upon a herd of five

[1] Rhys Davids, *Buddhist Birth Stories, or Jātaka Tales*, No. 18.

BUDDHA AND THE MORAL ORDER 13

hundred gazelles in a cavern he put out the eyes of them all. For that action he suffered the pains of hell for many hundred thousand years, and thereafter had his eyes put out five hundred times in as many human lives.[1]

Buddha had to go forward as well as backward in order to give full validity to his austere conception of the moral order. As in this life men enjoy and suffer for the good or evil done in former lives, so, he taught, must there be suffering and enjoyment in some future life or world for corresponding deeds done here. For the expression 'good or evil done' Buddhism has one word, 'Karma.' It will be convenient to use it for the longer phrase, as denoting merit and demerit, or character. The Buddhistic doctrine then is that the Karma of this life demands a future life, as this life presupposes and answers to the Karma of past lives. A 'future life,' I have said; by which *we* should, of course, understand our own life, implying personal identity, continuity of the soul's existence. Experts, however, are agreed that that is not the genuine thought of Buddhists. The soul for them is only a bundle of mental states without any substratum; therefore, like all composites, dissoluble and impermanent. Therefore,

[1] Burnouf, *Introduction à l'Histoire du Buddhisme Indien*, pp. 360-370. The hunter put out their eyes instead of killing them because he would not know what to do with so much dead meat. The blinded animals would not be able to escape, and could be killed at convenience.

though in popular conception transmigration means transmigration of the *soul*, for the disciple of Buddha it means transmigration of Karma, that is, of *character*. Mr. Rhys Davids, one of the best informed of our authorities, expresses this view in these terms: 'I have no hesitation in maintaining that Gotama did not teach the transmigration of souls. What he did teach would be better summarised, if we wish to retain the word transmigration, as the transmigration of character. But it would be more accurate to drop the word transmigration altogether when speaking of Buddhism, and to call its doctrine the doctrine of Karma. Gotama held that, after the death of any being, whether human or not, there survived nothing at all but that being's Karma, the result, that is, of its mental and bodily actions.'[1]

This transmigration or survival of character appears to us a very strange idea, but as Mr. Huxley has remarked,[2] something analogous to it may be found in the more familiar fact of *heredity*, the transmission from parents to offspring of tendencies to particular ways of acting. Heredity helps to make the idea of transmitted Karma more intelligible, and at the same time enables us in some degree to get over the feeling of its objectionableness on the score of morality. On first view, it seems an outrage on justice that my Karma should be handed on to

[1] *The Hibbert Lectures*, 1881, p. 92.
[2] *Evolution and Ethics*, p. 61.

BUDDHA AND THE MORAL ORDER

another person that he may bear the consequences of what I have done. If my soul survived death and passed into another form of incorporated life in which I, the same person, reaped the harvest of what I had sown in a previous life, no such objection would arise. But how, one is inclined to ask, can it serve the ends of the moral order, that one should sow in conduct what another reaps in experience? It is a very natural question, yet the thing complained of is essentially involved in moral heredity. Whether we like it or not, and whatever construction is to be put upon it, it is certainly an actual fact of the moral world.

While an analogy, instructive in some respects, exists between heredity and Karma, it would be a mistake to identify them. Heredity operates within the same species, every animal producing its kind; Karma roams through all species of animated being, so that the Karma of a man living now may be handed on some day to an elephant, a horse, or a dog. Heredity is transmitted by generation; according to the developed ontology of Buddhism Karma can work without the aid of a material instrumentality.[1] Heredity asserts its power in spite of great moral changes in the individual who transmits his qualities to his offspring. A saintly father who, by self-discipline, has gained victory over evil propensity may transmit, nevertheless, an inheritance of evil bias to

[1] Hardy, *A Manual of Buddhism in its Modern Development*, p. 395.

16 THE MORAL ORDER OF THE WORLD

his children. A Buddhist Arahat who, by sublime virtue, has attained Nirvana, escapes from the sway of the Karma law, and, though he may leave behind him a family born before he retired into the monastic life, he has no successor who takes upon him his moral responsibilities. Finally, in heredity the peculiarity of both parents, not to speak of atavistic or collateral contributions, are mixed in the character of offspring. Karma, on the other hand, is, as I understand, an isolated entity. Each man has his own Karma, which demands embodiment in an independent life for the working out of its moral results.

Karma then demands another life to bear its fruit. But how is the demand supplied? Now we know how Kant answered an analogous question, viz.: How is the correspondence between character and lot—that which ought to be and therefore sometime shall be—to be brought about? Only, said Kant, through the power of a Being who is head both of the physical and of the moral universe—God, a necessary postulate of the practical reason, or conscience. But in Buddha's system there was no god with such powers. The gods, in his view, far from being able to order all things so as to meet the requirements of Karma, were themselves subject to its sway. How then are these requirements to be met? The answer must be, that Buddhism assigns to Karma the force of physical causation. The moral postulate is turned into a

BUDDHA AND THE MORAL ORDER 17

natural cause. The moral demand literally *creates* the needful supply. Karma becomes a substitute for Kant's Deity. Similar confusion runs through the whole system.

Another source of the endless succession of existence must now be mentioned. It is *Desire*, the will to live. Desire for life originates new life. This Buddhistic tenet is a new form of the old Brahmanical account of the origin of the world, based on a hymn in the tenth book of the Rig-veda, where we find the theory that the universe originated in Desire naïvely hinted in the following lines :—

> 'The One breathed calmly, self-sustained, nought else beyond it lay.
> Gloom hid in gloom existed first—one sea, eluding view,
> That One, a void in chaos wrapt, by inward fervour grew.
> Within it first arose Desire, the primal germ of mind,
> Which nothing with existence links, as sages searching find.'[1]

The only difference between Brahmanism and Buddhism here is that in the former the desire which sets in motion the stream of existence is in Brahma, in the latter it is in individual sentient beings, the cosmological and pantheistic significance of the Brahmanical dogma being translated into an anthropological and ethical one.[2] How desire, either in Brahma or in the individual man, could have such power is, of course, an unfathomable mystery. Most

[1] Muir, *Sanskrit Texts*, vol. v. p. 356.
[2] Koeppen, *Die Religion des Buddha*, p. 294.

of us, I suspect, will agree with Mr. Rhys Davids when he bluntly declares that Buddha attached to desire, as a real, sober fact, an influence and a power which has no actual existence.[1]

But suppose we concede to desire all the power claimed for it, this question arises: Might it not be possible to give transmigration the slip, to break the continuity of existence, to annul the inexorable law of Karma, by ceasing from desire? Yes, joyfully, ecstatically, answered Buddha; and the reply is in brief the gist of the complementary doctrine of *Nirvana*. Karma and Nirvana are the great keywords of Buddhism. They represent opposite, conflicting tendencies. Karma clamours for continuance of being, Nirvana craves and works for its cessation. There is, as all must see, an antinomy here. Why should we cease to desire, if continuance of the stream of being is demanded by Karma? What higher interest can there be than that of the moral order? Ought not good men rather to cling to life for the very purpose of providing scope for the display of that order?

The precise meaning attached by Buddhists to the term 'Nirvana' has been the subject of much discussion. Some have taken it as signifying the annihilation of the soul, while others have assigned to it the directly opposite sense of a perpetuated life of the soul in a future state of bliss. The former of

[1] *Hibbert Lectures*, p. 113.

BUDDHA AND THE MORAL ORDER   19

these views can hardly be correct, seeing the cessation of soul-life takes place at death in the natural course of things, whereas Nirvana, whatever it be, is attained by moral effort. The latter view, while not without support in popular Buddhistic conceptions, is not in accordance with the genius of the system. Nirvana is, in the first place, a state of mind attainable in this life, the cessation of *desire* rather than of *existence*. According to Mr. Rhys Davids, the nearest analogue to it in Western thought is 'the kingdom of heaven that is within a man, the peace that passeth understanding.'[1] But this inward condition reached by the perfect man, the *arahat*, has an important objective result. It suspends the action of the law of Karma, breaks the chain of successive existence, prevents another life, bearing its predecessor's responsibilities, from coming into being. In the words of Mr. Davids, 'When the arahat, the man made perfect, according to the Buddhist faith, ceases to live, no new lamp, no new sentient being, will be lighted by the flame of any weak or ignorant longing entertained by him.'[2] It is another instance of the Buddhist habit of turning moral postulates into physical causes. Our first example was taken from Karma. Karma demands another life to bear its fruit; therefore, according to Buddhist ways of thinking, it produces the life required. Even so with Nirvana. It demands the suspension of the law of

[1] *Hibbert Lectures*, p. 31.   [2] *Ibid.*, p. 101.

Karma, therefore it ensures it. Hence, if all men were to become Arahats and attain Nirvana, the result ought to be the eventual extinction of animated being.

Other illustrations of the same mental habit are not wanting. The marvellous abstraction called Karma not only creates a succession of individual lives, but even a succession of *worlds* wherein to work out adequately the great problem of moral retribution. The cosmology of developed Buddhism is a grotesque, mad-looking scheme. But there is method in the madness. It is the moral interest that reigns here as everywhere, which, once it is perceived, redeems from utter dreariness pages concerning innumerable worlds in space and time that seem to contain but the idle dreams of an unbridled, fantastic Eastern imagination. For that which gives rise to the whole phantasmagory is the need of endless time to exhaust the results of Karma. The fruit of an action does not necessarily ripen soon; it may take hundreds of thousands of *Kalpas* to mature. What is a Kalpa? A great Kalpa is the period beginning with the origin of a world and extending beyond its dissolution to the commencement of a new succeeding world. This great Kalpa is divisible into four Kalpas, each representing a stage in the cosmic process of origination and dissolution. The four together cover a time of inconceivable length, immeasurably longer than would be the time required to wear away by the touch of a cloth of delicate texture, once in a hundred years, a solid rock sixteen miles broad and as many high. Yet, long as is the period of a great Kalpa, it may require many such to bring to maturity the fruit of an action done by a man during his earthly life of three-score years and ten. Therefore, as one world does not last long enough for the purpose, there must be a succession of worlds. Karma demands them, therefore Karma creates them. The Fiat of almighty Karma goes forth: Let there be worlds; and world after world starts into being in obedience to its behest. Worlds exist only for moral ends—to afford adequate scope for the realisation of the moral order.

There is something sublime as well as grotesque in this cosmological creation of the Buddhist conscience. And one cannot but admire the moral intensity which conceived it possible for an action, good or evil, to be quickened into fruitfulness after the lapse of millions on millions of years, during which it lay dormant. This long delay of the moral harvest gives rise to a curious anomaly in the Buddhist theory of future rewards and punishments. It is this: men who have lived good lives in this world may go at death into a place of damnation, and men who have lived here bad lives may pass into the heaven of the gods. The damnation in the one case is the late fruitage of some evil deed done in long bygone ages, and the bliss, in the other, the tardy recompense of a good deed done in a previous state of existence. This seems a perilous doctrine to preach, presenting as it does to the hopes and fears of men prospects for the near future which appear like a reversal of the normal law of retribution.

Thus far of Karma and Nirvana. I now add a brief statement on Buddhist conceptions concerning the experience and functions of a *Buddha*.

In view of the infinitely slow action of the law of retribution and the strangely incongruous experiences of intermediate states, one can imagine what an interminably long and endlessly varied career one must pass through whose ultimate destiny it is to become a *Buddha*—one, that is, perfectly enlightened, completely master of desire, sinless, and no more in danger of sinning. One wonders, indeed, how there ever could be such a being. The Buddhist creed certainly cannot be charged with representing the making of a Buddha as an easy thing. On the contrary, he is believed to have passed through many existences under many forms of being, and in various states of being: now an animal, then a man, then a god; at one time damned, at another time beatified; in one life virtuous, in another criminal; but on the whole moving on, slowly accumulating merits which are eventually crowned with the honours of Buddhahood.[1]

[1] Burnouf, *Introduction*, etc., p. 120.

One who has passed through such an adventurous history, and has at length arrived safely at the goal of perfect wisdom and goodness, must be a very valuable person when he comes into a world like this, full of ignorance, misery, and sin. What will be his function? What can he do for the race into which he has been born? For the Buddhist there is only one possible vocation for a Buddha. He cannot save men by vicarious goodness or suffering. Every man must be his own saviour, working out his salvation, as Buddha worked out his, through the ages and worlds, through beasthood, godhood, devilhood, to perfect manhood in some far-distant future æon. But a Buddha can tell men the way of self-salvation. He can preach to them the gospel of despair, declaring that life is not worth living, that birth is the penalty of previous sin, that the peace of Nirvana is to be reached by the extirpation of the will to live, and by gentle compassion towards all living creatures. This was how Gotama, the Buddha who was born in India some six centuries before the Christian era, occupied himself, after he became enlightened; and such must be the vocation of all possible Buddhas.

Of all possible Buddhas, I say, for to the followers of Gotama a plurality of Buddhas is not only possible but even necessary. Buddhist imagination has been busy here, as in the manufacture of worlds. The Christian knows of only one Christ, but the Buddhist knows of many Buddhas. The Buddhists of the

North, according to Burnouf, believing in an infinitude of worlds situated in ten regions of space, believe also in an infinite number of Buddhas, or candidates for the honour, co-existing at the same time. The popular pantheon includes two kinds of Buddhas: a human species, and another described as immaterial Buddhas of contemplation. The theistic school of Nepaul has an *Ur-Buddha*, a kind of divine head of all the Buddhas. But, according to the same distinguished authority from whom I have taken these particulars, primitive Buddhism, as set forth in the short, simple Sutras, knows only of human Buddhas, and of only one Buddha living in the world at the same time.[1]

Faith in a succession of Buddhas seems to be common to all Buddhistic schools. This faith has no basis in historical knowledge: it is simply the creature of theory. If asked to justify itself it might advance three pleas: possibility, need, necessity. Possibility, for it is always possible that in the long course of ages a man should make his appearance who has attained the virtue of Buddhahood. One actual Buddha proves the possibility of others. Looking at the matter *a priori*, one might be inclined to doubt whether in the eternal succession of existence even so much as one Buddha could ever appear. A candidate for the high distinction (called a Bodhisat) must become a proficient in the six great

[1] Burnouf, *Introduction*, pp. 97-107.

BUDDHA AND THE MORAL ORDER 25

virtues 'which conduct to the further shore': sympathy, purity, patience, energy, contemplation, wisdom. One can imagine a human being working at the heroic task in his own person, or through the successive inheritors of his Karma, during countless æons, in millions of existences, and after all failing in the task. The chances are millions to one against its ever being achieved. But then Gotama *was* a Buddha, and in presence of that one fact all *a priori* reasoning falls to the ground. The thing has happened once, and it may happen again and again. And it is very desirable that it should happen repeatedly. Need justifies faith. How important that in each new world as it arises a Buddha should appear to set the wheel of doctrine in motion, to unfold the banner of the good law, and so inaugurate a new era of revelation and redemption! It is abstractly possible, of course, that no Buddha might come just when one was most wanted, or that a Buddha might arrive on the scene when there was no urgent need for him, or that a multitudinous epiphany of Buddhas might take place at the same time; for the Buddhist theory of the universe knows of no Providence over all that can arrange for the appearance on the scene of its elect agents when their work is ready for them, and so plan that there shall be no waste of power. But even a Buddhist may hope that the fitness of things will somehow be observed; and for the rest the imperious demands of theory must be complied with. The way to Nirvana must be shown to the blind, and the competent leader must be forthcoming. *Stat pro ratione voluntas.*

But why cannot the one historic Buddha who was born in Kapilavastu in the sixth century before Christ meet all requirements? Well, for one reason, becoming, succession, is the supreme cosmological category of Buddhism, and it is not surprising that, in sympathy with the spirit of the system, the category was applied also to Buddhahood. There is an eternal succession of Kalpas, of destructions and renovations of worlds; why not also an unending series of Buddhas? But, granting that a succession of Buddha-advents is required by the genius of the system, why should it not be simply a series of re-appearances on the part of one and the same Buddha? Because all things in this universe are impermanent, Buddhas not excepted; nay, they more than all, for existence is a curse, and it is the privilege of a Buddha to escape from it absolutely, his own candle of life going out, and not lighting, by his Karma, the lamp of a new life in another. Gotama is to-day only a memory, and nothing remains of him for his disciples to worship except his bones scattered here and there over the lands.

This series of Buddhas, as already stated, is simply the creature of theory. Once more a moral postulate is turned into an efficient cause. Buddhas are needed at recurrent intervals, therefore Buddhas are forthcoming in spite of antecedent improbabilities. Of these Buddhas, countless in number, nothing is known, save in the case of one. Pretended knowledge simply makes the careers of all the rest a facsimile of the career of that one. All are born in middle-India; their mothers die on the seventh day after birth; all are in similar way tempted by Mara, and gain victory over the tempter; all begin to turn the wheel of the law in a wood, near the city of Benares; all have two favourite disciples, and so on. The story of these imaginary Buddhas is evermore but the monotonous repetition of the legendary history of Gotama.

In proceeding to offer some critical observations on the Buddhist conception of life and of the moral order, I must begin with the remark that the great outstanding merit of this religion is its intensely ethical spirit. In Buddhism virtue, in the Indian passive sense—self-sacrifice, sympathy, meekness—is supreme. It was indeed characteristic of ancient Indian religion under all forms to assign sovereign value and power to virtue in some shape. Even in the Veda, with all its naturalism, and its secular conception of the *summum bonum*, prayer, penitence, sanctity, wisdom, are represented as more powerful than the gods, as making men gods. But Buddhism rises to the purest conception of what virtue is, making it consist, not in meditation or self-torture, or work-holiness, but in inward purity and the utter uprooting of selfish desire. And, in opposition to Brahmanism, the new religion showed the sincerity and depth of its ethical spirit by treating caste distinctions as of subordinate importance compared with ethical qualities. It did not meddle with caste as a social institution, but it treated it as irrelevant in the religious sphere. It invited all, of whatever caste, to enter on the new path, believing all capable of complying with its requirements ; and in the new brotherhood all invidious distinctions were ignored. 'My law is a law of grace for all,' Buddha is reported to have said. Whether he uttered it or not, the saying truly reflects his attitude and the genius of his religion. It is in principle revolutionary, and, had the virtue of Buddhists not been of the quietistic type, treating all secularities as matters of indifference, it might have ended in the abolition of caste, as the Christian faith led to the eventual abolition of slavery.

One wonders why a moral consciousness so robust did not give birth to a reformed faith in God and in Providence. We have seen what it was equal to in connection with the doctrine of Karma. To Karma it assigned the functions both of creation and of providence. Karma is in fact a substitute for God. By the aggregate Karma of the various orders of living beings the present worlds were brought into existence, and their general economy is controlled. Karma creates and governs the world, because it postulates a world adapted to the working out of its requirements. Why not rather believe in a God who is at the head both of the physical and the moral worlds, and therefore able to make the two correspond? That surely is the true postulate of every system which makes the ethical supreme. Its failure to see this is the radical defect of the Buddhistic theory of the universe.

The failure was due to two causes.

First, the traditional gods of India were unworthy to hold their place in the faith and worship of men. When a severe moral temper began to prevail, sceptical reaction was inevitable. Reaction towards atheism is to be expected whenever a religious creed has degenerated into a set of dogmas in which the human spirit cannot rest; or when a creed, in itself pure, has become associated with an ignoble life. And a virtuous atheism of reaction is a better thing than the unvirtuous insincere theism or pantheism it seeks to replace. Buddhism was a virtuous atheism of reaction which sought to replace the prevalent Brahmanical pantheism. And as such it was relatively justified, a better thing than it found, if not an absolutely good thing.

But why remain in the reactionary stage? why not strive after a reformed idea of God? Why not go back to the Vedic idea of a Heaven-Father,

Dyauspitar, and charge it with new, ethical contents, so giving to the world centuries before the Christian era a Father in heaven, possessing moral attributes such as Buddha admired and practised—benignant, kind, gracious, patient, forgiving? The question leads up to the second cause of Buddha's theological shortcoming. It was due to his pessimistic interpretation of human life. Life being utterly worthless, how could a Father-God be believed in? Buddha's ethical ideal and his reading of life were thus in conflict with each other. The one suggested as its appropriate complement a benignant God over all; the other made the existence of such a Deity incredible: and the force on the side of negation proved to be the stronger. And yet the judgment on life which landed in virtual atheism was surely a mistake. All is not vanity and vexation of spirit. 'The earth is full of the goodness of the Lord,' declares a Hebrew psalmist. Why should Hebrews and Indians think so differently, living in the same world and passing through the same experiences of birth, growth, disease, decay, death? Do race, temperament, climate, geographical position, explain the contrast?

Out of this great error concerning life sprang another equally portentous, the idea of Nirvana as the *summum bonum*. Life, taught Buddha, is inherently miserable; therefore let wise men cease to desire it, and abstain from kindling with the taper of Karma the light of another life. Perfectly logical reasoning; but observe in what an antinomy the Buddhist is thus landed between Karma on the one hand and Nirvana on the other. Karma and Nirvana are irreconcilable antagonists. The one creates, the other destroys, worlds. Let Karma have its way, and the stream of successive existences will flow on for ever. Let Nirvana have its way, and men will cease to be, and the worlds will perish along with them. It is a dualism in its kind, as decided as that presented in the Persian religion, but with this difference: the Persian twin spirits are opposite in character, the one good, the other evil; the Indian antagonists, on the other hand, are both good, Karma representing the moral order,—righteousness, Nirvana, the *summum bonum*. It is a fatal thing when these two come into collision.

The Buddhist conception of Karma is as fantastic as its doctrine of Nirvana is morbid. Its atomistic idea of merit and demerit, as adhering to individual acts instead of to conduct as a whole, destroys the unity of character; and its theory of indefinitely delayed retribution is as baseless as it is mischievous in tendency. The resulting view of the world-process presents the spectacle of a moral chaos rather than a broad intelligible embodiment of sowing and reaping in the moral universe. It is unnecessary to point out how entirely diverse the world-process of Buddhist ethical theory is from that implied in the modern theory of evolution. In the evolutionary theory the world moves steadily onward from lower to higher forms of life till it culminates in man. On the Buddhist theory the universe is turned topsy-turvy. The higher may come before the lower, according to the requirements of the law of Karma. Man comes first of all, not at the end of the evolutionary process, as its crown and climax; for moral acts are the *prius* and cause of physical creation. There had been no world unless man, with his merit and demerit, had previously been. Under the modern conception physical causality and moral aims have their distinct value, under law to a supreme Cause who controls all, and makes the two worlds work in concert. Under the Buddhist conception physical causation counts for nothing; moral requirements alone find recognition: and the result is a fantastic see-saw, a wild fluctuation in the history of moral agents who may be gods at one time, men at another, beasts at a still later stage of their existence.

Yet, in spite of all its defects, theoretical and practical, the religious movement originated by Buddha may be numbered among the forces which have contributed in a signal degree to the moral amelioration of the world. Its ethical idea, if one-sided, is pure and elevated. It has helped millions to live sweet, peaceful lives in retirement from the world, if it has not nerved men to play the part of heroes in the world. It has soothed the pain of

BUDDHA AND THE MORAL ORDER

despair, if it has not inspired hope, and has thus, as Bunsen remarks, produced the effect of a mild dose of opium on the tribes of weary-hearted Asia.[1] This is all it is fitted to do, even at the best. The Buddhism even of Buddha was at most but an anodyne, sickly in temper while morally pure. The sickliness has been a more constant characteristic of the religion he founded than the purity. It has entered into many combinations which have marred its beauty, not even shrinking from alliance with the obscenities of Siva-worship.[2] But no religion can afford to be judged by all the phases it has passed through in the course of its development. Let us therefore take Buddhism at its best and think of it as kindly as possible. But what it gives is not enough. Men need more than a quietive, a soothing potion; militant virtues as well as meekness, gentleness, and resignation. The well-being of the world demands warriors brave in the battle against evil, not monks immured in cloisters, and passing their lives in poverty and idleness, wearing the yellow robe of a mendicant order.

[1] *Vide* his *God in History*, vol. i. p. 375.
[2] *Vide* on this Burnouf's *Introduction*, pp. 480-488.

LECTURE II

ZOROASTER: DUALISM

THE date of Zoroaster is very uncertain. Conjecture ranges over more than a thousand years, some making the prophet of the ancient Persians a contemporary of Abraham, while others bring him down as far as Hystaspes, the father of Darius I., *i.e.* to the sixth century B.C. The translator of the Gâthas, in the Sacred Books of the East, Mr. Mills, thinks that these poems, the oldest part of the *Avesta*, and believed to be from the mind if not from the hand of Zoroaster, may possibly have been composed as early as about 1500 B.C.; but that it is also possible to place them as late as 900 to 1200 B.C.[1] Taking the latest of these dates, the ninth century before the Christian era, as the period in which Zoroaster, or as he is now called, *Zarathustra*, made his appearance, it results that the man who is known to all the world as the promulgator of the dualistic theory preceded Buddha by three hundred years. If it had been necessary to be guided supremely by chronological

[1] *Vide* the *Introduction*, p. xxxvii.

ZOROASTER: DUALISM

considerations he should, therefore, have come first in our course. But for our purpose it does not greatly matter which of the two religious initiators has the honour of the first place. The movements they inaugurated are independent products of human thought brooding on the phenomena of life, proceeding from minds differently constituted and influenced by diverse environments.

The two men, however, were connected by very important links. They were kindred in race and in language, and they had a common religious inheritance. Indians and Persians were both of the Aryan stock. Their fathers lived together at a far-back time in the region north of Hindostan, whence they are believed to have migrated in two streams, one flowing southwards through the mountains towards India and the other westward towards Eastern Persia. Some time ago the theory was held that the separation was due to a religious rupture. The hypothesis was built on the facts that certain gods of the Vedic Pantheon appear degraded to the rank of demons in the Persian Sacred Book, the Avesta, and that the very name for a god in the Vedic dialect (*deva*) is, under a slightly altered form (*daeva*), in that book the name for a demon. It seemed a not improbable inference that the Zoroastrian movement was of the nature of a religious revolt which threw contempt on the common deities of the Indo-Iranian

36 THE MORAL ORDER OF THE WORLD

family.[1] Recent scholars reject this theory and invert the relation between geographical separation and religious divergence. Mr. Mills expresses the view now in favour in these terms: 'No sudden and intentional dismissal of the ancient gods is to be accepted with Haug, nor any religious schism as the cause of the migration of the Indians towards the south. The process was, of course, the reverse. The migrating tribes, in consequence of their separation from their brethren in Iran, soon became estranged from them, and their most favoured gods fell slowly into neglect, if not disfavour.'[2]

Whatever the cause of religious diversity may have been, there is no room for doubt as to its existence. The religious temper revealed in the Gâthas is widely different from that of the Vedic hymns, and still more from that of Buddha. The Vedic religion, as we saw, is a kind of healthy, cheerful, poetic naturalism, of which the beautiful hymns to the dawn (Ushas) may be taken as the typical expression. The Vedic worshipper cherishes no lofty conception of the highest good, nor does he brood too much on the sorrows of life and on its dark end in death. He seeks chiefly material things in his prayers, enjoys life cheerily while he may, and thinks of death as a sleep, without

---

[1] So Haug, *Die Gâthas des Zarathustra*. On his view *vide* Darmesteter, *Ormuzd et Ahriman*, p. 261 *f.*

[2] Introduction to translation of the Gâthas, p. xxxvi.

fear of aught beyond. By Buddha's time the Indian mind has made an immense advance in moral earnestness. Life now means much more than meat and drink; man's chief end is not to be happy, but to be good; sin and sorrow, the very occasional themes of reflection in the Veda, now monopolise attention. But the animal vigour and healthy energy of the Vedic Indian are gone, and in their place have come quietism and despair. The religion of the Gâthas sympathises with the moral intensity of Buddha as against the easy-going ways of the Vedic Indians; but, on the other hand, it is in touch with the manliness of the earlier phase of Indian character, as opposed to the sickly life-weary spirit of the later. There is a fervid spirituality pervading the Gâthas which reminds one of the Hebrew Psalter. The moral world, not the material, is what the seer has mainly in view. Of the Pagan enjoyment of nature, as it appeals to the senses, there is little trace. We find there nothing corresponding to the Ushas-group of hymns. Natural objects are seldom referred to, and never alone, or as the supreme objects of interest. When the Good Spirit is praised as the Maker of heaven and earth and all things therein: sun, moon, and stars, clouds, winds, waters, plants, He is also praised as inspirer of good thoughts.[1] The *summum*

[1] Mills' translation of the Gâthas, p. 113.

bonum for the poet of the Gâthas is the Kingdom of righteousness; fields, crops, flocks, have only the second place in his thoughts.

On the other hand, the morality of the Gâthas, unlike that of Buddhism, is virile, militant. It is a fight for the good against evil with all available weapons, material ones not excepted. The Zoroastrian has no idea of retiring from the world into a monastery, to give himself up to meditation on the vanity of things, and to that extirpation of desire which issues in Nirvana. His aim is to do his part manfully in the work of the world, tilling the fields, tending the flocks; and for the rest to fight to the death men of evil minds and evil lives whenever he encounters them.

Compared with Vedism the religion of the Gâthas is monotheistic, in *tendency* at least, if not in precisely formulated creed; compared with Buddhism it is theistic, believing not only in a moral order of the world, but in a moral order presided over by a Divine Sovereign. And the natural order and the moral are conceived as under one and the same divine control. The Good Spirit, Ormuzd (now written, *Ahuramazda*), is at once maker of the physical world, the source of piety, and the fountain of that reverential love which a dutiful son cherishes towards a father.[1] In the hymns of Zoroaster, as in the Hebrew Psalms, the glory of God appears

[1] The Gâthas, Yasna xliv. 7.

ZOROASTER: DUALISM

alike in the firmament which showeth His handiwork and in the moral law whose statutes make wise the simple.

But beside the Divine Head of the Kingdom of righteousness is Another, not perhaps of equal power and godhead, yet a kind of antigod, head of the Kingdom of evil and maker of whatever in the world is hostile to goodness. The Zoroastrian idea of God is practically dualistic, if not in the strict sense ditheistic. Ahuramazda has to submit to a rival, Ahriman (now called *Angra-mainyu*), the evil-minded, the Demon of the Lie. This dualism is not necessarily a pure invention of Zoroaster's. It may be the development of an unconscious dualism latent in the primitive religion of the united Aryan family.[1] Anthropologists tell us that dualism in crude forms was a characteristic of all primitive religions. It is *e.g.* a conspicuous feature in the religion of American Redmen from north to south.[2] Tylor gives the following curious example: 'North American tribes have personified Nipinukhe and Pipunukhe, the beings who bring the spring (nipin) and the winter (pipun): Nipinukhe brings the heat and birds and verdure, Pipunukhe ravages with his cold winds, his ice and snow; one comes as the other goes, and between them they divide the world.'[3] Traces of this 'early omnipresent dualistic

[1] Such is the view of Darmesteter, *Ormuzd et Ahriman*, p. 87.
[2] *Vide* Lang's *Myth, Ritual, and Religion*, vol. ii. p. 47.
[3] Tylor, *Primitive Culture*, vol. i. p. 300.

philosophy'[1] were to be expected in the original Aryan religion as elsewhere; and they are found in the Vedic Hymns as well as in the Gâthas.

In the Veda, however, the conflict is *physical*, not ethical. It is simply a vivid mythological representation of the phenomena of storms. The scene of warfare is the atmosphere, and the war is between Indra, the god of light and of rain, and Ahi, the serpent whose tortuous body, the clouds, hides the light, or Vritra, the bandit, who shuts up the light and the waters in his nebulous cavern.[2] It has been maintained that the Persian dualism was originally of the same type, and ingenious attempts have been made to discover support for the assertion in the Avesta.[3] This position, whether true or not, it is not necessary to call in question. The fact of importance for us is that at some time before the Gâthas were composed the physical conflict was transformed into a moral one, and the scene of warfare passed from the sky to the earth, and the subject of contest was no longer the light and the waters of heaven but the human soul. This is admitted even by Darmesteter, who strenuously maintains the primitive affinity between the Indian

[1] Lang, *Myth, Ritual, and Religion*, vol. i. p. 334; also vol. ii. p. 4, in reference to the crow and the eagle, the 'old ones' who made the world according to an Australian myth. 'There was continual war betwen these ornithomorphic creators. The strife was as fierce as between wolf and raven, coyote and dog, Ormuzd and Ahriman.'

[2] Darmesteter, p. 97.   [3] *Vide* Darmesteter's work above cited.

and the Persian forms of dualism. At what precise
time the transformation took place it may be impossible to determine, as also to what agency it
was due; enough for us that the great crisis in
the Persian religion was antecedent to the Gâthic
period. If the Gâthas, as is alleged, contain
survivals of the older type of dualism, they contain
also abundant traces of the transformed ethical
type. Ahura is an ethical divinity loving righteousness and hating iniquity. His rival also is an ethical
being, but of a sinister order; a lover of falsehood
and patron of wrong. And their respective subjects
are like-minded with the divinities they serve. And
the great fact for the sacred poet is the subjection
of the world to the dominion of two antagonistic
spirits, with the corresponding division of mankind
into two great classes, those who obey the Good
Spirit and those who are subject to the Evil Spirit.
If these lofty conceptions were not entirely new
creations, but transformations from lower forms of
thought, they are none the less marvellous, when
we consider how much is involved in the change
of physical deities into ethical deities. If the
transformation was the work of Zoroaster, single-
handed, he deserves to be ranked among the great
religious initiators of our race. If it was not the
work of one man, or of one generation, the gradual-
ness of the process does not make the result less
valuable. It was a great day for ancient Persia,

and for the world, when there dawned upon prophetic minds the idea of a Kingdom of the good under the dominion of a beneficent Spirit who required of men the culture of righteousness and the practice of mercy. If the bright vision had its dark shadow in a Kingdom of evil presided over by a rival deity, let us not undervalue it on that account. The Demon of the Lie only serves as a foil to show forth by contrast the virtues of Ahura. The sombre conception of an antigod, however crude and helpless from a philosophical point of view, at least evinces the resolute determination of the Persian sage to preserve the character of the good Spirit absolutely free from all compromise with evil, and from all moral contamination. To accomplish this laudable purpose is the *raison d'être* of the evil Spirit in the Zoroastrian creed. He is simply the negative of the good Spirit. He grows in the distinctness of his attributes and functions in proportion as the importance of keeping the divine idea pure is realised. He is whatever it is desirable that the truly divine should not be. In the primitive time before the separation, he was not known by name; then he became the personification and heir of the demons of the storm; then he assumed more definite shape as the antithesis of Ahura, and his character was outlined in malign completeness on the principles of analogy and contrast.[1]

[1] *Vide* Darmesteter, *Ormuzd et Ahriman*, chap. vi.

The thing to be emphasised, therefore, in the first place, in the religion of the Gâthas, is not the dualism, but the conception contained in them of the *Good Spirit*. This is a permanently valuable contribution to the evolution of religious thought. The character ascribed to Ahura is pure and exalted. Among the epithets employed to describe him, one specially strikes a thoughtful reader. Ahura is declared to be 'the Father of the toiling good mind,' and piety or devotion revealing itself in good deeds is called his daughter.[1] The application of the title 'Father' to the Divine Being is in itself worthy of note, and from the connection in which it is used we get a glimpse into the heart of the Divine Father. Observe who are His children. They are the men who toil, who take life in earnest, who with resolute will strive to do the work that lies to their hand. And what is the nature of that work? It is such as commends itself to the 'good mind,' work in which noble souls can be enthusiastic. That means something higher than tilling the fields and tending the flocks, though these useful labours are not despised. It means contributing to the store of righteousness and its beneficent fruits: in short, toiling for the kingdom of goodness. That is to say, the sons and daughters of Ahura are those who, in the language of Jesus, 'seek first the kingdom of God,' and heroically devote themselves to

[1] The Gâthas, Yasna xlv. 4.

its service. Through the children we know the Father, and perceive that He bears some resemblance to the Father-God Jesus made known to His disciples.

Further light is thrown on the character of Ahura by the doctrine of the *Amschaspands*. The name sounds very unattractive to our ears, but the thing is simple. The doctrine of the Amschaspands is simply the doctrine of the divine attributes. The Amschaspands are personified virtues of the good Spirit. They are six, or, counting Ahura Himself as one, seven. Their names are uncouth, and I shall not attempt to pronounce them, but according to Darmesteter they signify righteousness, the good mind, sovereign might, piety as it manifests itself in the souls of believers, health, and long life.[1] In this list there seems to be a mixture of physical and moral properties. Another thing still more notable is, the ascription to the Divine Being of what belongs to His worshipper—practical piety. We have already seen that the piety of good men is represented as the daughter of Ahura. But in the doctrine of the Amschaspands it is more than a daughter, even an essential ingredient in the character of Ahura. It almost seems as if the Deity of the ancient Persians were simply the immanent spirit of the holy commonwealth; He in it and it in Him, and all characteristic properties common to both. This

[1] Darmesteter, *l.c.*, p. 42.

ZOROASTER: DUALISM

might be called pantheism, were it not for the conception of an antigod, which is not consistent with a pantheistic theory of the universe. Mr. Mills suggests the designation, 'Hagio-theism,' to which he appends the explanatory title, 'a delineation of God in the holy creation.'[1]

This phrase does not cover the whole truth about God as conceived by Zoroastrians. Ahura is not merely the immanent spirit of the society of saints; He is, as already indicated, the Creator-spirit of the universe. His attribute of righteousness, *Asha*, denotes right order not only in the holy commonwealth but in the cosmos at large. This appears in Yasna xliv., which contains a series of suggestive questions addressed to Ahura which, in an interrogative form, set forth the poet's confession of faith concerning the relations of the good Spirit to the cosmic order. Two of these questions may be given by way of sample.

3. 'This, I ask thee, O Ahura! tell me aright:
>   Who by generation was the first father of the righteous order (within the world)?
>   Who gave the (recurring) sun and stars their (undeviating) way?
>   Who established that whereby the moon waxes and whereby she wanes, save thee?
>   These things, O great Creator! would I know, and others likewise still.

---

[1] The Gâthas, Introduction, p. xix.

46 THE MORAL ORDER OF THE WORLD

4. 'This I ask thee, O Ahura! tell me aright,
    Who from beneath hath sustained the earth and the clouds above that they do not fall?
    Who made the waters and the plants?
    Who to the wind has yoked on the storm-clouds, the swift and fleetest two?
    Who, O great Creator! is the inspirer of the good thoughts (within our souls)?[1]

The cosmic order and the moral order, then, are both alike ordained by Ahura. The courses of the stars; the alternations of light and darkness, day and night, sleep and waking hours; the daily succession of dawn, noon and midnight; the flow of rivers, the growth of corn and of fruit-trees; the exhilarating sweep of purifying breezes; the inspired thoughts of poets, saints, and sages, and the love which binds men together in family ties—these all have their origin in Ahura's wisdom and power.

This being so, what room and need, one is inclined to ask, in this universe, for a rival divinity? On first thoughts Angra-mainyu may seem an idle invention; but on second thoughts we are forced to admit that the conception, however crude, was very natural. Theories always have their ultimate origin in observation of facts. The fact-basis of the Persian dualism was *the observed presence in the world of two sorts of men*, diverse in spirit and in conduct, with incompatible interests and ever at war. They are the

---

[1] The Gâthas, Yasna xliv. The bracketed clauses in this and other quotations are explanatory expressions introduced by the translator.

ZOROASTER: DUALISM

good-minded and the evil-minded respectively; those who love truth and justice, and those who love falsehood and wrong. The existence of the two classes is recognised in the Gâthas in these quaint terms, 'He is evil who is the best one to the evil, and he is holy who is friendly to the righteous, as thou didst fix the moral laws, O Lord.'[1] The opposed classes come under the notice of the poet in a very realistic, obtrusive, and unwelcome manner in the form of two peoples, diverse in race, language, religion, and social condition. The good are represented by his own people, Aryans in race and language, worshippers of Ahura and tillers of the soil in fertile valleys by river-courses where flocks graze and grain grows. The evil are represented by obnoxious neighbours of the Turanian race,[2] nomads, worshippers of demons, too near the Aryan farmers for their comfort, ever ready to make incursions into their settlements and carry off the 'joy-creating kine' from the pleasant peaceful meadows.[3]

Behold an elect people, an Israel, in the far East, with Philistines on every side! The incessant conflict between them can be imagined. Invasion and rapine on the part of the demon-worshipping nomads, resolute defence of their property on the part of Zoroastrians. The bitterness of the increasing strife is reflected in the sacred poems by frequent reference, and by the terms of intense dislike applied to the

[1] Yasna xlvi. 6.   [2] *Ibid.*, 12.   [3] Yasna xlvii. 3.

foes of the children of light. In the conflict, material, moral and religious interests and motives are blended, and all three are surrounded with a common halo of sacredness. The defence of agriculture against the assaults of pagan nomads becomes a holy cause. Hence the personified abstraction, the 'Soul of the Kine,' becomes the poetic emblem, not only of the material interests of the worshippers of Ahura, but also of the spiritual. It is the 'Soul of the Kine,' representing the devout tillers of the land, that in the hour of distress raises a wailing cry to Ahura to send a strong wise man to teach them the true faith and lead them against their foes. Zoroaster was the answer to its prayer.[1]

No wonder that in these circumstances the idea of a divine antagonist to Ahura, head of the Kingdom of darkness, took possession of the mind of the poet and prophet who was sent in answer to the Soul of the Kine's prayer. For one of his intense mystic temper, Ahriman would seem the appropriate divine embodiment of the evil spirit active in the dark Turanian world. One can imagine how it might appear to him as a great revelation, throwing a flood of light on life's mysteries, to proclaim as an ultimate fact the existence of two opposed Spirits dividing the dominion of the world between them. This accordingly the hero, sent in answer to the distressed cry of the Kine's soul, is represented as doing in a

[1] Yasna xxix.

ZOROASTER: DUALISM

solemn address to an assembled multitude. 'Hear ye then with your ears,' thus he begins, 'see ye the bright flames with (the eyes of the) Better Mind. It is for a decision as to religions, man and man, each individually for himself.'[1] Then follows the great doctrine of dualism: 'Thus are the primeval spirits who as a pair (combining their opposite strivings), and (yet each) independent in his action, have been formed (of old). (They are) a better thing, they two, and a worse, as to thought, as to word, and as to deed. And between these two let the wisely acting choose aright. (Choose ye) not (as) the evil-doers.'[2]

That this doctrine of dualism would never have been heard of but for Turanian invasions of Aryan settlements, would be a very simple supposition. Alas! there was evil within the holy land as well as without, and there was a traditional instinctive dualism already in possession of the popular mind, and both these sources would contribute material for reflective thought on the mystery of good and evil and its ultimate explanation. But the doctrine would gain sharpness of outline from the existence of a Turanian environment, and the constant conflicts between the two hostile races would convert what might otherwise have been a mild philosophic theorem into a divine message coming from a heart on fire with a sacred enthusiasm and uttered in

[1] Yasna xxx. 2.   [2] Yasna xxx. 3.

words of prophetic intensity. Such is the character of the Gâtha in which the doctrine is proclaimed. The temper of the poet is not philosophic; it is truculent, Hebrew, Puritan. His utterance breathes at once the lofty spiritual tone and the vindictiveness of certain Psalms in the Hebrew Psalter. He contemplates with satisfaction the time when vengeance shall come upon the wretches who worship the Daevas.[1] His mind is dominated by the same broad antitheses that were ever present to the thoughts of Israel: between the elect people and the Gentiles, between light and darkness, truth and falsehood; and the light is very brilliant and the darkness very dark.

Yet the attitude of the Persian prophet towards the outside world is not exclusively hostile, as if those who had given themselves to the service of the Evil Spirit were incapable of change. Conversion is conceived to be possible. Conversions are expected even from the Turanians. With clear prophetic vision, reminding us of Hebrew Psalmists, the poet of the Gâthas anticipates a time when 'from among the tribes and kith of the Turanian those shall arise who further on the settlements of Piety with energy and zeal,' and with whom Ahura shall 'dwell together through his Good Mind (in them), and to them for joyful grace deliver His commands.'[2] The man who cherishes this hope has no wish to

[1] Yasna xxx. 33. [2] Yasna xlvi. 12.

ZOROASTER: DUALISM

enjoy a monopoly of Ahura's blessing. He harbours in his heart no pride either of election or of race. He is conscious, indeed, of possessing in the true faith a boon for which he cannot be too thankful. But he is willing to share the boon with any who have a mind to receive it, even if they come from the tents of the nomads. Race for him is not the fundamental distinction among men, as is caste for his kindred in India. The grand radical cleavage in his view is that between men of the Good Mind and men of the Evil Mind, and the fact attests the sincerity and depth of his devotion to the creed he proclaims.

That conversion is thought to be possible, even in unlikely quarters, is a point worth noting in that creed. Men, we see, are not conceived to be good or evil by necessity of nature and irrevocably; every man by an insurmountable fatality a child of Ahura, or a child of Ahura's antagonist; no change from bad to good possible, either through self-effort or through gracious influence of transcendent powers. Evil and good are objects of choice, and the man who makes a wrong choice to-day may make the better choice to-morrow. Such is the hopeful creed of Zoroaster.

But no optimistic expectations are cherished. Present experience does not encourage extravagant anticipations or universalistic dreams. Depressing facts stare one in the face: the obstinacy of unbelief, the rarity of conversions, and even within the pale of the chosen people the prevalence of grievous evil: arrogance among those of high degree, lying among the people, slothful neglect of needful toil;[1] and, worst of all, evil men not seen and believed to be the sinners that they are, posing and passing as children of light when they are in truth children of darkness.[2] To these moral faults have to be added perplexing social evils — bad men prospering, good men suffering frustration and misfortune. Surveying the whole, a man of earnest spirit addicted to reflection is more likely to fall a prey to dark doubt than to indulge in high hopes of rapid extension and steadily increasing sway for the kingdom of righteousness. Traces of such doubts are not wanting in the Gâthas. The poet asks such questions as these:—'Wherefore is the vile man not known to be vile?'[3] 'When shall I in verity discern if ye indeed have power over aught, O Lord?'[4] and he brings under Mazda's notice the perplexing facts of his own experience—unable to attain his wish, his flocks reduced in number, his following insignificant—beseeching him to behold and help if he can.[5] Here is matter enough surely for musing! Vile men, *e.g.* not known to be vile! Why cannot men be either one thing or another, decidedly good or decidedly evil? Why be evil and at the same time feign goodness? Alas! it is so advantageous some-

---

[1] Yasna xxxiii. 4.   [2] *Ibid.* xliv. 12.   [3] *Ibid.* xliv. 11.
[4] *Ibid.* xlviii. 9.   [5] *Ibid.* xlvi. 2.

times to have the name of being good; so easy to slide into the false ways of hypocrisy, especially in times of exceptional religious enthusiasm. When in the first fervour of a new faith believers have all things in common, Ananiases and Sapphiras are sure to arise. Again, has Ahura any real power? Ahura's good-will is not doubted, and that is well; for when, as in the case of the author of the 73rd Psalm, doubt arises in the mind whether God be indeed good even to the pure in heart, the feet are near to slipping.[1] But Ahura's power seems open to grave question. As things stand, the Evil Spirit seems to be in the ascendency. Openly wicked men abound, hypocrisy is rampant, all around the settlements of the worshippers of Mazda is the dark world of demon-worship. How can this be, if Ahura's power to establish the kingdom of righteousness be equal to his will? The personal afflictions of which the poet complains help, of course, to make these doubts and perplexities more acute. If Ahura be powerful, why does he not protect his devoted servant from plunder, and give him the success his heart desires in the propagation of the faith? Natural questions raising abstruse problems out of experiences which repeat themselves in all ages.

The poet of the Gâthas seems to have regarded the conflict between good and evil as eternal. The doctrine of dualism enunciated in the 30th Yasna

[1] Ps. lxxiii. 2.

54 THE MORAL ORDER OF THE WORLD

comes in as an answer to the question how the primæval world arose.[1] According to that doctrine, evil always has been and always will be. It never had a beginning, and never will have an end. There might be a time when men were not, but there never was a time when the transcendent Evil Mind was not. The two antagonist minds are both represented as 'primæval.'[2] And the prospect for the future is not one of the final conversion of all the evil-minded to goodness, but of the final judgment of the inveterately wicked. 'The swallowing up of sin and sorrow in ultimate happiness,' according to Mr. Mills, 'belongs to a later period. It is not Gâthic Zarathustrianism.'[3]

Of 'Zarathustrianism,' according to the Gâthas, I have endeavoured in the preceding statement to give a brief account. It remains to offer some observations on its general religious value, on its special contribution to the theory of the providential order, and on the influence which it has exerted on the subsequent history of religious thought.

The grand merit of this Persian religion is its thoroughgoing moral earnestness, its Hebrew passion for righteousness. In this respect Zoroaster is not unworthy to stand beside the prophets of Israel. As regards this fundamental characteristic, the meaning of the Gâthas, we are assured, remains unaffected by all the difficulties of syntax which make trans-

[1] Yasna xxviii. 12. [2] *Ibid.* xxx. 3. [3] The Gâthas, p. 26.

lation a hard task for experts.[1] The poet on every page appears an ardent admirer of the Good Mind; a passionate lover of justice, truth, purity, and kindness. Mr. Mills, who has rendered an important service by translating his hymns into English, pronounces an opinion on their value which may well be accepted as authoritative. It is in these terms: 'So far as a claim to a high position among the curiosities of ancient moral lore is concerned, the reader may trust himself freely to the impression that he has before him an anthology which was probably composed with as fervent a desire to benefit the spiritual and moral natures of those to whom it was addressed as any which the world had yet seen.'[2]

The Gâthic idea of God is the child of this intense ethical temper. The wise, good, beneficent Spirit called Ahura-mazda is a projection of the good mind which animates his worshipper. In our study of Buddhism we found, to our surprise, that his beautiful ethical ideal did not suggest to Buddha the conception of a Deity in which all he admired and sought to be was perfectly realised. The Persian prophet did not make this mistake. He saw in the good mind of man the immanence and operation of an absolute Good Mind. Hence his theology was as pure as his ethics. It was the bright reflection of a good conscience.

[1] *Vide* an article by Mr. Mills on 'Avestan Difficulties' in *The Critical Review* for July 1896. [2] The Gâthas, p. 1.

THE MORAL ORDER OF THE WORLD

The antigod proclaimed in the doctrine of dualism had a similar origin. It was a device to protect the character of Ahura from taint, and to heighten the brightness of its light by contrast with darkness. It may be a failure as a theory, but it does credit to the moral sentiments of its promulgator. Had he been less deeply impressed with the radical irreconcilable distinction between good and evil, he might have found it easier to believe that God was one not two, and so have divided with Hebrew prophets the honour of giving to the world ethical monotheism.

Passing now to the doctrine of the two gods, I remark concerning it, in the first place, that in promulgating it the Persian prophet was dealing seriously with a radical problem, the origin of evil. Of *moral* evil I mean, for it does not appear from the Gâthas that physical evil occupied a very prominent place in their author's thoughts. The question of questions for him was, Why are all men not under law to the good? To be good seemed so reasonable, so natural, to one whose own mind was good, to love truth, justice, and mercy so easy, that he could not but wonder why any should be otherwise minded. Evil appeared to him so unnatural, so unaccountable, that he was forced to seek its fountain-head not in man, but in a transcendent causality even within the region of the divine. A more serious view of the matter it is impossible to conceive.

But this short and easy solution will not bear

reflection. Obvious defects at once suggest themselves.

In the first place, the theory assigns too absolute significance to Evil by finding its origin and even its permanent home in the sphere of the divine. It has indeed been questioned whether Zoroaster really did this, whether his so-called dualism was dualistic in principle; that is, whether the Evil Spirit was co-ordinate with the Good Spirit, and not rather subordinate, even his creature.[1] But there is no trace of such a view in the Gâthas. The Good Spirit, as there conceived, could not create a spirit evil at the moment of his creation. He could only create a spirit who was at first good, then afterwards fell into evil—a being, *i.e.* like Milton's *Satan*. Such, however, is not the history of Ahriman as given in the Gâthas. He is evil from the beginning.

This idea of an absolute divine Evil is self-cancelling. It gives to Evil equal rights with the Good. If evil and good be alike divine, who is to decide between their claims? what ground is there for preferring either to the other? It comes to be a matter of liking, one man choosing the Good Spirit for his god, another the Evil Spirit, neither having a right

[1] The second of these alternatives is adopted by Harnack. *Vide* his essay on Manichæism at the end of vol. iii. of his *History of Dogma*, English translation. The opposite view was held by Hegel, who regarded the dualism of the Persian religion as a merit. The fault lay not in introducing the antithesis into the sphere of the divine, but in not providing for its being ultimately overcome. *Vide* his *Philosophie der Geschichte*, p. 182 (English translation, p. 186).

to call in question the other's choice. So it results that a dualism created by the over-anxious assertion of moral distinctions turns into its opposite, and makes these distinctions purely relative and subjective.

The account given of man's relation to this divine dualism, though simple and satisfactory at first sight, breaks down on further examination. It is represented as a matter of choice, 'a decision as to religions, man and man, each individually for himself.' The man of evil will, accordingly, chooses the Evil Spirit for his Divinity. But whence the evil will? Has the Evil Spirit waited till he was chosen before beginning to exert his malign influence, or has he been at work before in the soul of his worshipper predestining and disposing him to the bad preference? On the latter alternative, where is the freedom of will? If, on the other hand, the will be uncontrolled, and the choice perfectly deliberate and intelligent, a free preference of the worse mind by one who fully knows what he does, does this not involve a state of pravity which is final, leaving no room for change from the worse to the better mind, a sin against the Good Spirit which cannot be repented of or forgiven? Yet the Gâthic creed recognises the possibility of conversion.

The origin of evil cannot be explained so easily as the Persian sage imagined. The doctrine of the Twin Spirits raises more difficulties than it solves. Better leave the problem alone and confess that the origin of evil is a mystery. Or, if you will have a dualism, why not one such as Zoroaster's personal history might have suggested to him? One of the Gâthas obscurely hints at a temptation to a gross form of sensual indulgence.[1] How near the tempted one was to the discovery that the real antithesis was not between two divine Spirits eternally antagonistic, but between spirit and flesh in man; between the law in the mind and the law in the members! This form of dualism may not, any more than the other, go to the root of the matter, or utter the final word on all questions relating to evil. But it at least points to a real, not an imaginary, antagonism. And by placing the dualism within rather than without it gets rid of the hard line of separation between good men and bad men, drawn by a theory which lays exclusive emphasis on the will. In the light of this internal dualism we see that men are not divisible into the perfectly good and the perfectly evil, but that all men are both good and evil in varying proportions. There is a law in the members even of a saint, and there is a law of the mind consenting to good even in the most abandoned transgressor. The fact once realised tends to breed humility and sympathy. The good man becomes less satisfied with himself, and more inclined to lenient judgment on his fellow-men. What an immense advance in self-knowledge is revealed by

[1] Yasna li. 12.

comparing the Gâthas with the seventh chapter of St. Paul's Epistle to the Romans, and what a contrast between the hard severe tone of the Persian hymns and the benignant kindly accent of the words, 'Considering thyself, lest thou also be tempted'! Evil is not to be explained away by smooth phrases; but there is comfort in the thought that few commit that sin against the Holy Ghost which consists in a perfectly deliberate and intelligent preference of evil to good; that most sins are sins of ignorance and impulse committed by men who are carried headlong by desire or habit, and deluded by a show of good in things evil.

On the historic influence of the Persian theory, only a few sentences can be added. The religion of Zoroaster is almost extinct, its only adherents now being the Parsees in India, amounting to about one hundred and fifty thousand; an insignificant number compared with the four hundred millions professing Buddhism, and suggesting the thought that, with all its fair promise, this ancient faith must have had some inherent defect which foredoomed it to failure. It is not easy to believe that under the providential order a religion fitted to render important service to mankind would be allowed so completely to sink out of sight. The subsequent career of Zoroastrianism, while it was the religion of the Persian people, was not favourable to permanent influence and extensive prevalence. It developed into the worship of fire, and of the Haoma plant, and of spirits innumerable, of diverse grades, names, and functions, and into elaborate ceremonial for the purpose of securing ritual purity. Dualism widened out into a species of refined polytheism, and the ethical, supreme at first, became lost among the details of a sacerdotal system.

The direct influence of Persian dualism has been supposed to be traceable specially in two quarters: in the later religious ideas of the Hebrews, and in the Manichæan religion which made its appearance in the third century of our era. As to the latter, to speak of it first, the main interest it possesses for us is the hold which it took of the youthful mind of Augustine, and the influence which through him it has exercised on Christian theology. It used to be regarded as certain that the religion of Mani was a revival of Zoroastrianism modified by Christianity. Recent investigation, however, has brought about a change of view; and the theory now in favour is that the basis of Manichæism is to be sought in the old Babylonian religion; that it is a Semitic growth with a mixture of Persian and Christian elements. It resembles Zoroastrianism in so far as it also teaches a dualistic theory of the universe. But the Manichæan dualism is not ethical, but physical. The great antithesis in the creed of Mani is that between light and darkness, not as emblems of good and evil, but as themselves good and evil. Religious knowledge consists in the knowledge of nature and its elements, and redemption in a physical separation of the light elements from the darkness. Human nature belongs mainly to the realm of darkness, while not without some sparks of light. The ethics of the system are ascetic, inculcating abstinence from all that belongs to the dark region, such as fleshly desire. However repulsive to us this strange religious conglomerate may appear, it must have met the mood of the time, for it spread rapidly, and became one of the great religions of the period.[1]

Going back now to the alleged influence of Persian thought on the religious ideas of Israel after the period of the Exile: the chief instance of this has been found in the conception of *Satan*. Satan has been supposed to be Ahriman transferred from Persia to Palestine. It is a plausible but by no means indisputable hypothesis. The question is mixed up with critical theories as to the dates of those Old Testament books in which Satan occurs as a personal designation. These are Job, Zechariah, and 1 Chronicles. If these books were written during or after the Exile, the Persian origin of the Satan idea would be at least possible. But even among critics of the freest type there is diversity of opinion as to their dates. Thus Renan places the Book of Job as far back as the eighth century B.C. He is equally

[1] *Vide* the article by Harnack referred to on p. 57, note.

decided as to the non-identity of Satan with Ahriman, giving as his reason that Satan does nothing except by the order of God, that he is simply an angel of a more malign character than the rest; sly, and inclined to slander; by no means to be identified with the genius of evil existing and acting independently.[1] More significant, perhaps, is the function assigned to Satan in 1 Chronicles. He there performs an act which in an earlier book, 2 Samuel, is ascribed to God. In Samuel Jehovah tempts David to number the people, in Chronicles Jehovah's place is taken by Satan.[2] It is a ready suggestion that the Chronicler, writing at the close of the Persian period of Jewish history, made the alteration under the influence of Persian ideas as to what it was fit that God should do. To tempt men to evil was not, from the Persian point of view, suitable work for the Good Spirit; such a malign function properly belonged to his rival. That familiarity with Persian ways of thinking gave rise to the scruples betrayed in the alteration made on the older narrative is an allowable conjecture.

However they are to be explained, the scruples manifestly existed, and this is the thing of chief interest for us. We see here, if not Persian dualism, at all events a species of dualism originating in a feeling kindred to that which gave rise to the doctrine of the 'Twin Spirits.' The Chronicler's

[1] *Le Livre de Job*, p. xxxix.
[2] *Vide* 2 Samuel xxiv. 11, and cf. 1 Chronicles xxi. 1.

feeling obviously was that to tempt is an evil work which may not be ascribed to God. The feeling represents an advance in some respects on the older less scrupulous way of thinking, which would have found no stumbling-block in the robust prophetic sentiment, 'I form the light and create darkness; I make peace and create evil.'[1] The scruple of the later time grew out of an intensified sense of moral distinctions: wherever this sense becomes acute, dualism in some form is likely to reappear. Hence we are not done with dualism even yet. Though the Zoroastrian religion is all but extinct, its conception of an antigod is not a thing of the distant past. As we shall see, at a later stage in our course, it is being revived under a new form in our own time.[2] There is much in the world to tempt one who believes in a good God to take up with the dualistic hypothesis. Yet surely it cannot be the last word. The broad strong creed contained in the prophetic oracle above cited expresses, not only the rough belief of an unrefined moral consciousness, but also the ultimate conviction in which alone the heart can find rest. Perhaps the prophet had the Persian dualism in view when he made the bold declaration. While respecting the moral earnestness in which that dualism had its source, he deemed it, we may suppose, only a half truth, and therefore supplied the needed correction by representing God as the creator

[1] Isaiah xlv. 7.　　　[2] *Vide* Lecture X.

both of light and of darkness. However hard to hold, this is the true creed. The dominion of the world cannot be divided between two, whether we call them Ormuzd and Ahriman, Jehovah and Satan, God and Devil, or by any other names. God must be God over all, and His providence must be all-embracing.

LECTURE III

THE GREEK TRAGEDIANS: NEMESIS

STUDENTS of the religions of mankind insist on the importance of distinguishing between the mythical and the truly religious elements in belief. In all stages of culture, among the lowest and most backward peoples as among the most advanced, the two elements are found to co-exist. They are of very different value. In the mythical element the absurd and the immoral abound. The religious element, on the other hand, is a comparatively pure and rational sentiment, everywhere essentially the same; faith in a Power working for righteousness, and more or less benign in its dealings with the children of men.[1]

In no case is it more necessary to bear this distinction in mind than in dealing with the religion of Greece. The mythology of that religion earned for itself a bad reputation by those grotesque and licentious features on which the early Christian Fathers were wont to dilate in an apologetic interest. The tendency of apologists generally has been to think of these features of ancient Pagan religions too

[1] *Vide* Lang, *Myth, Ritual, and Religion*, vol. i. pp. 328, 329.

exclusively, in forming an estimate of their worth. Hence the fact complained of by Professor Max Müller, that while we have endless books on the mythology of the Greeks and Romans, we have comparatively few on their religion, that is, their belief in a wise, powerful Eternal Ruler of the world.[1] Since that distinguished scholar made his complaint, thoughtful students of Greek literature have become more alive to the fact that such a belief in a Divine Moral Order had a large place in the minds of the wisest Greek thinkers, and really constituted their proper religious creed. The modern spirit inclines to give that belief the position of prominence in its estimate of Hellenic religion, and to regard the mythology as a thing which grew out of a primitive nature-worship, for which the Greeks of a later age were not responsible, and towards which they assumed varying attitudes of reverent receptivity respectful tolerance, or sceptical contempt.

Mythology and religion, in the sense explained, are intimately combined in Greek Tragedy. The myths and legendary tales of the heroic age are the warp, and the ethical and religious sentiments of the poet are the woof, of the immortal dramas of Æschylus, Sophocles, and Euripides. The warp is essentially the same in all three, yet the colour varies more or less in each of them. The individuality of each of the great dramatists comes out in his manner of

[1] Vide *Science of Language*, vol. ii. p. 413.

reproducing the tradition, as also in the attitude he assumes towards the whole stock of myths and legends handed down from antiquity. For Æschylus they are truth to be accepted with reverent faith; for Sophocles they are fiction to be received and used with artistic decorum; for Euripides they are ridiculous tales to be regarded with sceptical scorn and handled with critical freedom. The woof varies as well as the warp. When we compare the three tragedians with each other, we can trace a certain advance in their respective conceptions of the moral order of the world. This was to be expected in the case of men possessing exceptionally high intellectual and moral endowments. None of them was likely to be a simple echo of his predecessor. Every one of them, Æschylus not excepted, was likely to have some new thought to utter on the high themes which occupied their minds in common. Development in all respects, indeed, may be looked for; in dramatic art, in the personal attitude towards mythology, and in the individual views concerning the providential order.

Progression has been recognised in the two first of these three departments. As to the artistic side I cannot go into details, but must content myself with a brief general indication, based on the instructive statement of Mr. Symonds in his *Studies of the Greek Poets*. Mr. Symonds says: 'The law of inevitable progression in art from the severe and animated embodiment of an idea to the conscious elaboration of merely æsthetic motives and brilliant episodes, has hitherto been neglected by the critics and historians of poetry. They do not observe that the first impulse in a people towards creativeness is some deep and serious emotion, some fixed point of religious enthusiasm or national pride. To give adequate form to this taxes the energies of the first generation of artists, and raises their poetic faculty, by the admixture of prophetic inspiration, to the highest pitch. After the original passion for the ideas to be embodied in art has somewhat subsided, but before the glow and fire of enthusiasm have faded out, there comes a second period, when art is studied more for art's sake, but when the generative potency of the early poets is by no means exhausted.' The author goes on to indicate how, during these two stages, the mine of available ideas is worked out, and the national taste educated, so that for the third generation of artists the alternatives left are either to reproduce their models—a task impossible for genius—or to seek novelty at the risk of impairing the strength or the beauty which has become stereotyped. 'Less deeply interested in the great ideas by which they have been educated, and of which they are in no sense the creators, incapable of competing on the old ground with their elders, they are obliged to go afield for striking situations, to force sentiment and pathos, to subordinate the harmony of the whole to the melody of the parts, to sink the prophet in the poet, the hierophant in the charmer.' Æschylus represents the first stage in this progression, Sophocles the second, Euripides the third. Mr. Symonds compares the three poets to the three styles of Gothic architecture, Æschylus representing the rugged Norman, Sophocles the refined pointed style, Euripides the florid flamboyant manner. 'Æschylus,' he says, 'aimed at durability of structure, at singleness and grandeur of effect. Sophocles added the utmost elegance and finish. Euripides neglected force of construction and unity of design for ornament and brilliancy of effect.'[1]

The advance in the second respect, *i.e.* in the attitude assumed towards the legends which formed the stock-in-trade of dramatic art, from the reverence of Æschylus through the artistic reserve of Sophocles to the outspoken rationalism of Euripides, has been duly recognised by such recent writers as Verrall and Haigh.[2] But the third aspect of the onward movement—for our purpose the most important of all —that exhibited in the respective conceptions of the three great tragedians on the subject of the moral order and relative phenomena, has not received as yet, at least so far as I know, the full acknowledgment and distinct formulation to which it is entitled.

---

[1] *Studies of the Greek Poets*, 1st series, pp. 206-208.

[2] *Vide* Verrall's *Euripides the Rationalist* (1895), and Haigh's *The Tragic Drama of the Greeks* (1896).

That development here also can be verified, seems to me beyond doubt. It is just such a progression as might have been expected. When stated, the law of advance is so simple and natural as to appear self-evident, and scarcely in need of verification.

The law in question is as follows :—

Æschylus, coming first, believes firmly in the unimpeachable retributive justice of Providence. His doctrine is kindred to that of Eliphaz in Job: 'Remember, I pray thee, who ever perished being innocent? or where were the righteous cut off?'[1] Sophocles, coming next, while not questioning the general truth of the Æschylean doctrine of Nemesis, sees clearly and states frankly that there are exceptions both ways; bad men prospering, good men suffering grievous misfortune. Antigone, Œdipus, Philoctetes are some of the conspicuous examples of afflicted innocence. Such facts the poet, while constrained to acknowledge their existence, does not profess to understand; he simply reckons them among the mysteries of human life. Euripides goes one step further; the suffering of innocence is for him as well as for Sophocles a fact, but not altogether a mysterious one: he perceives a ray of light amid the darkness. He knows and notes that there is not merely such a thing as innocence involuntarily suffering unmerited evil, but also such a thing as innocence voluntarily enduring

[1] Job iv. 7.

evil, at the prompting of love and in devotion to a good cause. Such self-sacrifice did not appear to him, I think, a violation of the moral order, but rather the manifestation of that order under a new form. This law of progress in the reading of moral phenomena, kept well in view, will help us to appreciate better the distinctive lessons to be learnt from the Greek Tragedians concerning the providential order of the world.

A few general statements of fact may here be premised.

The story of the rise, progress, and uses of the Greek Tragic Drama cannot here be told. Suffice it to say that the drama served the same purpose for the Greeks that the sermon does for a Christian community. It did this and more. The statement of Professor Blackie is not far from the truth, that 'the lyrical tragedy of the Greeks presents, in a combination elsewhere unexampled, the best elements of our serious drama, our opera, our oratorio, our public worship, and our festal recreations.'[1] The drama was for the Greek the chief medium of ethical and religious instruction. The three most celebrated dramatic preachers were those already named: Æschylus, Sophocles, and Euripides. Æschylus was born 525 B.C., Sophocles about 497 B.C., and Euripides 480 B.C. Æschylus took part in the war against the Persians and made the defeat

[1] Translation of Æschylus, vol. i. Introduction, p. xlviii.

of the mighty foe by his countrymen the subject of one of his tragedies. He and his brother-poets wrote many tragic dramas, only a few of which have been preserved; of Æschylus seven, of Sophocles seven, and of Euripides eighteen. Their themes were taken for the most part from the traditional tales of the gods and the legendary history of the heroic age of Greece. Homer was their Bible. Æschylus is reported to have said that his tragedies were only slices cut from the great banquet of Homeric dainties. The siege of Troy with relative incidents supplied abundant topics for the dramatic preacher who, with the true preacher's instinct, was ever careful to point the moral lesson suggested by his story. Among the legends which offered ample opportunity for moralising were those relating to the fortunes of Agamemnon, the leader of the Greek host against Troy, and of his family. The main events are: the sacrifice of the daughter of Agamemnon, Iphigenia, at Aulis, to obtain a fair wind to carry the fleet to Troy; the murder of Agamemnon on his return home from the ten years' siege, by his own wife, Clytemnestra; and the murder of her in turn by her son Orestes. Æschylus and Euripides both handle these themes with great power, though with characteristic differences in the mode of treatment. Three of the extant plays of Æschylus are devoted to them: the *Agamemnon*, the *Libation-Bearers*, and the *Eumenides*, *i.e.* the

74 THE MORAL ORDER OF THE WORLD

Furies who haunted Orestes when he had killed his mother. The first and the last of the three show the genius of the poet at its best. With them is worthy to be associated the *Prometheus Bound*, whose theme is unique, and whose story, as we shall see, presents a curious problem with reference to the doctrine of Æschylus concerning the moral order, which I now proceed to illustrate.

The message of Æschylus, broadly stated, is that the gods render to every man according to his works, that men reap in lot what they sow in conduct. In teaching this doctrine he was by no means merely echoing traditional opinion. The older view was that quaintly expressed by Herodotus, that Deity is envious;[1] that is to say, that the gods inflict misery on men not only because they do wrong, but also because they are more prosperous than befits the human state. In a passage in the *Agamemnon* Æschylus refers to this ancient belief as still current, intimates his inability to acquiesce in it, and, though conscious of standing alone,[2] boldly declares his conviction that

> 'Whoso is just, though his wealth like a river
> Flow down, shall be scathless : his house shall rejoice
> In an offspring of beauty for ever.'[3]

---

[1] *Historia*, i. 32. Τὸ θεῖον πᾶν φθονερόν.

[2] Nägelsbach, in *Nachhomerische Theologie*, p. 50, l.ads proof that Æschylus really stood alone in his view—that he was, as he says, μονόφρων.

[3] Blackie's translation of Æschylus, vol. i. p. 47.

THE GREEK TRAGEDIANS: NEMESIS 75

Thus, while, by comparison with Sophocles and still more with Euripides, representing an antiquated theory, Æschylus was himself an innovator, inaugurating a new type of thought on the subject of the moral order. His contribution was an important step onwards in the evolution of providential theory. It aimed at the moralisation of belief concerning the divine dealings with men, by lifting these out of the low region of caprice or jealous passion into the serener atmosphere of fixed ethical principle. It was a doctrine worth preaching with all the enthusiasm that a new and [noble faith can inspire, and Æschylus lost no opportunity of illustrating and enforcing it.

The *Persians* is the only piece among the remains of the ancient drama which draws its material from the history instead of the mythology of Greece. Æschylus may have been tempted to make it an exception because of the splendid opportunity it afforded of illustrating his doctrine of retribution. This drama is a sermon on the ruin that overtakes pride, as exemplified in the disastrous failure of the ambitious attempt of the Persian despot to subdue Greece. The mood of the preacher is that of a Hebrew prophet announcing the doom of Babylon or Tyre, or of Carlyle when he wrote *The French Revolution*. 'To him, as to the old Hebrew prophets, history is a revelation of the will of providence; and the ruin of armies, and the overthrow of nations, are but examples of the handiwork of God.'[1] The gist of the whole dramatic spectacle is given in these few lines:

> 'For wanton pride from blossom grows to fruit,
> The full corn in the ear, of utter woe,
> And reaps a tear-fraught harvest';

or still more tersely in the brief sentence:

> 'Zeus is the avenger of o'er-lofty thoughts,
> A terrible controller.'[2]

The sway of the principle of Nemesis in *individual experience* is pithily proclaimed by Æschylus in these sentences:

> 'Whatsoever evil men do, not less shall they suffer.'[3]

> 'Doubt it not, the evil-doer must suffer.'[4]

> 'Justice from her watchful station
> With a sure-winged visitation
> Swoops, and some in blazing noon
> She for doom doth mark,
> Some in lingering eve, and some
> In the deedless dark.'[5]

These oracles show the punitive aspect of the moral order, which is the thing chiefly insisted on by the poet. But he is not unmindful of the action of Providence in rewarding the good, however humble their station: witness this cheering reflection:

---

[1] Haigh, *The Tragic Drama of the Greeks*, p. 104.
[2] *The Persians*, 816-819 and 823-824; Plumptre's translation.
[3] Οὐ τοῖς κακοῖς τὸ δρᾶμα τοῦ πάθους πλέον, *Agam.* 533 (vide *Sales Att.*).
[4] Δράσαντι δήπου καὶ παθεῖν ὀφείλεται, *Fabula Incerta*.
[5] *Choëphoræ*, 61-65; Blackie's translation.

THE GREEK TRAGEDIANS: NEMESIS

> 'Justice shineth bright,
> In dwellings that are dark and dim with smoke,
> And honours life law-ruled.'[1]

To call in question or deny the doctrine set forth in these and similar utterances Æschylus accounts an impiety. Hear his emphatic protest in the *Agamemnon*:

> 'One there was who said,
> The gods deign not to care for mortal men
> By whom the grace of things inviolable
> Is trampled under foot.
>   No fear of God had he.'[2]

The devout poet not only believes in the punishment of sin, but that the penalty may come in a later generation:

> 'I tell the ancient tale
> Of sin that brought swift doom.
> Till the third age it waits.'[3]

Laius sins, Œdipus his son sins and suffers, Eteocles and Polyneikes his grandsons fall by each other's hands.

He believes that there is heredity of moral evil, sin propagating itself, and entailing a curse upon offspring:

> 'But recklessness of old
> Is wont to breed another recklessness,
> Sporting its youth in human miseries,
> Or now, or then, whene'er the fixed hour comes.'[4]

---

[1] *Agamemnon*, 747-749; Plumptre's translation.
[2] *Ibid.*, 360-364; Plumptre's translation.
[3] *The Seven against Thebes*, 739-741; Plumptre's translation.
[4] *Agamemnon*, 737-740; Plumptre's translation.

78 THE MORAL ORDER OF THE WORLD

But he also believes that there is mercy as well as severity in the visitations of divine justice. Suffering is disciplinary as well as punitive, when rightly taken:

> 'For Jove doth teach men wisdom, sternly wins
> To virtue by the tutoring of their sins.
> Yea! drops of torturing recollection chill
> The sleeper's heart; 'gainst man's rebellious will
> Jove works the wise remorse:
> Dread Powers! on awful seats enthroned, compel
> Our hearts with gracious force.'[1]

Wholesome doctrine all this; but are there no exceptions, no cases of good men suffering and bad men thriving? What Æschylus may have taught on this question in his many lost tragedies we cannot guess, but his extant plays contain one instance of a good man or demigod suffering, without, as we should judge, any sufficient reason. I refer to the Titan Prometheus, chained to a rock for thousands of years because he had been a benefactor to men. What view Æschylus took of the remarkable legend: whether he regarded Prometheus as a real offender suffering just punishment, or as an exception to his own rule, we have not the means of deciding, as the *Prometheus Bound* is the second of three connected dramas on the same theme, and is the only part of the trilogy that has been preserved. Guesses have been made at the nature of the solution which would be given in the concluding part, the

[1] *Agamemnon*, 170-177; Blackie's translation.

Prometheus Unbound. Mr. Symonds holds that
Æschylus regarded the hero as a real transgressor,
that the vilification of Jove as a despot in the
Prometheus Bound is to be understood in a dramatic
sense, and that in the concluding play the Titan
was shown to be really and gravely in the wrong;
guilty of obstinacy eminently tragic, as displaying at once culpable aberration and at the
same time the aberration of a sublime character.[1]
This is a legitimate supposition, but not the only
one possible. Is it not conceivable that in the final
piece the poet represented Jove as adopting an
apologetic rather than a self-justifying tone, as in
reference to the destroying flood we find the sacred
writer putting into Jehovah's mouth the words, 'I
will not again curse the ground any more for man's
sake,'[2] and admitting that he had treated the Titan
with undue severity? Or, granting that to the end
the poet held the hero to be guilty, and tried to show
how, does it follow that, in the words of Mr. Symonds,
'if we possessed the trilogy entire we should see that
Prometheus had been really and grandly guilty'?[3]
Might we not rather have seen the poet trying hard
to prove that, and failing? What if it was a case
not capable of solution on the principle of just
retribution? a case, like that of Job, of too deep

[1] *Studies of the Greek Poets*, 2nd series, pp. 173-188.
[2] Genesis viii. 21.
[3] Symonds' *Studies of the Greek Poets*, 2nd series, p. 188.

import for the Eliphaz theory to cope with, and coming under some other, deeper law?

There is a law, known to us, under which the Titan's experience might with some measure of reason be classified, the law, viz. according to which the world's greatest benefactors are the greatest sufferers. Prometheus, as exhibited by Æschylus, is a signal benefactor. He is what writers on primitive religions call a *culture-hero*, one whose vocation is to teach ignorant untutored races the rudiments of civilisation. He taught rude primitive men the use of fire—stole fire from heaven for their benefit; taught them to speak and to think; instructed them in house-building and ship-building, in medicine, divination, and smelting ore, in the art of using the stars for fixing the order of the seasons: in short, enabled them to pass from the brutish ignorance of the Stone Age, as it is now called, when

> 'no craft they knew
> With woven brick or jointed beam to pile
> The sunward porch; but in the dark earth burrowed
> And housed, like tiny ants, in sunless caves,'[1]

to the intelligence and culture of civilised humanity. The same hero who has been such a benefactor to men had previously done signal service to Zeus, helping him in his war against Kronos and the Titans, and securing for him his celestial throne. Here surely was one who had deserved well at the

[1] *Prometheus Bound*, 457-461; Blackie's translation.

hands of both gods and men! Yet what is his fate? To be chained for long ages to a rock in a Scythian wilderness. The attempt to show that such signal service followed by such barbarous treatment illustrates the justice which makes conduct and lot correspond, must be desperate. One would rather say that such an experience belonged to a morally chaotic age when Zeus had not begun to be just, when in the exercise of a newly-attained sovereignty he could not afford to be either just or generous, but had to be guided in his action by selfish policy rather than by equity, treating as enemies those who had been his greatest friends. The radical defect of the legend from a moral point of view is that the reign of Zeus, the fountain of Justice, has a beginning, involving as a necessary consequence that justice has a beginning also. The divine monarch is thereby subjected to the exigencies of an Eastern despot, whose first use of power is to destroy his rivals, and also those to whom he has been much indebted. How one who was so earnest in proclaiming the reality of a just moral order as Æschylus could be attracted by so uncouth and grim a story, it is as difficult to understand as it is to conjecture how he treated it. Was his motive to meet an objection to his favourite theory, to answer an imaginary opponent asking: On your view, what do you make of the Prometheus legend? And was his answer, in effect, this: 'That is an old-time story; all that happened before the moral order was settled; no such thing could happen now'? How the legend itself arose is another puzzling question. Was it a survival from savage times, modified and transformed in the long course of tradition?[1] Or had it for its fact-basis the observation that benefactors of men often have a hard lot?

The *Eumenides*, not less than the *Prometheus Bound*, possesses a peculiar interest in connection with the Æschylean doctrine of Nemesis. If the latter be an instance of apparently flagrant injustice belonging to a rude age before the moral order was settled, to be explained away or apologised for, the former supplies an instance illustrating the difficulty of applying the principle of retributive justice when right seems to be on both sides. Orestes slays his mother, Clytemnestra, for murdering his father, her husband, Agamemnon. He acts on the counsels of the Delphic oracle, and the Erinnyes pursue him for the deed. Divine beings take opposite sides; Apollo advising the action, the Furies driving to madness the actor. Which of these is in the right? Is Orestes a hero or is he a criminal? or is he both in one? How is the principle of retributive justice to be applied? Must the scales be evenly balanced, inclining to neither side? So it would appear, from

[1] According to Lang (*Myth, Ritual, and Religion*, ii. 31), Mani, the culture-hero of the Maoris, stole fire from heaven, like Prometheus, for his people, among other services, such as inventing barbs for spears and hooks.

the issue of the trial of Orestes before the Areopagus in Athens, which is that the votes for acquittal and for condemnation are equal, Athene giving her casting vote in favour of the accused. The equality in the vote is significant. It is a virtual confession that there are cases in which the theory of retributive justice breaks down; when it is impossible to say how on that theory a man is to be treated; when he cannot be treated either as a well-doer or as an evil-doer without overlooking an essential element in the case; and when the only possible course is a compromise in which the accused gets the benefit of the doubt. The compromise is suggested by Athene, the goddess of *wisdom*, who votes for Orestes and strives to appease and soothe his relentless pursuers. They, however, are characteristically reluctant to be appeased, a point of instructive import in connection with the theory of Nemesis. The Erinnyes of Æschylus are a marvellous creation. They are more than a powerful artistic representation of a legendary group of avenging deities. They possess psychological significance as symbols of the punitive action of conscience. In this point of view certain features in the dramatic presentation are noteworthy. The Furies pursue Orestes, the slayer of his mother, not Clytemnestra, the murderess of his father; he being noble-minded, she thoroughly bad.[1] They

[1] The formal explanation of this fact is that the Furies pursued only when the blood shed was that of kindred; but Mr. Symonds truly

are unwilling to yield to the counsels of wisdom, repeating their wild song of relentless pursuit before yielding to the persuasions of Athene. They do at last submit. But, though constrained to surrender their victim, they are treated with great respect as a power making for righteousness justly inspiring wholesome dread. All this is a parable embodying weighty spiritual truth. The nobler the nature, the more it is liable to become the prey of an evil conscience for acts which, justifiable under a certain aspect, do violence to tender natural affection. A mother may deserve to die, but it is not for a son to be the executioner; and if he be a man of fine nature, he cannot play that part with impunity. Maddening remorse will be the penalty. And that remorse will not be easily exorcised by wise reflection on the ill desert of the dead and the irrevocableness of the deed. It will keep saying, You killed your *mother*. But remorse, though obstinate, need not be unconquerable. The greatest offender may take comfort in the thought that his sin is not unpardonable, and the time comes to many who have been in a hell of torment when they are able to grasp this consoling truth. But though now at rest, they never regret the misery they have passed through. They look back on it with satisfaction as

observes that 'in a deeper sense it was artistically fitting that Clytemnestra should remain unvisited by the dread goddesses. They were the deities of remorse, and she had steeled her soul against the stings of conscience' (*Studies of the Greek Poets*, 1st series, p. 191).

an expiation for their sin. Remorse is the penalty for wrong done to the best feelings of our nature. It is penalty enough. No need for added pains to punish the man who has suffered mental agony through conflict between feelings, both in their own place good, the sense of justice and the affection of love. That agony satisfies the moral order. It is also justified by the moral order. For Orestes is indeed an offender. He should have consulted his conscience, not the Delphic oracle. No need for any other oracle than conscience to tell him that his mother must suffer for her crime by other hands than his.

In passing from Æschylus to Sophocles we become conscious of a considerable change in the moral atmosphere. He is less of a theologian, more of an artist, than his predecessor. The human interest of his story counts for more with him than problems in ethics and religion. He does not deny the Æschylean theory of retribution: on the contrary, he accepts and re-echoes it, but only half-heartedly, with less depth of conviction and fainter emphasis of utterance. He sees that there are many exceptions to the theory, many instances in which no intelligible moral law can be detected; human experiences in which a reign of chance rather than of moral order seems to prevail. Life appears to him a mystery too deep and complex to be explained by any cut-and-dried theory such as that which insists on a uniform correspondence between conduct and lot.

Such being the attitude of Sophocles, we do not expect to find in his dramas either such splendid exemplifications, or such memorable statements, of the law of Nemesis, as we meet with in the pages of Æschylus. Yet sufficient, if not signal, homage is done to the law by occasional sayings such as the few samples which follow.

Œdipus at Colonus thus addresses his friends:

> 'If thou honourest the gods, show thy reverence by thine acts; and remember that their eyes are over all men, regarding both the evil and the good.'[1]

Creon in *Antigone* asks:

> 'Dost thou see the gods honouring evil men?'[2]

The swift punishment of wrong is proclaimed in the same drama in these terms:

> 'Lo, they come, the gods' swift-footed ministers of ill,
> And in an instant lay the wicked low.'[3]

Slow punishment is hinted at in these words from *Œdipus Colonëus*:

> 'The gods see well, though slowly, when one turns from their worship to the madness of impiety.'[4]

Sometimes the expression of this faith is coloured

---

[1] *Œdipus Colonëus*, 277-281, translation from D'Arcy Thomson's *Sales Attici*. [2] *Antigone*, 288.
[3] *Ibid.*, 1104-1106; translated by Plumptre.
[4] *Œdipus Colonëus*, 1536-9.

THE GREEK TRAGEDIANS: NEMESIS   87

by a tinge of doubt. Thus Philoctetes, maddened by a sense of wrong, exclaims:

> 'Perdition seize you all!
> And it shall seize you, seeing ye have wronged
> Him who stands here, if yet the gods regard
> Or right or truth. And full assured am I
> They do regard them.'[1]

Two different, if not incompatible, points of view are combined in these words spoken by Athene to Ulysses:

> 'All human things
> A day lays low, a day lifts up again.
> Yet still the gods love those of temperate mind,
> And hate the bad?'[2]

The sombre sentiment expressed in the first sentence of this extract recurs with significant frequency in the pages of Sophocles. The fleeting, unstable nature of human fortune, irrespective of character, is a trite theme with him. Thus in *Œdipus Tyrannus* the chorus sing:

> 'Ah, race of mortal men,
> How as a thing of nought
> I count ye, though ye live;
> For who is there of men
> That more of blessing knows,
> Than just a little while
> In a vain show to stand,
> And, having stood, to fall?'[3]

---

[1] *Philoctetes*, 1035-39.   [2] *Ajax*, 130-133.
[3] 1186-1193; Plumptre's translation.

In a fragment preserved from an unknown drama the changefulness of life is likened to the phases of the moon:

> ' Human fortunes, good and ill,
> Never stand a moment still;
> To a wheel divine they 're bound,
> Turning ever round and round;
> The moon of our prosperity
> Wanes and waxes in the sky;
> Plays her fickle and constant game,
> Aye a-changing, aye the same:
> See! her crescent of pale light
> Gathers beauty night by night;
> Till, when sphered in perfect grace,
> Gradual she dims her face;
> Lies anon on heaven's blue floor
> A silver bow, and nothing more.' [1]

The phases of the moon, however brief their period, still run through a regular course. The misery of human life, as depicted by Sophocles, includes subjection to the caprice of chance not less than to periodic change. The Messenger in *Antigone* thus delivers his opinion:

> ' I know no life of mortal man which I
> Would either praise or blame. It is but chance
> That raiseth up, and chance that bringeth low,
> The man who lives in good or evil plight,
> And none foretells a man's appointed lot.' [2]

In a fragment from a lost drama, one of the

---

[1] *Fabula Incerta*, translated by D'Arcy Thomson in *Sales Attici*, p. 81.
[2] 1156-1160; translated by Plumptre.

THE GREEK TRAGEDIANS: NEMESIS

dramatis personæ sums up his philosophy of life in these pithy terms:

> 'Say not thou of weal or woe :
> 'Tis big, or little, or not at all :
> For mortal blessings come and go,
> As flit sun-shadows athwart a wall.'[1]

This is dismal enough: human experience without any traceable order or law, given up to the dominion of hazard, so that anything may happen to any man at any moment. But there is something more dismal still: human experience subject to an *evil* order, reversing the awards of the moral order, and assigning prosperity and adversity with sinister indifference to desert. That our poet was keenly alive to the existence of phenomena of this sort appears from another fragment out of the same drama from which our last quotation is taken. I give it in the version supplied by Mr. Symonds:

> ''Tis terrible that impious men, the sons
> Of sinners, even such should thrive and prosper,
> While men by virtue moulded, sprung from sires
> Complete in goodness, should be born to suffer.
> Nay, but the gods do ill in dealing thus
> With mortals ! It were well that pious men
> Should take some signal guerdon at their hands;
> But evil-doers, on their heads should fall
> Conspicuous punishment for deeds ill-done.
> Then should no wicked man fare well and flourish.'[2]

These sentiments concerning the changefulness and chancefulness and moral confusion of life make,

[1] *Aletes*: Thomson's translation; rather free.
[2] Symonds, *Studies of the Greek Poets*, 2nd series, p. 273.

on the whole, a depressing impression. They are pessimistic in tone, though it is not to be supposed that the poet had any intention to teach a full-blown pessimistic theory. He took life as he found it; and he found it dark enough, so dark that in gloomy moments a thoughtful man might be tempted to doubt whether it were worth living. A reflection of this despairing mood may be found in these lines from a choral ode in *Œdipus at Colonus*:

> 'Happiest beyond compare
> Never to taste of life;
> Happiest in order next,
> Being born, with quickest speed
> Thither again to turn
> From whence we came.'[1]

And in this from *The Maidens of Trachis*:

> 'On two short days, or more, our hopes are vain;
> The morrow is as nought, till one shall show
> The present day in fair prosperity.'[2]

Yet we must never forget that the man who made his dramatic characters utter such sombre sentiments, also put into the mouth of Antigone that grand declaration concerning the eternal unwritten laws of God that know no change, and are not of to-day nor yesterday, and that must be obeyed in preference to the temporary commandments of men.[3] One who believes in these eternal laws of duty, as expressing the inmost mind of deity, and that reckons com-

---

[1] 1223-1228; Plumptre's translation.
[2] 943-946; Plumptre's translation.   [3] *Antigone*, 455-459.

pliance with them at all hazards the supreme obligation, cannot with propriety be classed with pessimists, though that Antigone should suffer for her loyalty to these sovereign behests may appear to him a great mystery. If he does not understand Antigone's fate, he at least sees in it a moral sublimity which redeems life from worthlessness and vulgarity. Nay, the nobleness of her self-sacrifice seems to bring him to the threshold of a great discovery: that such a life cannot be wasted, but must possess redemptive value. What but this is the meaning of these words spoken to Antigone by her father Œdipus: 'One soul acting in the strength of love, is better than a thousand to atone.'[1] A single utterance like this may not justify the conclusion that the poet had fully grasped the principle of vicarious atonement, but it does show that the idea was beginning to dawn on his mind.

It is now, happily, quite unnecessary to waste time in defending *Euripides* against the prejudiced criticism of scholars who, taking Sophocles as the model, see in him nothing but artistic blemishes, or the still more prejudiced diatribes of religious philosophers who, biassed by pet theories, see in him nothing but an impious scoffer. We can afford to smile at the oracular verdict pronounced upon him

[1] Vide Plumptre's 'Essay on the Life and Writings of Sophocles,' vol. i. of his translation, pp. lxxvii.-xcix.

by Bunsen, that his theory of the universe is that of *Candide*, and that the religion of Æschylus and Sophocles was as repugnant to him as that of the Psalms and Prophets was to Voltaire.[1] The man whose dramatic productions have been a delight to poets like Milton, Goethe, and Browning, can dispense with the patronage of learned critics; and as for his religious and ethical bent, it is sufficiently guaranteed by the fact of his belonging to the Socratic circle. It will be well to come to the study of his sentiments on the topics which concern us with this fact in our minds, and to remember that when a play of Euripides was to be put upon the stage Socrates was ever likely to be one of the spectators. Euripides was doubtless a sceptic in reference to the mythology of Greece, but that in no way impugns the sincerity and depth of his ethical and religious convictions. He believed in God if not in the gods, he reverenced moral law, and he had no doubt as to the reality of a moral order, though it may be that he did not rest his faith therein on the same religious foundation as Æschylus. It may be well to offer a few vouchers of this last statement before going on to notice the more distinctive con-

[1] *God in History*, ii. 224. For a chillingly unappreciative estimate of Euripides vide *Religion in Greek Literature*, by Dr. Lewis Campbell, 1898. According to this author, Euripides was simply a melodramatist whose task was rather to interest than to instruct; his connection or sympathy with Socrates is regarded as doubtful; the examples of self-devotion which brighten his pages are spoken of as recurring 'with almost monotonous frequency.'

tribution of this great Master of song to the doctrine of Providence.

The *Hercules Furens* contains an explicit testimony to the Power-not-ourselves making for righteousness. Just before, it is true, the chorus have made a rather profane and senseless complaint that the gods have not given to the good, as the unmistakable stamp of their worth, the privilege of being a second time young, so that they might be as easily recognised as the stars at sea by sailors.[1] But for this inconsiderate outburst the poet makes ample amends by putting into the mouths of the chorus this distinct confession of faith in the moral order:

> 'The gods from on high regard the wicked and the good.
> Wealth and prosperity try the hearts of men, and lead them on to the ways of unrighteousness;
> For he that is prosperous saith within himself: surely the evil days will never come:
> Therefore driveth he furiously in the race; and heedeth not the limits of the course;
> And he striketh his wheel against a stone of stumbling; and dasheth in pieces the chariot of his prosperity.'[2]

This also from *Ion* has the ring of conviction in it. It is the last word in a drama replete with beautiful wise thought:

> 'Let the man who worships the divine beings be of good cheer, when his house is visited with misfortune. For in the end the worthy obtain their deserts and the wicked, as is meet, shall not prosper.'[3]

---

[1] *Hercules Furens*, 646-660.
[2] *Ibid.*, 753-760; Thomson's translation.   [3] *Ion*, 1620-1623.

Artemis in *Hippolytus* declares that 'the gods have no pleasure in the death of the righteous, but they destroy the wicked with their children and homes.'[1]

Euripides is familiar with such great truths of the moral order as these: that confession takes a burden off the heart,[2] and that in all human thought and action God co-operates.[3] But it is specially to be noted that he has some insight into the 'method of inwardness,' a glimpse, that is to say, of the truth that the rewards and punishments of human conduct are to be sought not merely or chiefly in the sphere of outward life, but in the state of the heart. He understands, at least dimly, that to be spiritually-minded is life and peace. Witness this hymn of Hippolytus to Artemis:

> 'For thee this woven garland from a mead
> Unsullied have I twined, O Queen, and bring.
> There never shepherd dares to feed his flock,
> Nor steel of sickle came: only the bee
> Roveth the springtide mead undesecrate:
> And Reverence watereth it with river-dews.
> They which have heritage of self-control
> In all things, not taught, but the pure in heart—
> These there may gather flowers, but none impure.
> Now Queen, dear Queen, receive this anadem,
> From reverent hand to deck thy golden hair;
> For to me sole of men this grace is given
> That I be with thee, converse hold with thee,
> Hearing thy voice, yet seeing not thy face.
> And may I end life's race as I began.'[4]

---

[1] *Hippolytus*, 1329-30. [2] *Ion*, 874-6. [3] *Supplices*, 736-8.
[4] *Hippolytus*, 73-87. The translation is by Arthur S. Way, *The Tragedies of Euripides in English Verse*, vol. i. p. 127.

That the penalty of wrongdoing is also to be sought within seems to be hinted at in this fragment from a lost drama:

> 'Think you that sins leap up to heaven aloft
> On wings, and then that on Jove's red-leaved tablets
> Some one doth write them, and Jove looks at them
> In judging mortals? Not the whole broad heaven,
> If Jove should write our sins, would be enough,
> Nor he suffice to punish them. But Justice
> Is here, is somewhere near us.'[1]

These extracts seem to bring us within measurable distance of New Testament ethics. But we get nearer still to Christian thought along a different path. The light of that day whose dim dawn we descried in Sophocles shines on the pages of Euripides. He sees the glory and the power of *self-sacrifice*. He understands that the good man's life is not self-centred, but rather is a fountain of benefit to all around. In the *Children of Hercules*, which contains one of the most signal examples of sacrifice, he opens with this sentiment put into the mouth of Iolaus, the nephew of Hercules: 'This has long been my opinion: the just man lives for his neighbours, but the man whose mind is bent on gain is useless to the city, hard to conciliate, good only to himself.'

The novelty of this point of view—living for others the mark of goodness—may be seen by comparing

[1] Fragment from *Melanippe*, translation from Symonds, 2nd series, p. 293.

the behaviour of Iphigenia, daughter of Agamemnon, when she is being sacrificed at Aulis, as described by Æschylus, with the account given of the same scene by Euripides. In the *Agamemnon* of the earlier poet the sacrificed maiden is simply a reluctant victim, casting at those who offered her to the gods a piteous, piercing glance, and unable, though wishing, to speak.[1] In the *Iphigenia in Aulis* of Euripides, on the other hand, the daughter of King Agamemnon, after a struggle with natural feeling, rises at length to the heroic mood of self-devotion, and seeks to reconcile her outraged mother to the inevitable by such arguments as these: Greece looks to me; on me depends the prosperous voyage of the fleet to Troy and the destruction of that city; I shall have the happy renown of having saved my country; I may not be too attached to life, for as a common boon to the Greeks, not for yourself only, you bore me.[2] The opportunity it affords him of exemplifying this mood is the chief, if not sole, source of the poet's interest in the whole story. He has no faith in the oracles of soothsayers which pronounced the sacrifice necessary, no faith in the gods who demanded it, no faith in its efficacy, no faith even in its reality; for in his presentation of the legend the victim is rescued and appears afterwards as a priestess in *Tauris*. But he has faith in self-sacrifice as the highest virtue, and he loses no opportunity of

[1] *Agamemnon*, 230-235.   [2] *Iphigenia in Aulis*, 1347-1365.

THE GREEK TRAGEDIANS: NEMESIS 97

eulogising it, as in the instances of Menœkeus in the *Phœnissæ*, who, in accordance with the prophecy of Tiresias, kills himself to save Thebes,[1] and of Polyxena in *Hecuba*.[2]

The most pathetic instances, however, are those of *Macaria* and *Alcestis*. In the case of Macaria, the daughter of Hercules, the element of voluntariness is very conspicuous. The oracle demands that some one shall die, but does not indicate the particular victim. Theseus, though willing now, as at all times, to defend the cause of the innocent, refuses to give any of his family as a sacrifice for the Heraclidæ. In this crisis Macaria comes to the rescue and offers herself. Iolaus, guardian of the children of Hercules, approves her spirit, but to soften the rigour of a hard fate proposes that the victim should be determined by lot. To which Macaria replies in these remarkable terms: 'I will not die by lot, for there is no merit in that. Do not speak of it, old man. But if ye choose to take me, ready as I am, I willingly give my life for these, but not under compulsion.'[3]

The most signal example of self-sacrificing love is supplied in the beautiful tale of Alcestis related in the tragedy of the same name. Admetus, king of Pheræ, in Thessaly, is sick and about to die. Apollo, who had formerly served the king as a

[1] *The Phœnician Damsels*, 990-1015.
[2] *Vide* lines 339-375.
[3] *Heraclidæ*, 547-557.

herdsman, in reward for past kindness asks and obtains from the Fates a respite for Admetus, on condition that he find some one willing to die for him. The king asks all his friends in turn to do him this service, but in vain. At last his wife, Alcestis, hearing how matters stand, offers to grant the boon all others had refused. She sickens and dies accordingly. Hercules arrives shortly after, and, on learning what has happened, goes to the tomb of the deceased, brings her back to life and restores her to her husband.

In his *Symposium* Plato alludes to this story as illustrating the doctrine that love is ever ready to do anything that may be required of it for the good of the object loved, even to die in its behalf (ὑπεραποθνήσκειν). He could not have chosen a better example. Love was the sole motive of Alcestis. She does not nerve herself to the needful pitch of heroic fortitude by considerations of patriotism or posthumous fame. She makes no fuss about the matter, nor does the poet make it for her. She is not brought on the stage resolving to die, and telling what has helped her to adopt such a resolution. The curtain is lifted on a woman lying sick on a couch. She speaks but once, to bid farewell to her husband, and to utter her last wishes. Her praises are sung for her, not by her. An attendant relates with enthusiasm her behaviour on the morning of her last day, in terms of exquisite

THE GREEK TRAGEDIANS: NEMESIS 99

pathos. The choral odes referring to her noble action are singularly beautiful. One declares that Alcestis will be a theme of song to the poets of Greece in all after ages; another sings of the inevitable dominion of death, and then of the consolations of posthumous fame in these glowing terms:—

> 'Deem not she sleeps like those devoid of fame,
>   Unconscious in the lap of earth;
> Such homage as the gods from mortals claim
> Each traveller shall pay her matchless worth,
> Digressing from his road; and these bold thoughts,
> Expressed in no faint language, utter o'er her grave:
> "She died to save her Lord, and now
> She dwells among the blest.
> Hail, Sainted Matron! and this realm befriend."'[1]

The love of Alcestis is beautiful, but the occasion of her self-sacrifice does not command our respect. Indeed, none of the occasions of self-sacrifice in the dramas of Euripides do this. They are, in other instances, the result of superstition; in the one before us, of selfishness. Why could Admetus not die himself, after having lived sufficiently long? Probably Euripides had no more respect for the occasion than we have; no more respect, I may add, than he had for the legend that Alcestis was brought back to life by Hercules. There is probably truth in the view of Mr. Verrall that the poet did not believe that Alcestis was really dead.[2] His

[1] *Alcestis*, 1007-1014; Wodhull's translation. Cf. Way's translation in *The Tragedies of Euripides in English Verse*, vol. i. p. 51.
[2] Verrall's *Euripides the Rationalist*, p. 75.

point was that Alcestis was *willing* to die. And as for the occasions of self-sacrifice, he took this one, and all the rest, as they were furnished to him by tradition. They were welcome as giving him the opportunity of preaching his favourite doctrine that the spirit of self-devotion is the soul of goodness.

This doctrine was an important contribution to ethics. How far Euripides was aware of the extent to which life afforded natural and most real opportunities for the display of the self-sacrificing temper of love we have no means of knowing. It may be assumed that it was a subject possessing keen interest to his mind, and that he was a close observer of all illustrative phenomena. It may also be assumed that in utilising the traditional data supplied by heroic legends he had something more important and specific in view than to illustrate the 'pluck,' as it has been called ($εὐψυχία$), of Greek men and women.[1] Not the physical virtue of 'pluck,' though that element might have its place, but the high moral virtue of self-devotion, was his theme. And, seeing that virtue awakened in his soul such an ardent enthusiasm, he could not have found it hard to believe that a moral order which afforded large scope for its exercise was not an evil order but rather a beneficent one, which might have been

[1] Symonds, *Studies of the Greek Poets*, 1s. series, p. 212. Mr. Symonds sees in the value set on $εὐψυχία$ by Euripides a reflection of the advancing tendencies of philosophy containing the germ of the Stoical doctrine of $καρτερία$.

appointed by a benignant deity. It has indeed been denied that Euripides had any such belief, while his merit in proclaiming the vicarious nature of love is fully acknowledged. Professor Watson remarks: 'It is only in Euripides that we find something like an anticipation of the Christian idea that self-realisation is attained through self-sacrifice. In Euripides, however, this result is reached by a surrender of his faith in divine justice. Man, he seems to say, is capable of heroic self-sacrifice, at the prompting of natural affection, but this is the law of human nature, not of the divine nature. Thus in him morality is divorced from religion, and therefore there is over all his work the sadness which inevitably follows from a sceptical distrust of the existence of any objective principle of goodness.'[1] I am not satisfied that this is a well-grounded judgment. The spirit of Euripides, I believe, was the spirit of Socrates, the martyr, and the devout believer in a beneficent deity. There may be sadness in his writings, but there is neither cynicism nor pessimism. An admirer of heroic love cannot be a pessimist. He sees in love's sacrifice not merely the darkest, but the brightest feature in the world's history. All that is needed to make him an optimist is that he have faith in a God in harmony with his own ethical creed: admiring self-sacrifice; yea, himself capable of it. That Euripides

[1] *Christianity and Idealism*, p. 39.

had fully found such a God I do not assert. That he was on the way to the discovery I cannot doubt. The idea of God as the absolutely good was familiar to the Socratic circle, as we learn from the Dialogues of Plato, and such a man as Euripides could neither be unacquainted with it nor fail to perceive its value. It is true that in his pages, as in those of his brother-dramatists, the dark shadow of a morally indifferent Fate (Μοῖρα) now and then makes its appearance, as in these lines:

> 'A bow of steel is hard to bend,
>   And stern a proud man's will;
> But Fate, that shapeth every end,
>   Is sterner, harder still;
> E'en God within the indented groove
> Of Fate's resolve Himself must move.'[1]

This utterance points to a species of dualism, a conflict between a benignant Providence and a blind force which exercises sway over both gods and men. There is a dualism in Plato also. A certain intractableness in matter resists the will of the Good Spirit so that he cannot make the world perfect, but only as good as possible.[2] But the thing to be thankful for in Plato is the clear perception that the will of God is absolutely good, if his power be limited. Euripides also, I think, had a glimpse of this truth.

---

[1] D'Arcy Thomson's *Sales Attici*, p. 213, based on a chorus in the *Alcestis* (962-981). For a literal translation *vide* Way, *The Tragedies of Euripides*, vol. i. p. 49.

[2] *Vide* Lecture X.

LECTURE IV

THE STOICS: PROVIDENCE

THE system of thought and the way of life which go by the name of Stoicism constitute a phenomenon not less remarkable in its fashion than the ethical wisdom of the great Greek tragedians. Zeno, Cleanthes, and Chrysippus, the founders of the school of the porch, are in some respects as notable a triad as Æschylus, Sophocles, and Euripides. Their distinction, however, lies, not like that of the three poets, in literary genius, but in moral intensity. Their thoughts of God, man, duty, and destiny, and the life in which these found practical embodiment, present the best religious product of Greek philosophy. There is room indeed for doubt whether that philosophy can be credited with the exclusive parentage of so worthy an offspring. The influence of Socrates is of course very manifest in the ethical spirit of the Stoics. But something more than Socrates seems to be discernible there: something new, foreign; a stern temper in striking contrast to Hellenic lightheartedness; a seriousness reminding us more of the gravity of a Hebrew prophet than of the gaiety of a Greek philosopher.

This first impression is seen to be more than a passing fancy when it is considered that the early masters and scholars of Stoicism were actually, for the most part, strangers from the East, and not a few of them natives of Semitic towns or colonies. Zeno, the first founder, was from Citium, a Phœnician colony in Cyprus, and he commonly went by the name of 'the Phœnician,' a fact which bears witness to his Semitic origin. Thus the hypothesis readily suggests itself that race enters as a factor in the genesis of Stoicism, that the peculiarities of this new phase of Greek philosophy are the unmistakable product of Semitic genius. This view has been adopted and earnestly advocated by such competent writers as Sir Alexander Grant[1] and Bishop Lightfoot.[2] Their high authority cannot lightly be disregarded; but if we do not feel able to share their confidence as to the certainty of this racial theory, we shall do well at least to lay to heart the ethical affinity which it is adduced to explain. The Stoic temper and the Semitic temper are kindred. The Stoic philosophy is, so to speak, Hebrew wisdom transplanted into Greek soil; like the latter, intensely ethical in spirit, and practical in tendency. In both we discern the same leading characteristics: 'the

[1] *Vide* his *Ethics of Aristotle*, 3rd edition, vol. i. Essay VI.
[2] *Vide* his *St. Paul's Epistle to the Philippians*, Dissertation II.

recognition of the claims of the individual soul, the sense of personal responsibility, the habit of judicial introspection, in short the subjective view of ethics.'[1]

Stoicism was at once intensely ethical and intensely individualistic. It contemplated the universe from the view-point of the individual man, and the thing of supreme interest for it in the individual man was his moral consciousness. The latter feature, as we have seen, may be traced partly to the influence of Socrates, partly to the influence of the Semitic spirit; the former was the natural result of the complete breakdown of the political life of Greece due to the Macedonian conquest. It is necessary to note the time at which the Stoical movement made its appearance. Like all great spiritual movements, it came when the world was prepared for it and needed it. It was the offspring of despair in more senses than one, but very specially of political despair. When public life offered no opportunities, what could a thoughtful man do but retire within himself, and concentrate his energies on the discipline of his own spirit? And yet the same circumstances which brought about this contraction of interest led also to a great expansion. If the glory of Greece had vanished, *humanity* remained; in place of the *city*, the philosopher had the *wide world* as a home for his soul. And so it

[1] Lightfoot on *Philippians*, p. 272.

came to pass that the system of thought which most worthily met the need of the time was cosmopolitan in spirit as well as individualistic. The Stoic, while intensely conscious of himself as a moral personality, was also not less conscious of belonging to a great human brotherhood. It has been reckoned among the contradictions of Stoicism that, 'with the hardest and most uncompromising isolation of the individual, it proclaims the most expansive view of his relations to all around.'[1] In reality, however, these two contrasted qualities are but complementary aspects of the same fundamental point of view. The ethical is universal; the ethical individual is but a particular embodiment of that which constitutes the essential element common to humanity. The same combination of individualism with universalism appears in the later prophetic literature of Israel under similar outward circumstances, national misfortune opening the eyes of Hebrew seers and Greek sages alike to the inner world of the soul and the outer world of mankind.

Stoicism was not the only philosophy in Greece at the beginning of the third century before the Christian era. Philosophic activity in the post-Aristotelian period gave rise to three rival schools—that of the Stoics, that of the Epicureans, and that of the Sceptics. All three had the same fundamental characteristic of subjectivity, retirement within the self, and the same general temper of self-sufficiency,

[1] Bishop Lightfoot on *Philippians*, p. 296.

or independence of outward things. The two first-named schools, to confine our attention to them, differed in their conception of the chief good. The Stoics placed it in *virtue*, the Epicureans in freedom from disagreeable feelings, or, in one word, in *pleasure*. The mere co-existence of a school having 'pleasure' for its watchword lends added emphasis and significance to the Stoic position. It is not necessary to judge severely the philosophers of the garden, and to impute to them all the abuses to which their leading tenet too easily gave rise. Epicurus did not undervalue virtue; he maintained that there could be no true pleasure dissociated from virtue. Seneca states the point at issue between him and the masters of the porch in these terms, 'whether virtue be the cause of the highest good, or itself the highest good.'[1] With the Stoics he espouses the latter alternative, and repudiates with indignation not merely the placing of virtue under pleasure, as a lower category and mere means to pleasure as an end, but the comparing of virtue with pleasure at all. 'Virtue,' he says, 'is the despiser and enemy of pleasure; leaping away as far as possible from it, it is more at home with labour and pain than with that effeminate good.'[2] The Roman representative of Stoicism may be accepted as a true interpreter of the respective attitudes of the two opposed systems. Taking them

[1] *De Beneficiis*, lib. IV. cap. ii.   [2] *Eodem loco*.

at his estimate, one cannot but feel that the Stoic, whatever his defects, has the nobler bearing. Much depends on what you put first. It is a great thing to say: virtue, duty, is first; especially when you know that others are saying something very different. Then your doctrine means: virtue first, all else, whatever is comprehended under enjoyment, second; virtue first and at all hazards, be the consequences what they may; pleasure or pain, it is all one. This is a heroic programme, and the man who is able to carry it out will certainly live to better purpose than the man whose programme is: enjoyment the *summum bonum*, but enjoyment obtained on the most rational and virtuous methods possible.

The Stoic, while sternly opposed to making pleasure the chief good, did not refuse it a place, under any form, in human experience. He held, however, that the only pleasure or happiness worth having was that connected with right conduct. Virtue, in his view, was its own reward, and vice its own penalty. Virtue is self-sufficient; nothing else is needed to make a wise man happy. This doctrine makes the wise man entirely independent of everything outside his own will. The good man is satisfied from himself, and perfectly free from all dependence on outward good. Outward goods, so-called, are really things indifferent. There is nothing good but the absolute good, a good will; nothing evil but the absolute evil, an evil will. Health,

THE STOICS: PROVIDENCE

riches, honour, life, however much valued by ordinary men, fall under the category of the indifferent, for every one who knows the secret of the blessed life.[1] This view of outward good kills *passion*. The passions are the result of wrong estimates of external good and evil. From the irrational estimate of present good arises the passion of pleasurable feeling, of future good that of desire; out of a false conception of present evil comes sorrow, and of future evil, fear.[2] The wise man, subject to no illusions, is passionless. He feels pain, but, not regarding it as an evil, he suffers neither torment nor fear; he may be despised and evil-treated, but he cannot be disgraced; he is without vanity, because honour and shame touch him not; he is not subject to the passion of anger, nor does he need this irrational affection as an aid to valour; he is even devoid of sympathy, for why should he pity others for experiences which are matters of indifference to himself?[3]

Nothing is more characteristic of Stoicism than this doctrine of *apathy* as the distinctive mood of wisdom. Mr. Huxley tells us that he finds it difficult to discover any very great difference between

[1] Zeno reckoned among the ἀδιάφορα life, death, honour, dishonour, pain, pleasure, riches, poverty, disease, health, and the like. *Vide* Stobæus, *Eclogæ*, vol. ii. 92.

[2] The Stoics, with Zeno at their head, reckoned desire, fear, pain, and pleasure the four chief passions. *Vide* Stobæus, *Eclogæ*, ii. 166.

[3] *Vide* Zeller, *Die Philosophie der Griechen*, iii. pp. 216, 217, where vouchers for these details are given.

the *Apatheia* of the Stoics and the *Nirvana* of Buddhists.[1] The one does readily suggest the other to our minds, and the two words do denote states of soul essentially the same. But the calm retreat of passionless peace is reached by different paths in the two systems. It is a case of extremes meeting, a common result arrived at by entirely opposite interpretations of life, that of the Buddhist being pessimistic, while that of the Stoic was optimistic. Life is full of misery, said the Buddhist; from birth to death human existence is one long unbroken experience of sorrow and vexation of spirit, therefore extinguish desire and so escape finally and for ever from pain. The so-called ills of life, said the Stoic, do not deserve the name; the so-called goods of life are no better entitled to the designation: treat all alike with disdain and so possess your soul in serenity. The relation of the two systems to objects of desire is diverse. Buddhism is ascetic, ever engaged in the work of extirpating desire. Stoicism finds its inner satisfaction 'in ignoring not in mortifying desires.' The Stoic's attitude is 'nonchalance, the charter of his self-sufficiency.'[2] The diversity in temper goes along with a corresponding diversity of view in regard to the universe at large. The Buddhist deemed the existence of the world,

---

[1] *Evolution and Ethics*, p. 76.
[2] *Vide* Rendall's translation of *Marcus Aurelius Antoninus to Himself*, introduction, p. xlii. (1898).

THE STOICS: PROVIDENCE

as of the individual man, an evil. As a man is born because he has done wrong in a previous state of existence, so the world exists to afford scope for the law of moral retribution displaying itself in the apportionment of rewards and penalties. The Stoic, on the other hand, took an optimistic view of the world. He believed in the rationality of the universe. Therefore he defined virtue alternatively as living according to our own reason, or as living in accordance with the nature of things, in harmony with the laws of the cosmos. The Buddhist view of birth and death as evils, and penalties of sin, would never enter his mind, or seem other than an absurdity if suggested by another person. He would have said: birth and death both belong to the universal order, therefore they are not evil. The natural order was to be accepted loyally, without demur. The will of nature, said Epictetus, can be learned from what is common to all. How do we take the death of another man's wife or child? We say it is human. Say the same as to your own.[1] Faith in nature, with frank submission to its appointments, was part of the piety of Stoicism.

This faith, as held by the Stoics, was associated with and buttressed by a physico-theological system of thought. Though before all things practical, ethical philosophers, they had their science of nature, which was at the same time their theology. Their

[1] *Enchiridion*, cxxxiii.

physics were not original, being to a very large extent simply an appropriation of the opinions of the pre-Socratic philosopher Heraclitus, who taught that fire, or æther, was the original substance of the universe, identified this primæval fire with God, to whom he ascribed the properties at once of matter and of mind, and represented the history of the world as a gradual transformation of the primæval fire into the elements, and of the elements into the primæval fire; that is, as consisting in an endless alternation of world-making and world-burning. The theological aspect of this cosmological speculation is what chiefly concerns us. In the hands of the Stoics the resulting idea of God is a strange mixture of Materialism, Pantheism, and Theism. God, like all things that really exist, is material and the source of all matter. He is one with the world which is evolved out of His essence, as in the theory of Spinoza; God and Nature are the same thing under different aspects. Yet, unlike Spinoza, the Stoics introduced into their idea of God theistic elements reminding us of the characteristic conceptions of Socrates, who regarded the world teleologically, plied the argument from design for the existence of a good God, and asserted the reality of a benignant providential order, having man for the special object of its care. In these respects the Stoics were disciples of Socrates, as in their physics they were followers of Heraclitus.

THE STOICS: PROVIDENCE

Accustomed as we, in modern times, are to sharply defined contrasts between materialistic, pantheistic, and theistic theories, we are apt to wonder how such heterogeneous elements could ever have been brought together in even the crudest attempt to form an idea of God. Unless we be on our guard we may draw from the materialism of the Stoics very mistaken and prejudicial inferences as to their view of Deity, confounding them with those who cherish a purely mechanical idea of the universe and have no faith in the exceptional significance of man arising out of his spiritual nature; whereas, in truth, as to these vital questions their creed was the same as that held by modern theists. The two forms of materialism, as has been pointed out by a French writer on Stoicism, are not only distinct, but of opposite tendency. 'While the materialism of our day wishes to recognise the existence of the corporeal and sensible only, to get rid for ever of the ideal realities and inaccessible essences, the physics of the Stoics made everything material in fear lest the spiritual realities should vanish. The modern materialist says: "All is body, therefore thought is nothing but a mode of body." The Stoic said: "All is body, and thought being corporeal is a substance, more subtle without doubt, but as real as are the objects our senses perceive." It is not to withdraw the world from the watchful authority of a sovereign intelligence, but rather to give to that supreme reason efficacious power everywhere present that the Stoics conceived God as co-extensive with the universe.'[1]

We must take ancient thought about God as we find it, looking indulgently on the materialistic dross, and giving full value to the theistic gold. If we keep in view the Semitic origin of the founders of Stoicism, we shall remember that speculative consistency was not to be expected of them, and that ethical wisdom was more in their line than cosmological theory. It is difficult to say in what precise relation such theory as they did promulgate stood to the ethical doctrines which constitute the chief ground of their claim to serious consideration at this date. Did the ethical system, first formulated, create a desire for a congruous and confirmatory theory of the universe, or did the masters of the school bring to their ethical studies such a theory cut-and-dried, and always at hand to give direction to thought in the answering of puzzling questions? Were ethical problems first solved and then God conceived in harmony with the solutions, or was the idea of God first fixed, then employed to control moral judgments? The question has special interest in reference to the Stoic doctrine concerning things indifferent. That doctrine seems a paradox, and it is natural to ask, Would the men who promulgated

[1] F. Ogereau, *Essai sur le Système Philosophique des Stoïciens*, p. 297.

THE STOICS: PROVIDENCE

it have adopted so extreme a position as that pain, disease, privation, dishonour, are not evils, unless they had been required to do so by their theological creed? Was it not a case of *a priori* reasoning? 'The soul of the world is just; the world in all its arrangements is rational, because the work of a Supreme Reason. The Providence of God, like God Himself, must be perfect; therefore it must ever be well with the good; therefore human happiness must depend on the state of the soul, not on outward experiences, which, whether pleasant or the reverse, are to be regarded as of no account.' That they argued thus is not inconceivable. But it is against this view that in their doctrine of the indifferent the Stoics were not original any more than in their materialistic physics, or in their teleological conception of the world. In this, as in some other important respects, they were disciples of the Cynics. Speaking generally, the Stoics were original in the spirit rather than in the matter of their teaching. They borrowed freely from all preceding schools, and blended the separate contributions into a harmonious system under the inspiration of their characteristic moral enthusiasm. This fervour saved them from being pure eclectics, and converted what might otherwise have been a mere patchwork of opinions into a living organism of thought, in which all parts of the system acted and reacted on each other. When the body of Stoical doctrine is thus conceived, the question above formulated is superseded. It is no longer a question of exclusive action of the ethics on the theology, or of the theology on the ethics. Each in turn influenced the other. Belief in a benignant Providence confirmed the doctrine of the *adiaphora*, and this doctrine made that belief easier.

Assuming that such a relation of interaction existed between the doctrines of Providence and of things indifferent in the minds of the Stoical teachers, we may regard them as making an important contribution to the solution of the problem, How is the providential order to be justified in view of the facts of human experience? It is an anticipation of what Mr. Matthew Arnold calls the Christian 'method of inwardness'; the method, that is to say, of seeking happiness within, in the state of the heart, rather than without in the state of fortune. The Stoics taught: It must always be well with the good man; his felicity lies in a well-ordered mind, which is life and peace. The outward ills which befall him are of little account; at the worst, they are light, easily tolerable afflictions. This is obviously a decided advance upon the Old Testament view, whether we have regard to the more ancient theory championed by Eliphaz in the Book of Job, according to which outward lot and conduct uniformly correspond—no innocent person perishing—or to the modified conceptions of prophets like Jeremiah, which recognised

THE STOICS: PROVIDENCE

suffering on the part of the righteous as a fact, but as a fact full of mystery and furnishing ground for surprise and complaint.[1] It is equally an advance on the ideas of the elder Greek tragedians, Æschylus and Sophocles, which correspond respectively to those of Eliphaz and Jeremiah. It falls short, on the other hand, of the lofty thought enunciated in the oracles of the second Isaiah, and re-echoed by Euripides, that the sufferings of the good are not a dismal fate involuntarily endured, but the free self-sacrifice of love cheerfully offered for the benefit of others.[2] Stoicism had not humanity enough to rise to such a conception. Even when recognising the existence of such instances of heroism, it would look rather to the benefit accruing to the hero himself than to that accruing to others. In discoursing on the benefits derivable from all external ills, even death, Epictetus uses as an illustration the story of Menœkeus, on which he makes this comment: 'Think you, Menœkeus reaped little benefit when he devoted himself to death? Did he not preserve his piety towards his country, his magnanimity, his fidelity, his generosity? Had he preferred to live would he not have lost all these, and acquired instead the opposite vices—cowardice, meanspiritedness, lack of patriotism, ignoble love of life?'[3] The point made is, in its own place, not unimportant. It

---

[1] *Vide* Lectures VI. and VII.   [2] *Vide* Lecture III.
[3] *Dissertationes*, Book iii. c. 20, 1.

is something to be able to say that outward ill, so far from robbing the good of happiness, may even promote the increase of that happiness by strengthening the virtue which is the sole fountain of all true felicity. But when that alone is said in connection with instances of self-sacrifice, a lesson is missed of far greater importance for the vindication of the providential order than the merely homeward-bound view of affliction as useful to the individual sufferer.

The method of inwardness, as pursued by the Stoics, is open to the objection that it makes the way to peace too much of a short cut. They minimised unduly the outward ills of life. It sounds very philosophic to say: To the good no real evil can happen, as to the evil no real good; and to ply the sorrow-laden with such admonitions as these: 'A son has died; it depends not on the will of man, therefore it is not an evil. Cæsar has condemned you—an involuntary event, therefore not evil; you have been led to prison—so be it. Jove has done all these things well, because he has made you able to bear such things, made you magnanimous, provided that no real evil should be in such experiences, made it possible for you to be happy in spite of such experiences.'[1] Men within the school might make themselves believe that such considerations were conclusive, but those outside could not be expected to acquiesce. It is not reasonable to ask men to accept

[1] Epictetus, *Dissertationes*, iii. 8.

bereavement, condemnation by a judicial tribunal, imprisonment, as matters of indifference, because involuntary so far as the sufferer is concerned. Men naturally wish to know how such events are to be construed with reference to the will of the Supreme. And when it is considered that the masters of the school were wont to point to suicide as a door of escape always open for the unhappy, it becomes doubtful if even they were satisfied with their own philosophy. Why fly from life if outward ill be illusory? If there be a benignant Providence at work in human experience, why not live on through all possible experience, rejoicing evermore, praying without ceasing, in everything giving thanks?

Dissatisfaction with the Stoic justification of Providence finds forcible expression in Cicero's *De Natura Deorum*, where, after the creed of the porch has been sympathetically expounded by one interlocutor, Balbus, another, Cotta, is introduced sharply criticising it. Among the trains of reflection put into Cotta's mouth the following has a prominent place. If the gods really care for the human race they ought to make all men good; at least they ought to look after the interest of those who are good. But do they? Is it not the fact that there are many instances of good men suffering undeserved calamity, and of bad men prospering? The argument winds up with the remark: 'Time would fail if I wished to recount the examples of good men overtaken with bad fortune and of evil men favoured with good fortune.' Of course the case of Socrates receives prominent mention. 'What,' asks the sceptic, 'shall I say of Socrates, whose death, as I read, always brings the tears into my eyes? Surely if the gods pay any attention to human affairs they exercise very little discrimination.'[1]

Here is the age-long problem of the sufferings of the righteous stated, if not solved in the pages of the philosophic Roman orator. The early Stoics, far from solving the problem, hardly even stated it, their exaggerated doctrine concerning the indifference of outward ill preventing them. What grand possibilities of sublime wrestling with an apparently unfathomable mystery they thereby missed we know from the Book of Job. Suppose Zeno, Cleanthes, and Chrysippus had occupied the place of Eliphaz, Bildad, and Zophar, what would they have said to the sufferer? Something like this: 'We hear, friend, that the Sabæans have stolen your oxen and asses, and that your flocks of sheep have been destroyed by lightning; vex not yourself, these are merely outward events independent of your will, therefore no evils, to be treated as if they had not happened by a wise man. We hear, moreover, that your sons and daughters have been suddenly killed, amid their festivities, by a tornado. It is a somewhat unusual and startling event; still, such things do occur now

[1] Lib. iii. cc. 32, 33.

and then, and form part of the order of nature; they happen indifferently to all, irrespective of character; and when they happen they are purely external events, therefore indifferent. For the rest: consider that your children have been restored to the peace of the pre-natal condition, and say to yourself: "When I begot them I knew that they would have to die."[1] We not only have heard, we see, that you are afflicted in your own person with a loathsome disease, wasting and painful. This is harder to bear than all the other ills, but the apathetic wise man is equal to the task. Consider, Job: Pain has its seat in the body, why should it disturb the peace of your mind?' What would the man of Uz have thought of such consolations? Would they have appeared to him an improvement on the solemn homilies in vindication of divine justice addressed to him by the friends who had come to condole with him? Which is the more trying to patience—to be told: 'You suffer much, therefore you must be a very bad man'; or to be told: 'You are, we are sure, a very good man, but you know you do not really suffer?' Perhaps there is not much to choose between them. Let us be thankful that the author of Job kept aloof from the pedantries alike of Eliphaz and of Zeno; that he conceived of his hero as at once an exceptionally good man and an exceptionally miserable man. For

---

[1] *Ego quum genui, tum moriturum scivi.* Seneca, in *Ad Polybium Consolatio*, cxxx.

by this sharp antithesis between conduct and lot the problem of Providence in the individual life was adequately stated, and a need for earnest discussion created; and if, after all that was said in the debate, the problem remained unsolved, it was at least kept open for other attempts by the ruthless sweeping away of premature superficial solutions. The Stoic solution was probably not before the writer's mind. Had it been, we can imagine what his sound Hebrew sense would have had to say about it: 'Destitution, sorrow, pain, are not to be charmed away by fine phrases. They are grim realities. They happen to men under the Providence of God, and some account of them must be given if faith in the justice and goodness of God is not to make shipwreck.'

The later Stoics did make some attempt to supply a *rationale* of the sufferings of the good, on the assumption that these were real. Epictetus offered as his contribution the idea that tribulation promotes the development of heroic character. In an apologetic discourse on Providence he asks: 'What sort of a man would Hercules have been had there not been lions and hydras and stags and wild boars and unrighteous savage men to fight with, and drive out of the world? What would he have been doing, had not such beings existed? Spending his whole life nodding in luxury and idleness, without any chance of using his arms, strength, power of endurance, generous disposition.' The moral of the life of

THE STOICS: PROVIDENCE

Hercules is thus pointed: 'Come then, thou also, look at the powers given thee, then say to Jove, Bring any trial you please, for, lo! I have been equipped by thee for beautifying myself by the things which happen.' To such as are of a different temper, preferring to sit and groan and complain in presence of difficulties, he addresses the remonstrance: 'I can show you that you have been provided with talents and opportunities for the exercise of magnanimity and fortitude; show me, if you can, what occasion you have for complaining and finding fault.'[1]

In his treatise *De Providentia* Seneca presents some distinctive points of view. The aim of this work is not to treat of Divine Providence in general, but to discuss the special question, Why, if the world be under a providential guidance, do so many evils overtake good men? It abounds in fine thoughts felicitously expressed, which, for the most part, must here be left unnoticed. I can refer only to what may be called the *spectacular* aspect under which the subject is prominently, though not exclusively, presented. Two thoughts fall under this category. The first is that the sufferings of the good are a pleasing sight to the gods; the second, that they make an important revelation of character to the sufferers themselves and to their fellow-men. As to the former, Seneca remarks: 'I do not wonder if

[1] *Dissertationes*, i. 6.

sometimes the gods are seized with a desire to see great men struggling with calamity.'[1] He represents the gods as, like generals, placing the best men in the posts of danger, and he counsels those so placed to console themselves with the reflection: God has deemed us worthy to be employed as a means of ascertaining how much human nature can bear.[2] The use of trial for the revelation of character to men is thus set forth: You are a great man; but how shall I know, if fortune give you no opportunity of displaying your virtue? I judge you miserable because you never have been miserable. You have passed through life without an adversary. Nobody will know what you could have done, not even you yourself. There is need of trial for the knowledge of ourselves. No one learns what he is good for except by being tried.[3] You know the steersman in a tempest, the soldier in battle.[4] Calamity is the opportunity of virtue.[5] Fire proves gold, misery brave men.[6] To other men the manifestation of a heroic spirit conveys a lesson of endurance. The suffering hero is born to be an example.[7]

The general theory of Providence taught by the early masters of the school might have been satis-

---

[1] *De Providentia*, cap. ii.   [2] *Ibid.*, cap. iv.
[3] *Ibid.*, cap. iv.
[4] *Ibid.*, cap. iv.: 'Gubernatorem in tempestate, in acie militem intelligas.'
[5] *Ibid.*, cap. v.: 'Calamitas virtutis occasio est.'
[6] *Ibid.*, cap. v.   [7] *Ibid.*, cap. vi.

factory enough, if they had not done their best to render it nugatory by dividing men into two classes, one of which did not need God's care, and the other did not deserve it. There was no lack of emphasis in their assertion of the doctrine that God cares for men. After God, they argued, there is nothing in the world better than man, and nothing in man better than reason. Therefore God must have reason. The divine reason finds its proper occupation in caring for the world, providing for its permanence, furnishing it with all things needful, and adorning it with beauty; but above all in caring for man. The world was made for beings endowed with reason, gods and men. The care of God for man is apparent in the structure of his body and the endowment of his mind, and in the subservience of the vegetable and animal creation to his benefit. Not to see the evidence of divine care, especially in the mind of man, is to be devoid of mind. As for the body, it is enough to refer to the hand, with its marvellous capacity of art, in the use of which men can produce a second nature in the nature of things.[1]

Most acceptable doctrine; but when we view this richly endowed being more closely, and consider the account given of the use he makes of his reason, our faith in his being the object of divine care is somewhat shaken. Human beings, we are told, consist of

[1] *Vide* Cicero, *De Natura Deorum*, lib. ii., in which an account of the teaching of the early masters on God and Providence is given.

two classes: wise men and fools. The wise are those who follow the dictates of reason; the fools those who disregard these dictates, and are blindly led by false opinion and passion. The fools, it appears, form the great majority; almost the whole mass indeed. And the fools are perfect fools. The wise men also are perfectly wise. There is no shading; there are no degrees of folly and wisdom. Virtues and vices respectively go in groups; he that has one virtue or vice has all, and each in perfection. This idealising way of viewing character is not peculiar to Stoicism, but the tendency to apply the category of the absolute to ethical distinctions was never carried to greater extravagance than by the Masters of the Porch. It reached its highest point of fantastic idealisation in the delineation of the Wise Man. The Wise Man of Stoic theory cultivates all the virtues; does all things rightly; is prophet, poet, orator, priest; is perfect in character, and endowed with a felicity not inferior to that of the gods; is a free man and a king. He is invulnerable, not because he cannot be struck, but because he cannot be injured. Nothing hurts divinity; no arrow can reach the sun.[1] He is absolutely self-reliant, and totally indifferent to popular judgment. As the stars move in a contrary direction to the world, so he goes against the opinion of all.[2] He neither asks

[1] Seneca, *De Constantia Sapientis*, cap. iv.
[2] *Ibid.* cap. xiv.

nor gives sympathy. In the proud consciousness of virtue he feels no soft indulgence towards the bad, but severely leaves them to endure the just penalty of their folly.

This man needs not God's care. He is a god himself. He is even superior to the gods in some respects, *e.g.* in patience. They are beyond, he is above, patience. He does not need even so much as to believe in God. Like Buddha, he can do without gods. The ethics of Stoicism have no need for a theistic foundation; they would suit the agnostic better than the theist. The Stoic wise man is absolutely self-sufficient, and does not need to care whether there be such a thing as a deity, a providence, or a hereafter. He talks piously about the gods, and about their care of men; but this is merely the accident of his position, the tribute he pays to the time in which he lives. He might cast off his creed like a suit of old garments, and it would make no difference. The Stoic temper can survive Stoic theology. The temper is indeed likely to survive the theology, for it is apt to be the death of it. That temper is much more hostile to true faith in divine Providence than the belief in fate, destiny, and the inexorable reign of law which formed a part of the Stoic system of thought. The reign of physical law in no way excludes a providential order of the world, which simply means that the world, while mechanically produced, has an aim to which the whole cosmos is subservient and each part in its relation to the whole. But the proud self-sufficiency of the sage stultifies the whole theory of a providential aim guiding the mind of God, by making man, the crown of creation, independent of God.

The Stoic scorn for fools tends in the same direction. Who can believe that God cares for a race who, having received the gift of reason, almost without exception make no use of it, and seem incapable of being cured of their folly? The true disciple of the porch did not believe it. His maxim was: 'God cares for the great and neglects the small.'[1] The sentiment, as put into the mouth of Balbus, the advocate of Stoicism, by Cicero, means that divine favour is not to be judged by outward chances such as the destruction of a crop by a storm. We are not to think that a man has been neglected by God because such misfortunes befall him, if he be endowed with the truer and more enduring riches of virtue. The inner treasures are the great things; the outer goods of fortune are the small. But for the genuine Stoic the adage was apt to bear another sense, viz. that God cares for great men and neglects small men. In his exposition of the doctrine of Providence, Balbus maintains that the gods care not only for the human race, but for individual men, for men in the great divisions of the earth—Europe,

[1] *Magna dii curant, parva negligunt.*—Cicero, *De Natura Deorum*, lib. ii. cap. lxvi.

THE STOICS: PROVIDENCE

Asia, and Africa; and also for men living in Rome, Athens, Sparta, and, among these, for particular men named.[1] But the men named are all more or less famous, concerning whom, and others like them, it is affirmed that they could never have been the men they were without divine aid. There is no mention, even in a general way, of insignificant men as the objects of God's care; no hint that even the hairs of their heads are all numbered. The pathos of the doctrine of Providence, as taught by Jesus, is wholly lacking in these grandiose demonstrations. 'Magna Dii curant, parva negligunt' is the keynote of the Stoic's providential psalm of praise.

Returning to the wise man of Stoic imagination, the question arises, Where are men answering to the description to be found? The Stoics themselves were obliged to admit that their number was few; but they ventured to name Socrates, Diogenes, and Antisthenes among the Greeks, and Cato among the Romans, whom the modern historian Mommsen bluntly calls a fool.[2] The wise man of Stoicism is in truth only an ideal. But he is none the less important as an index of the spirit of the system. There can be no better guide to the genius of a religion or a philosophy than its moral ideal. The

---

[1] Cicero, *De Natura Deorum*, lib. ii. cap. lxvi. Balbus alludes to the fact that Homer assigns to the leading heroes, Ulysses, Diomede, Agamemnon, Achilles, divine companions in their trials and dangers.

[2] Mommsen, *The History of Rome*, vol. iv. part ii. p. 448; English translation by Dr. Dickson.

wise man of Stoicism is as vital to it as the Buddha to Buddhism, or the perfect man who studies the law day and night to Judaism. The modifications which Stoicism underwent in course of time tended to gain for it wider currency, but they are not the most reliable indication of the true temper of its teachers. It is by the esoteric doctrine of Buddhism, the law for the monk, rather than by its exoteric doctrine, the law for the laity, that its true character is known. In like manner the apathetic sage, passionlessly yet passionately following reason, is the *beau ideal* of Stoicism, the revelation of its inmost soul. Suppose, now, we saw the ideal realised in a few rare specimens of humanity, what would they look like? Like the blasted pines of the Wengern Alp, standing near the summit of the pass, leafless, barkless, sapless; chilled to death by the pitiless icy winds of winter blowing off the glaciers. Compare this picture with that of the righteous man of Hebrew poetry: 'He shall be like a tree planted by the rivers of water,' with its leaf ever green and bringing forth fruit in its season.[1] How poor a character the cold, unsympathetic wise man of Stoicism appears compared even with the tender-hearted saint and sage of Buddhism! Between the Stoic wise man and the Jesus of the Gospels, the friend of publicans and sinners, no comparison is possible. Can we wonder that Stoicism, with all its

[1] Psalm i.

earnestness, remained an affair of the school? No system of religious thought can make way in the world which has no place in its ethical ideal for pity; no gospel for the weak. The Stoic was a Greek Pharisee who thought himself better than other men, and despised all whom he deemed his inferiors. He had his reward. He enjoyed to the full his own good opinion, and failed to win the trust and love of his fellow-men.

In the foregoing paragraph I have referred to *modifications* of the Stoic system as originally constructed. These were much needed in connection with three salient features : the exaggerated conception of the wise man, the doctrine that pain is no evil, and the connected doctrine of apathy. Shading was introduced into the first by substituting, in the place of the ideal wise man, the man who, though he hath not attained nor is already perfect, yet is advancing onwards towards the goal. In connection with the second it was found necessary to introduce distinctions among the things which rigid theory had slumped together as indifferent, and to divide these into three classes—the things to be desired, the things to be avoided, and the intermediate class of things neither to be desired nor to be avoided, to which the title 'indifferent' is properly applicable. In the first class were included such physical endowments as were favourable to virtue—bodily health, riches, honour, good descent, and the like. Finally, the apathy of theory was toned down by a gracious permission to the wise to indulge natural feeling to a certain measured extent; to rejoice in prosperity and grieve under bereavement, to commiserate the unfortunate, and to give play to the sentiment of friendship.

It was, as might have been expected when Stoicism became naturalised in the Roman world, towards the beginning of the Christian era, and from that time onwards, that it underwent this humanising transformation. The austere Roman nature presented a promising stock whereon to graft the philosophy of the porch, but Roman good sense was not likely to adopt without qualification the paradoxes and subtleties of Greek theorists. While welcoming the system in its main outlines, and especially in its characteristic temper, Roman disciples supplied at the same time the needful corrective. Cicero, one of the earliest Roman admirers, if not an abject disciple, of Stoicism, reveals in his writings the common Roman attitude. In the second of his *Tusculan Questions*, having for its theme how to bear grief, he treats as a mere extravagance the doctrine of Zeno, that pain is no evil. 'Nothing is evil, he teaches, save what is base and vicious. This is trifling. You do not by saying this remove what was troubling me.'[1] Seneca, coming a century later, about the begin-

---

[1] *Tuscul. Quæst.*, lib. ii. cap. xii.

ning of our era,[1] rebukes the pride of the Stoic wise man by frank confession of personal moral infirmity, and by equally frank proclamation of the evil bias of human nature. 'We have all sinned,' he sadly owns, 'some gravely, others less grievously; some deliberately, others under impulse, or carried away by evil example. Some of us have stood in good counsels with little firmness, and have involuntarily and reluctantly lost our innocence. We not only come short, but we will continue to do so to the end of life. If any one has so well purged his mind that nothing can any more disturb and deceive it, he has still come to innocence through sin.'[2] This confession occurs in a treatise entitled *De Clementia*, and it is meant to suggest a motive for the exercise of mercy, a virtue to which Stoics were not prone. As one reads the penitent acknowledgments of the Roman courtier he is reminded of the Pauline sentiment: 'Considering thyself, lest thou also be tempted.'[3]

With not less emphasis than Cicero, Seneca dissents from the Stoic doctrine concerning pain. 'I know,' he says, 'that there are some men of severe rather than brave prudence who assert that the wise man will not grieve. They must speak of what they have never experienced, else fortune would

---

[1] Cicero was born 106 B.C., Seneca probably a few years before the commencement of our era.
[2] *De Clementia*, cap. vi.   [3] Galatians vi. 1.

have shaken out of them this proud wisdom, and driven them in spite of themselves to a confession of the truth. Reason demands no more than that grief be free from excess.'[1] Some have doubted whether Seneca could have referred in such unsympathetic terms to a sentiment so characteristic of Stoicism, and have found in the passage quoted a ground for calling in question the authenticity of the work in which it occurs, the *Consolatio ad Polybium*. But the plea for the legitimacy of grief takes its place beside that for the exercise of mercy, as an appropriate feature of Roman Stoicism.

Epictetus, the Phrygian, was of sterner stuff than Seneca. He had been a slave before he became a teacher; he was lame and of a sickly constitution. This hard lot had bred in him the temper of an out-and-out Stoic, or even of a Cynic; so that he was ready to accept without abatement the dogma: Pain no evil. But the same severe experience had opened his naturally generous heart to a sympathy with the weak more akin to Christianity than to Stoicism. In his teaching God is not the God of the wise only, but of all, wise and foolish alike. No human being is an orphan, for God is a Father exercising a constant care over all.[2] On the ground of the universal Fatherhood of God he inculcates humanity in the treatment of slaves. To one who

[1] *Ad Polybium Consolatio*, cap. xxxvii.
[2] *Dissertationes*, III. xxiv. 1.

THE STOICS: PROVIDENCE

is represented as asking: 'How can you put up with a slave who, when you call for hot water, pays no attention or brings water lukewarm?' he replies: 'Slave! can you not bear with your own brother who takes his origin from Jove, as a son born of the same seed as yourself?'[1] so giving to the idea that men are God's offspring, in the hymn of Cleanthes, a breadth of application which its author in all probability did not dream of.

In two respects the later Roman Stoicism was no improvement on the earlier, viz.: the practice of suicide and the view entertained of the future life. The former is one of the most perplexing features of the system. It is hard to reconcile with Stoic principles either the wish or the temptation to put an end to one's life. The Stoic had unbounded faith in the will of the universe, which for him was revealed in events. With Epictetus he would say: 'Desire nothing to happen as you wish, but wish things to happen as they do';[2] and with Marcus Aurelius: 'Whatever is agreeable to thee, O universe, is agreeable to me; nothing is early or late for me that is seasonable for you.'[3] Is it not a corollary from this that one should be content to let life last as long as it can, viewing the mere physical power to last as an indication of God's will? Was it not an illogical as well as an unworthy proceeding on the part of Zeno and

[1] *Dissertationes*, I. xiii. 1. [2] *Enchiridion*, cap. viii.
[3] *Meditationes*, Book iv. cap. xxiii.

Cleanthes to inaugurate the bad fashion of taking the work of putting a period to their lives out of the hands of nature? Then what need or temptation to pursue this self-willed course could arise for one who believed that disease and pain and all things that tend to produce life-weariness are no real evils? Yet the legitimacy of suicide was maintained by all Stoics, not excepting Seneca, Epictetus, and the Emperor Aurelius. 'If you do not wish to fight,' said Seneca, 'you can flee; God hath made nothing easier than to die.'[1] 'God hath opened the door,' said Epictetus; 'when things do not please you, go out and do not complain.'[2] 'If the room smokes I leave it,'[3] was the homely figure under which the Stoic ruler of Rome still more cynically expressed the right of men to renounce life when they were tired of it.

That Stoicism gave an uncertain sound on the future life is not surprising. A firm, consistent doctrine on that subject could hardly be expected from a philosophy whose theory of the universe was a heterogeneous combination of materialism, pantheism, and theism. Even the founders of the school do not seem to have been of one mind on the subject. Zeno thought that the souls of men might survive death and maintain their separate existence till the general conflagration,

[1] *De Providentia*, cap. vi. [2] *Dissertationes*, lib. iii. cap. viii.
[3] *Meditationes*, v. 29.

THE STOICS: PROVIDENCE

when, with the rest of the universe, they would be absorbed into the primæval fire. Chrysippus restricted the honour of such a survival to the wise. The Stoics of the Roman period seem to be in doubt whether, even in the case of the wise, death will not mean final extinction of being. To the question, How can the gods suffer good men to be extinguished at death? Marcus Aurelius replies: 'If it be so then it is right, if it be not right then the gods have ordered it otherwise.'[1] To a mother grieving over the loss of a beloved son, all the consolation Seneca has to offer is such as can be extracted from reflections like these: 'Death is the solution and end of all griefs, and restores us to the tranquillity in which we reposed before we were born. Death is neither good nor evil. That can be good or evil which is something, but that which is itself nothing and reduces all things to nothing, delivers us to no fortune.'[2]

But let our last word concerning the Stoics be one of appreciation. They have added to the spiritual treasures of the human race a devout, religious tone and a serviceable moral temper. The religious tone finds characteristic expression in the hymn of Cleanthes, in some utterances of Epictetus, and in the general strain of the *Meditations* of Aurelius.

---

[1] *Meditationes*, xii. 5.
[2] *Ad Marciam Consolatio*, cap. xix. But there are passages to a different effect in Seneca's writings.

138 THE MORAL ORDER OF THE WORLD

The keynote of Stoic piety is struck in the opening sentences of the hymn. 'Thee it is lawful for all mortals to address. For we are thy offspring, and alone of living creatures possess a voice which is the image of reason. Therefore I will for ever sing thee and celebrate thy power.'[1] The sayings of Epictetus breathe throughout the spirit of childlike trust in God, of thankfulness for the blessings of Providence, and of cheerful submission to the divine will. The prevailing mood finds culminating utterance in the closing sentences of one of his discourses on the providential order. 'What then, since most of you are blind, were it not needful that some one should perform this function (of praise), and on behalf of all sing a hymn to God? For, what else am I, an old man, good for except to praise God? If I were a nightingale, I should do the part of a nightingale, if a swan, the part of a swan; but being a rational creature I must praise God. This is my work and I do it. I will keep this post as long as I may, and I exhort you to join in the chorus.'[2] The same spirit pervades the *Meditations* of the Stoic Emperor, only in them the note of sadness predominates.

The ethical temper of Stoicism is not faultless. It is too self-reliant, too proud, too austere. Never-

[1] From translation by Sir Alexander Grant in *Oxford Essays*, 1858, p. 96.
[2] *Dissertationes*, lib. i. cap. 16.

THE STOICS: PROVIDENCE

theless it is the temper of the hero, whose nature it is to despise happiness so-called, to curb passion, and to make duty his chief end and chief good. A little of this temper helps one to play the man, and fight successfully the battle of life, especially at the critical turning-points in his experience. If the mood pass with the crisis, and give place to a softer, gentler mind, no matter. It is well to go from the school of the porch to the *Schola Christi*. But Stoicism has much in common with Christianity; this above all, that it asserts with equal emphasis the infinite worth of man. It backs man against the whole universe. In view of the importance of the doctrine we can pardon the extravagance with which it is asserted, and even think kindly of the Stoic wise man. The very existence of a man like Epictetus, a slave yet recognised within the school as a good man and a philosopher, helps us to measure the distance that had been travelled in the direction of Christian sentiment since the time of Plato and Aristotle. To both these philosophers the very idea would have appeared a profanity.[1]

[1] *Vide* Bosanquet, *Civilisation of Christendom*, p. 43.

LECTURE V

DIVINATION

IT is not unfitting that a study of Divination in its bearing on the providential order should form the sequel to our discussion of the opinions of the Stoics on the same theme. For the philosophers of the porch took a prominent place among the defenders of the reality of divination, and of its importance as a manifestation of the divine care for men. Zeno, as we learn from Cicero, sowed the seeds of the doctrine, Cleanthes adding somewhat to the store of seminal utterances, while the third of the great founders, Chrysippus, dealt with the subject in a more elaborate manner in two books, adding another on oracles, and a fourth on dreams. The tenets of these masters became the orthodox tradition of the school, which was followed without dissent till Panætius, who introduced the Stoic philosophy to the knowledge of the Romans, about a century and a half before the Christian era, ventured to hint a modest doubt far from welcome to other members of the sect.[1] It happens, however, that, while few

[1] Cicero, *De Divinatione*, lib. i. cap. iii.

DIVINATION

of the Stoics called in question the accepted doctrine on divination, some of them have bequeathed to us sayings which, possibly without any intention on their part, can be used with effect in undermining that very faith in the diviner's art which the originators of the school had made it their business to propagate. On this ground also it is suitable that the topic should be taken up at this stage.

The Stoic interest in divination was mixed up with the general conceptions of the school concerning God and Providence. The three topics—God, Providence, and Divination—formed a closely connected group in their minds. Belief in any one of the three was held to imply belief in the rest, so that each of them in turn, assumed as admitted, might be used to prove the others. According to the purpose in view it was argued now, if there be anything in divination then there are gods; and at another time, if there be gods then divination must be a reality. Cicero has given us in short compass the logic of the Stoics in plying the latter of these two complementary arguments. It is as follows. 'If there be gods, and yet they do not make known to men beforehand the things which are to come to pass, either they do not love men, or they do not know what is going to happen, or they think that men have no interest in knowing what is going to happen, or they think it beneath their dignity to reveal the future, or such revelation is beyond their power. But they do love us, for they are beneficent, and friendly to the human race: they are not ignorant of things which they themselves have ordained; it is our interest to know what is going to happen, for we will be more cautious if we know; the gods do not account revelation of the future beneath their dignity, for nothing is more becoming than beneficence; and it is in their power to know the future. Therefore it cannot be affirmed that gods exist, yet do not by signs reveal the future. But there are gods, therefore they give signs. But if they give signs they must also put within men's reach the science of their interpretation, for the one without the other would be useless. But this science is divination. Therefore divination is a reality.'[1] Thus reasoned Chrysippus, Diogenes, and Antipater; acutely if not irrefutably.

Belief in divination was not the monopoly of a school or a nation, but a common feature of all ancient ethnic religion. 'What king,' asks the apologist of the belief in Cicero's treatise, 'what king ever was there, what people, that did not employ the diviner's art?'[2] That art had great vogue, especially in Greece and Rome. The fact, it has been suggested, is to be accounted for by the consideration that these energetic peoples naturally found the chief interest of religion in its

[1] Cicero, *De Divinatione*, lib. i. cap. xxxviii.
[2] *Ibid.*, lib. i. cap. xliii.

bearing on this life.[1] But this remark holds true not merely in reference to the Greeks and Romans; it applies to pagans generally. Absorbing concern for the temporal is a characteristic of all peoples in a rudimentary moral condition. 'After all these things do the Gentiles seek.' Their very prayers are for material benefits, as one can see in the Vedic hymns. The *summum bonum* of crude religions consists in the gifts of fortune. And wherever these gifts are chiefly sought after, the arts of divination will flourish. Who will show us any good in store for us in the future? is the question on the lips of many, and wherever keen curiosity as to the secrets of to-morrow prevails, there will always be men offering themselves who profess ability to meet the demand, by drawing aside the veil of mystery which hides things to come from human eyes.

Divination may be regarded as a primitive form of revelation, and when placed under this category it gains in dignity. Nothing can be more natural, rational, and praiseworthy, on the part of beings endowed with reason, than the desire to know God. Show me Thy glory, show me Thy ways, show me Thy will, are prayers of which not even the wisest and most saintly have cause to be ashamed. What is there better worth knowing than the nature,

[1] A. Bouché-Leclerq, *Histoire de la Divination dans l'Antiquité*, vol. i. p. 3.

144 THE MORAL ORDER OF THE WORLD

thoughts, purposes of the great mysterious Being who made and sustains this world? But all depends on the kind of knowledge sought. There are two kinds of knowledge which a son may desire to have concerning his father. He may wish to know his father's thoughts about right and wrong, what he approves and what he disapproves, what he loves and admires, and what he hates and despises, that he may order his own life so as to win the commendation of one whom he instinctively reveres. Or he may wish to know how much his father is worth, and what share of his fortune will fall to his own portion by his will when he dies, and to what extent a life of pleasure will thus be put within his reach in the years to come. The one kind of knowledge is the desire of a noble-minded son, the other of a son the reverse of noble-minded. Equally diverse in character may be the revelations men seek concerning God. The devout wish of one man may be simply to know God's spirit, His thoughts towards men, whether they be gracious or the reverse, to be assured of His goodwill, and to be informed as to the kind of conduct that pleases Him. With this knowledge he will be content, living a life of trust and obedience, and for the rest leaving his times, his whole future, in God's hands, without curiosity or care as to what to-morrow may bring. The eager desire of another man may be to obtain just that kind of knowledge concerning God's purposes about which the first-named person is wholly indifferent, detailed information as to coming events in his future experience: when he is to die, how and where, the ups and downs in his way of life, the good and evil, fortune and misfortune, in his lot. The first kind of knowledge alone deserves the name of revelation. It is ethical in character, and it makes for a life of righteousness and wisdom. The second kind of knowledge, if attainable, is of no moral value, and bears no worthy fruit in conduct. The desire for it has its root in secularity of mind, and the real or imaginary gratification of it can only tend to a more abject bondage to the secular spirit.

The agent of revelation in connection with the higher kind of knowledge above described is the *prophet*, in connection with the lower the *diviner* or *soothsayer*. The characters of the two types of agents are as diverse as their occupations. The prophet is a man of simple, pure, unworldly spirit. He has a consuming passion for truth. His one desire is to know God as manifested in the world He has made, and in the history of mankind, and with absolute sincerity and unreserve to make known to others the vision he has seen. He has also a passion for righteousness as, in his judgment, the highest interest of life, and he makes it his business to preach the great doctrine that a people doing justly must prosper, has nothing to fear from the future, can defy all adverse fortune. But the diviner: what sort of a man is he? By the impartial testimony of history, a repulsive combination of superstition, greed, fraud, pretension, and ambition. Anything but a simple-minded man is the soothsayer; rather is he dark, enigmatical, inscrutable. 'Worthless, and full of falsehood are the utterances of soothsayers,' asserts vehemently Euripides.[1] 'The whole tribe of diviners are covetous,'[2] declares, with no less emphasis, Sophocles. With this scorn and contempt of the Greek tragedians harmonises the tone in which Hebrew prophets ever speak of the fortune-telling tribe in their Semitic world.

Yet we must not judge of all who, in primitive times, believed in and practised divination, by the depraved character of the professional diviner of a later age. The two kinds of knowledge above contrasted might be combined as objects of desire in the religious consciousness, and both might be sought in perfect simplicity of heart. Why should not God communicate both to them that loved Him; reveal to them the law of duty as summed up in the Decalogue, and make known also the good and evil that were to befall them in the future? The law of chastity was written on the heart of Joseph, as his behaviour in the house of

[1] *Helena*, 745, 746. [2] *Antigone*, 1036.

Potiphar attests. He feared God from his youth, and set moral duty above all considerations of advantage. But Joseph was also a dreamer of dreams, which he regarded as divine intimations of coming events in his own life; and he was an interpreter of the dreams of others, in which he found pre-intimations of years of plenty and of famine in the near future of the land of Egypt. Joseph had the prophet's love of righteousness, yet he could divine. In those simple times men would view his divining talent as the natural result of his righteousness. To whom should the secret of the Lord be revealed but to them that feared Him, to a Joseph or to a Daniel? The Stoics said that the wise man alone can divine.[1] That sentiment was a survival of the feeling of far back antiquity. In the mouth of the Stoics it seems an anachronism, for by their time it had been made manifest that the ways of the diviner and the ways of wisdom and goodness were apt to lie far apart, and that lovers of wisdom, like Sophocles and Euripides, were inclined to show their bias by expressing abhorrence for the diviner's character, and their unbelief in the value of his pretended revelations. But in claiming the diviner's vocation for the wise, the Stoics were simply repeating the verdict of the tragic poets in a different form. They acknowledged the degeneracy, but refused to despair of the art.

[1] *Vide* Stobaei, *Eclog.*, lib. ii. 238.

They aimed at reform rather than destruction. 'Divination,' they said in effect, 'is a sorry business as actually practised, but put it into the hands of the wise man and all will be well.' Perhaps so, but what if the wise man declined the honour? That is what we should expect from the wise man as conceived by the Stoics.

The *media* of revelation at the diviner's disposal were manifold. He could range over the wide region of the *fortuitous*, the *unusual*, and the *marvellous*, assumed to be specially significant. Whatever in the heavens or the earth, or beneath the earth, or in the aërial spaces, was fitted to arrest attention or awaken the sense of mystery and awe, might be expected to yield significant omens to those who had the eye to see and the ear to hear. The whole world was full of signs, hinting meanings bearing on the fortunes of men, and revealing to those who could understand the secrets of the past and the present, and above all of the future. There were signs in the stars, in the thunder-storm, in the flight and song of birds, in the murmur of the wind among the leaves of an oak-tree, in the livers of sacrificial victims, in the visions of the dreamer, and in the utterances of madmen. The question was not, where could the voice of God be heard, but where could it not be heard? There was a plethora of revelation, and it was a matter of taste to which department in the

DIVINATION

ample compass of the soothsayer's art any one might devote himself. There was room and need for specialisation, that every sort of divination might have its experts. If one method of ascertaining the divine will went out of fashion, it did not greatly matter, another was sure to take its place. One people might learn from another. The Chaldæans were the masters of astrology. The Greeks had their far-famed Delphic oracle. The Etruscans were the inventors of fulgural divination and of haruspicy.

Among the most ancient and most interesting forms of divination was that of *augury,* which sought to ascertain the will of the gods by observing the flight and the song of birds. Its prevalence and popularity in Greece from an early period is attested by the fame of Tiresias and Calchas in mythological story, and by the use of the Greek name for a bird, ὄρνις, in Athenian speech, as a generic name for all presages. The chief place among the birds of fate was assigned to the eagle, the vulture, the raven, and the crow; but before all to the high-flying birds of prey which appear to reach heaven.[1] These messengers of Zeus, on whose cries and movements so much was believed to depend, filled the breasts of simple-minded beholders with superstitious awe. Even free-thinking philosophers, living after the

[1] *Vide* Nägelsbach, *Die nachhomerische Theologie des Griechischen Volksglaubens,* p. 164.

150 THE MORAL ORDER OF THE WORLD

commencement of the Christian era, like Celsus and Porphyry, ascribed to the eagle and other omen-bearing birds greater importance than to man. The feeling of more ancient times is happily reflected in the *Ion* of Euripides. The foundling of that name is temple-sweeper in the shrine of Apollo his father, at Delphi. One of his menial duties is to keep the birds from defiling the sacred edifice. But they come one after another; now an eagle, now a swan, now some other winged creature, from Mount Parnassus, or the Delian lake, or the banks of the Alpheus. Ion warns them off, bids them return to their accustomed haunts, even threatens them with an arrow from his bow. But he has not the courage to carry out his threat; boy though he be, he is restrained by religious awe. 'I am afraid to kill you, who announce to mortals the messages of the gods.'[1] Euripides had no faith in divination in any form, but augury had a romantic side which would appeal to him as a poet.

The same thing cannot be said of *haruspicy*, that form of divination which sought divine omens in the bowels of slaughtered animals. This contribution to the resources of the soothsayer's art is as unromantic and unpoetical, not to say repulsive, as can be conceived. One can with difficulty imagine a people

[1] κτείνειν δ' ὑμᾶς αἰδοῦμαι
τοὺς θεῶν ἀγγέλλοντας φήμας
θνατοῖς.—*Ion*, 179, 180.

like the Greeks adopting it, not to speak of originating it. Its proper home was among the Etruscans, but it soon migrated to Rome, where it found a congenial harbour among a prosaic, utilitarian race. Cicero, no believer in divination, thought the best way of making this art ridiculous was to tell the grotesque story of its discovery, which was to the following effect. A certain person named Tages suddenly arose in a deep-drawn furrow in a field which was being ploughed, and spoke to the ploughman. This Tages was described in the Etruscan books as a boy in face but with an old man's wisdom. The ploughman, amazed at the apparition, expressed his surprise with a shout which drew a crowd to the spot, to which the stranger with the boy's face and the old man's mind communicated the rudiments of the haruspicine art. What need, adds the narrator, of a Carneades or an Epicurus to refute such absurdities? Who can believe in a creature, call him god or man, ploughed up in a field?[1] The conception is certainly grotesque enough, and it seems to imply a lurking feeling that the art which formed the subject of this strange being's course of instruction could never have entered into the mind of any ordinary human being. And yet, to do the Etruscans justice, it must be owned that if there was any reality in divination, and if the assumptions on which it rested had any validity, the inspection of entrails was just

[1] *De Divinatione*, lib. ii. cap. xxii.

as natural, and rational, as any other divinatory practice. All who offered sacrifices to the gods had a vital interest in making sure that the victims would be acceptable, and so obtain the benefit sought. External qualities, such as freedom from blemish, or the possession of certain marks, could be ascertained while the animal was living, but the interior of the body could be inspected only after death.[1] But why inspect the interior if the exterior was in order? Because it was one of the assumptions on which divination rested that the *unusual* was significant. Suppose, now, some peculiarity was discovered, possibly by accident, in the liver of a dead animal intended for sacrifice. How natural the thought: 'This means something. What if a victim with this peculiarity were unacceptable to the deity we desire to propitiate? It may seem a small matter, but nothing is small in the ritual of sacrifice, on which so much depends.' The moment these thoughts entered the mind of a priestly functionary the art of haruspicy was on the point of being born.

One would think that the *stars* were too far away to run any risk of falling within the diviner's cognisance. Yet astrology prevailed in the East generally, and especially in Chaldæa, and in Egypt, from a very early time. It spread to the West about the beginning of the Christian era, and, in spite of severe discouragement at the hands of the

[1] So Nägelsbach, *Nachhomerische Theologie*, p. 167.

Imperial government, it steadily gained ground, until it finally eclipsed all other forms of divination, including haruspicy. Even since the era of modern science dawned, some distinguished students of nature have not been insensible to its fascinations. Nor, when we reflect on the matter, is this difficult to understand. The only postulate required to start the astrologer on his career is that the stars, fixed and wandering, like the sun and moon, are there for the service of man. The service rendered by the sun is immense. His light and heat are the life of the world. The moon is emphatically the lesser light, yet she does in a humbler way for the night what the sun does more perfectly for the day : yields light to guide the path of men. What then is the function of the stars, so multitudinous in number? The light they give, notwithstanding their vast number, is insignificant ; they must therefore have been set in the sky for some other purpose than that of illumination. Or rather, may one not say: If they also are to be regarded as luminaries, the light they give must be not that which is appreciable by the physical eye, but that rather which addresses itself to the contemplative mind brooding over the mysteries of human life? May the motions and positions of the stars not give a clue to the diversity of human experience? Suppose we try. Let us divide the starry sphere into twelve divisions, or houses, like twelve liths of an orange, six above the horizon, and six below, assigning to each a distinctive character and its own measure of influence on human destiny. Then let us observe the position of these houses at the birth-hour of this or that human being, say the child of a king, or of a prince or a sage, and let us watch throughout the years which follow how far the actual career of those whose nativity was cast corresponds with what the astrological indications led us to expect. If in the life-histories of some notable men remarkable correspondences are discovered, then the hypothesis that the positions of the heavenly bodies, if they do not exert a causal influence upon, do at least help us to predict, the course of human destiny, may be regarded as established. This conception of the movements of the stars as in a pre-established harmony with the changes in man's life has a certain magnificence about it which appeals to the imagination; and we can easily understand how it should commend itself to the Stoics, with their pantheistic theory of solidarity binding together all parts of the universe, and even to an astronomer like Kepler.

The far-famed *Delphic Oracle* supplies an instance in which the natural medium of revelation was a subterranean influence in the form of an intoxicating vapour, which, when inhaled by the priestess sitting on the tripod over the chasm whence the exhalation proceeded, inspired her with the gift of prophecy. The *unusual* character of the phenomenon seemed to point it out as available for divining purposes, and the alleged effect, in an age when divination was believed in, would be regarded as amply justifying expectation. The solitude of the spot and its sublime surroundings, hemmed in by mountain precipices, were fitted to create on susceptible minds the impression that here, if anywhere, the gods might be expected to speak to men. In the Homeric hymn to the Pythian Apollo that god is represented as seeking for a spot where he may found an oracle, and on coming to Crissa under Mount Parnassus, as finding there a place manifestly marked out for the purpose by its seclusion and by the grandeur of its environment.[1] The wisdom of his selection was proved by the event. The oracle of Delphi became renowned throughout Greece and beyond, and eclipsed all other means of ascertaining the divine will. It was not the only oracle in Greece. There were oracles of gods, demons, and heroes; and in particular one at Dodona, sacred to Zeus, whose prestige lay in its great antiquity. Its divine signs were the sound of the rushing wind among the leaves of an oak, the murmur of a spring at its foot, and a caldron or pan of bronze suspended on its branches with a chain that knocked in the breeze against its side and spoke divine messages to the devout ear. In the old times of orthodox Pagan faith they were wont to speak of the basin that is never silent, and when a new faith

[1] Ilgen's *Hymni Homerici*, p. 13.

had come in its adherents said in triumph: 'The oak speaks no more,' 'the caldron prophesies no more.' But Delphi outshone Dodona, and still more did it extinguish the light of individual diviners of the type of Calchas and Tiresias. It grew to be the centre of a wealthy religious corporation, and it became an important factor in the political history of Grecian states, through the answers which it gave to those who sought its guidance in affairs of grave import. These answers were rendered more imposing by being delivered at first in, or translated into, hexameters. The poetry, if it came from the lips of the Pythia, must be put to the credit of the inspiring god; for the qualification for being a good Pythian prophetess was to be entirely passive under divine influence, a mere mechanical mouthpiece of Apollo. The time came when poetry gave way to plain prose, and the fame of the oracle began to decline. It fell into disrepute when Greece lost its independence under Macedonia and Rome. From that time it ceased to be a political power, and degenerated into an establishment for carrying on the trade of vulgar soothsaying.

This decline became a subject of anxious reflection to devout adherents of the old religion. In an essay on the cessation of oracles, Plutarch offers tentative solutions. It was a natural subject of discussion for one who had studied philosophy at Delphi, and had an opportunity of observing how the glory of the oracle had departed in the age in which he lived, the first century of our era. In that essay Plutarch makes one of his interlocutors say: 'Is it wonderful if, with iniquity abounding, not only as Hesiod foretold, reverence and justice have forsaken the earth, but also the Providence of the gods, which provided the oracles, hath everywhere departed?' Another, in a similar strain, suggests that Providence having given men, as a benevolent parent, many other things, had refused them oracles for their sins. An entirely distinct theory is hinted at when the view is enunciated by a third party in the discussion that not God but demons are the cause of the cessation. Demons, unlike the gods, are subject to change, decay, senility, and religious institutions in which they act as the agents of Deity may share their subjection to transiency. Cicero, discussing the same topic, in his work on Divination, ignores this distinction between gods and demons, and treats the theory as subjecting the gods to the category of decay, and therefore as false and untenable. Age, he contends, cannot affect the divine, meaning to hint that the oracle, had it been really divine, would have been eternal, and that the simple explanation of its decay was that men began to be less credulous.[1]

This brings us face to face with the question, Is divination a reality, or is it only a great delusion? The knowledge of the future which the diviner

[1] *De Divinatione*, lib. ii. cap. lvii.

promises to put within men's reach by his art is tempting, if there be such a thing; but is there? Reflection suggests doubts of various sorts: as to the possibility, the rationality, the certainty, the utility, and the moral tendency of the foresight thus acquired. On the first of these points Cicero presses believers in divination with a dilemma. Fortuities, he argues, cannot be foreseen, therefore there is no divination; fatalities can be foreseen, because certain; therefore again there is no divination, because divination has to do with the fortuitous.[1] The reasoning is addressed to the Stoics, who believed both in fate and in divination, and is intended to convince them of the inconsistency of their position. The Stoics were acute logicians, and would have their own way of getting out of the difficulty. Their idea of the matter seems to have been this: that, from the beginning, the world was so ordered that certain signs, discoverable in different parts of nature, as in the stars of heaven, or in the livers of animals, should precede certain events, so that the law of connection between sign and event being once ascertained, from the observed sign the event could be predicted.[2] This view, while recognising the superficial aspect of fortuitousness in the system of signs, regards them as, not less than the events, pre-ordained, and certain. It implies further that both signs and events, while

[1] *De Divinatione*, lib. ii. cap. x.   [2] *Ibid.*, lib. i. cap. lii.

DIVINATION

teleologically connected, may have physical causes. The doctrine practically amounts to the assertion that a fixed physical order and a providential order are not mutually exclusive, but are simply different aspects of the same universe. So stated, the position of the Stoics is not easily assailed, and on the whole it may be admitted that divination is not to be got rid of by short-hand metaphysical argumentation. The conception of a system of interpretable signs inwoven into the frame of nature, intended by Divine Providence to serve the purpose of revealing the future, is not on the face of it absurd.

But abstract possibility is one thing, probability, or rationality, is another. In the theory of divination the *unusual* is supposed to be the appropriate region of the significant. If you want to find the signs whose accurate interpretation yields the knowledge of future events, you must seek them above all among the rarer phenomena of nature. This proposition, while commending itself to men living in a pre-scientific age as natural and reasonable, is nevertheless very open to criticism. It is easy to see, of course, how the unusual should be regarded as the sphere of the divinely significant when the unusual was conceived as that which had no natural cause. Then a portent, such as that of a mule having offspring, naturally passed for a vehicle of special divine revelation. Against this popular way of thinking, Cicero taught that every event has a natural cause, and that, though *praeter consuetudinem*, it is not *praeter naturam*. A mule bearing offspring a miracle because it does not happen often![1] If it could not have happened it would not; if it could, it is not a miracle.[2] Thus viewed, the unusual can have no special significance as compared with the usual. The only question is whether it can have even as much significance, not to speak of more. That there is a revelation of God and of His will in nature is every way credible. But what sort of revelation is to be expected, and where is it chiefly to be looked for? If the knowledge desired be that of special events in the future, as procured by the diviner's art, then the unusual is necessarily the significant, because there is nothing in the usual to attract attention. That the sun rises every day can mean nothing for any individual man or people, but that the sun undergoes eclipse at a critical juncture may be very ominous in reference to an impending event, such as a battle. If, on the other hand, the knowledge sought be that of general laws, as revealing Divine Reason and Divine Beneficence, then the usual is the significant and the unusual the non-significant, or that in which significance is obscure. Though both alike due to physical causes, the usual and the unusual are nevertheless both capable of being the vehicle of revelation; but if the revelation desired be of the

[1] *De Divinatione*, lib. ii. cap. xxviii. [2] *Ibid.*, lib. ii. cap. xxii.

DIVINATION

nature last described, then the advantage lies not with that which happens rarely, but with that which happens regularly. I would sooner trust the lark's song on a summer morning as a revelation of the truth that the earth is full of the goodness of the Lord, than believe that the issue of a battle depended on the crowing of a cock, or the fortune of war on the dropping of grain on the ground from the greedy mouths of sacred chickens.[1] It is what one can learn from the rule rather than from the exception, from the fixed order of nature rather than from what seem breaches of that order, or random chances subject to no order, that is important. The Psalmist understood this when he wrote: 'The heavens declare the glory of God ... in them hath He set a tabernacle for the sun. ... His going forth is from the end of the heaven, and his circuit unto the ends of it: and there is nothing hid from the heat thereof.'[2] The sun in his daily course, not in the rare eclipse, is for the Psalmist the declarer of the Divine glory. And, granting for a moment that the two kinds of revelation are possible, a general revelation of the glorious reason, wisdom,

[1] Observation of the feeding of the sacred chickens was another of the prosaic forms of divination in use among the Romans. The more greedily the chickens ate the more of the food would fall to the ground, and this was regarded as a favourable omen. The omen was technically called *tripudium*—terripavium, suggesting that the quantity which fell from the mouth of the fowl was enough to make the earth quake. Vide Cicero, *De Divinatione*, lib. ii. cap. xxxiv.

[2] Psalm xix. 1-6.

justice, and goodness of God, and a special revelation of particular events concerning the future fortunes of individuals and peoples, there can be little question in rightly conditioned minds as to which of the two is the more important. The diviner may possibly have his place, but it is far in the background as compared with that of the prophet. The prophet also has something to say on the future fortunes of men and nations, but the special events he takes an interest in are simply concrete exemplifications of great moral principles. The general ethical revelation of God is for him the thing of supreme value.

The lack of *certainty* in the diviner's revelation is a grave drawback. Not much is gained by the existence of a system of interpretable signs. All turns on the interpretations. Who is to be the interpreter? Who is to fix the principles of interpretation? Are they to be determined by guessing to begin with, and then by verifying the guesses by subsequent observation? Take dreams, for example. Some appear utterly trivial, some grotesque; few reveal plainly what they are supposed to mean. How shall we know which have any meaning, and how shall we find out the import of those which have, seeing their significance is for the most part enigmatical? Cicero compares the gods, making so-called revelations through dreams, to Carthaginians or Spaniards speaking in the Roman Senate without an interpreter;[1] and he lays down the peremptory principle that if the gods want men to know, the signs they give ought to be clear, and if they do not want men to know they ought not to give any signs at all, not even occult ones.[2] There is force in his contention. To what purpose fill the world with an elaborate system of premonitory signs which are as hard to interpret as hieroglyphics, and by their obscurity offer a too tempting opportunity to the pretender and the quack?

Supposing the difficulty of interpretation to be got over, the next question that arises is, *cui bono*? Is it useful to know beforehand what is going to befall us? Is it not rather a merciful arrangement that the future is hidden from our eyes by a thick veil, so that we can live in hope even when tragic experiences lie before us? Does not that very divine care for men which is the major premiss of the argument in support of divination really raise a presumption against it? May we not argue: 'Yes, God does care for man, therefore He keeps the times and seasons in His own power, so that neither men nor angels know the day or hour.' 'Would Pompey, think you,' asks Cicero, 'have rejoiced in his three consulships, and his three triumphs, if he had known that he was to be murdered in an Egyptian solitude, after losing his army, and that after his

[1] *De Divinatione*, lib. ii. cap. lxiv.
[2] *Ibid.*, lib. ii. cap. xxv.

164 THE MORAL ORDER OF THE WORLD

death things were to happen which cannot be spoken of without tears?'[1]

On the relation of divination to the moral order I shall have an opportunity of speaking in next Lecture; meantime I offer a few observations on its *moral tendency*. Moral tendency is not to be put in the forefront in criticising a system, but when evil results are as prominent as they certainly are in the history of divination, it is legitimate to refer to them as raising a grave doubt whether the diviner has any claim to be regarded as the instrument of a beneficent Providence. Roman annals report damning facts against the astrologers. They were expelled from Rome in A.D. 139, as a public nuisance and danger to the State. Tacitus describes the Mathematicians as a race of men treacherous to the powerful, deceitful to those whose hopes they fed; a race which would always deserve to be under the ban, and which nevertheless would always receive encouragement.[2] A Christian bishop of early date describes the same class of men as making kings disappear by promising to their murderers impunity.[3] Shakespeare recognised the justice of the accusation in reference to the whole soothsaying tribe when he made the salutation of the witches on the blasted heath, 'All hail, Macbeth! that shalt be king hereafter,' bear its natural fruit in murder.

---

[1] *De Divinatione*, lib. ii. cap. ix.
[2] *Historiæ*, i. 22.   [3] Hippolytus, *Ref. Hær.*, lib. iv. 7.

DIVINATION

Such facts help us to understand, if not to sympathise with, the stern injunction in the legislative code of Israel: 'Thou shalt not suffer a witch to live.'[1]

Without insisting on the crimes of fortune-tellers of all grades and descriptions, it may be affirmed that the decline of faith in divination was bound to keep pace with the growth of the moral consciousness. In this connection the influence of the Stoics deserves to be considered. For it is true of them, as was remarked at the commencement of this Lecture, that they were destroyers of the faith in divination which they preached. They played two mutually antagonistic parts. They furnished divination with a theoretic basis, and they supplied scepticism with conclusive arguments against its reality and value. The foundations of faith were sapped by sayings uttered by leaders of the school. Among these may be reckoned that which affirmed that the wise alone could divine. This saying, on the lips of the Stoics, had not the depth of spiritual meaning that belongs to the Beatitude: 'Blessed are the pure in heart, for they shall see God,' but it looks in the same direction. For what is the wise man of Stoicism? He is one who sets little store on the goods of fortune, in comparison with the supreme good of virtue. If such a man alone can divine, the trade of the diviner will be in danger of falling out

[1] Exodus xxii. 18.

of fashion. He will not care either to be himself a diviner or to be a consulter of diviners. He will regard the future events of outward fortune as not worth ascertaining, and though the world be full of signs by which these events can be predicted he will not take the trouble either to discover or to interpret them. Ultimately this mood must end in scepticism as to the existence of such interpretable signs; for why credit the gods with taking pains to provide means for obtaining a knowledge of the future which wise men do not value? Probably this feeling was the source of the doubt of Panætius.

A disintegrating spirit lurks in certain sayings of Epictetus on the subject of divination. Here is one of them: 'When you are about to consult the oracle you do not know what is going to happen, but you do know what *sort* of a thing, if you be a philosopher; for if it be one of the things that do not depend on ourselves, of necessity it is neither good nor evil. Therefore do not bring to the soothsayer either desire or aversion.'[1] From consulting in this indifferent mood to not consulting at all is but a short way. The doctrine, 'All things outward indifferent,' must end in the doors of the oracle being closed. It does not go so far as Paul's doctrine, 'All things work for good,' which is still more hostile in spirit to the practice of divination; but another saying of Epictetus shows that he had reached that point also.

[1] *Enchiridion*, cap. xxxix.

It is: 'If the raven utter an unlucky cry do not be disturbed; you can make all things lucky if you like.'[1] One who has reached this position is practically a Christian in temper. There are no unlucky days for him; he knows no fear concerning the future. He takes no thought for the morrow; his motto is that of the Psalmist: 'My times are in Thy hand.'[2] How completely Epictetus had attained to this moral attitude appears from his answer to the question, What is ominous? 'Do we not call those things ominous which are significant of coming evil? Then cowardice is ominous, meanspiritedness, mourning, grief, impudence.'[3]

But of all the sayings of the Phrygian sage bearing on the present topic, the most important are those in which he defines a class of things about which we may not consult the diviner. 'Many of us,' he says, 'neglect many duties through unseasonable resort to divination. What can the diviner foresee except death, or danger, or disease, or something of that kind? But if it be my duty to incur danger, or risk my life for a friend, what room is there for divination? Have I not a diviner within which tells me the nature of good and evil, and shows me the signs of both? What need is there, besides, for haruspicy and augury?'[4] The use of these in such a case he elsewhere pronounces not

---

[1] *Enchiridion*, cap. xxiv.
[2] *Psalm* xxxi. 15.
[3] *Discourses*, lib. iii. cap. xxiv. 8.
[4] *Ibid.*, lib. ii. cap. vii. 1.

only needless, but wrong. 'When friend or country has to be defended with risk, do not consult the oracle. For if the prophet tell thee that the state of the entrails is inauspicious, that points to death, wounds, or exile. But after he has spoken, reason has something to say, viz., that with friend and country danger must be faced. Wherefore come to the greater, Pythian prophet, who thrust out of the temple a man who was not willing to help a friend in danger of his life.'[1] In short, the doctrine of this Stoic teacher is: 'In matters of duty consult conscience, not the oracle; before doing your duty do not wish to know whether there are to be any disagreeable consequences.' Cicero had already taught the same high lesson. He praised the man who, when fidelity to a cause was at stake, used the auspices of virtue and did not look to the possible event, and he laid down this golden rule: duty is to be learned from virtue itself, not from auspices.[2]

Under such teaching as that of Epictetus, the diviner's occupation is gone. The upshot is this: in reference to matters of outward fortune it is not worth while consulting the diviner; in reference to matters of duty it is not lawful to consult him. It is heroic doctrine, and therein lies the diviner's opportunity. Few, even in Christian communities, have made up their minds once for all to do their duty whatever betide. Many, before

[1] *Enchiridion*, cap. xxxix.   [2] *De Divinatione*, cap. xxxvii.

deciding on their line of action, wish to know what the consequences are going to be. In the old Pagan world men of this time-serving type would have made a pilgrimage to Delphi to get a prophetic forecast of the future. In these Christian ages, when the oracles have long ceased to speak, and the astrologers and augurs are no more, the worldly-wise man must be his own diviner. He must try to guess the future by a sagacious instinct, or carefully study the signs of the times; watch the forces at work, estimate their relative strength, calculate the probable resultant, and, when all this has been done, make up his mind how he is to act. In the rule, what he decides on is just the opposite of what he ought to do, and would do if he took counsel with the wisdom that is associated with moral simplicity. Of course, he is satisfied in his own mind that no other course was open in accordance with the dictates of prudence. He is the wise man in his own esteem, the man who does the right at all hazards being the fool. He *is* the world's wise man, but not God's. He is the Pagan sage, not the Christian. He lives on the Pagan level, and takes the spirit, if not the art, of the diviner for his guide. That spirit will never die out till men generally value worldly good less and ethical good more. When food and raiment, and all that they represent, have indeed been relegated to the second place, then fortune-telling, and fortune-guessing, and

170 THE MORAL ORDER OF THE WORLD

fortune-hunting, and fortune-worshipping will finally disappear.

With divination, say some in our time, Providence and Prayer must go. According to the author of an elaborate history of Divination in Antiquity, 'he who believes in Providence and Prayer accepts all the principles on which ancient divination rests.'[1] Surely not *all* the principles! Some of them, of course, he does accept, *e.g.*, that there is a god, and that he cares for man. These cover the doctrine of Providence and Prayer, but they are not the specific principles involved in the theory of divination. Besides the general truth of God's care for man, that theory assumes that the divine care, if real, must show itself by revealing to men the secrets of the future. That assumption, we have seen, is very disputable for various reasons; and, moreover, it implies a false estimate of the relative importance of the good and evil of outward lot, as compared with the good and evil of inward state. That assumption therefore must go. But though it goes, the more comprehensive truth of God's care for man may remain, and if it remain the belief in Providence and the practice of Prayer are justified. When the theory of divination is abandoned, what happens to that belief and that practice is not rejection, but purification or transformation. A divine

[1] A. Bouché-Leclercq, *Histoire de la Divination dans l'Antiquité*, vol. i. p. 104.

care still exists, but it shows itself in a worthier way; petitions are still offered to a benignant divinity, but for higher benefits. That Providence and Prayer must pass away with Divination is as little true as that, with divination, everything of the nature of *prophecy* must disappear. How far from being the case this is, we know from the history of prophecy in Israel. There were diviners in Israel as elsewhere. But the time came when the men of moral insight saw that their skill was a pretence and their arts mischievous. What then? Why, the great ethical prophets appeared, laughing to scorn the diviner and all his ways, and showing the people a more excellent way through their noble passion for righteousness, and their grand doctrine that the only path to prosperity was to do God's will. Even so, when the diviner has been turned adrift there remains a doctrine of Providence which stands in the same relation to that which was associated with the practice of divination as the Hebrew prophet bore to the soothsayers of the Semitic world. The decay of divination signifies, not that belief in Providence is growing faint, but rather that it is being perfected. *Absolute trust in Providence kills the curiosity out of which springs the diviner's art.* The believer in God is so sure of His goodwill that he does not want to know what is going to happen; enough for him that all will certainly go well. The case of Prayer is similar. When divination ceases, prayer for outward good as the *summum bonum* must certainly come to an end, but not prayer in every form. What happens is that the lower, Pagan type of prayer gives place to the higher, whose chief desire is that God's will may be done, and that His kingdom may come.

A concluding reflection may appropriately be added here. We can now in some measure understand what a formidable barrier the practice of divination presented to moral and religious progress. It found men in possession of crude ideas of God, Providence, and the highest good and chief end of man, and its whole tendency was to keep them from getting any further. It addressed itself to a secular mind, and it worked steadily towards complete enslavement to secularity. Its power was strengthened by its plausibility. What more natural than to place the *summum bonum* in earthly good fortune; what more tempting than the wish to know beforehand what sort of fortune the future was to bring; what a willing ear those who cherished this wish would lend to men who came to them and said: 'By the kindness of the gods we are able to communicate to you the knowledge you desiderate'! What weary centuries of fruitless experiments and disappointed hopes it would require to convince men inclined to believe in it that the whole system was an imposture! Perhaps this result could never have been reached, unless a new religion had come capable of lifting men at once into a higher, purer world of religious thought and moral aspiration. Till the new faith came, anything that could help to break the diviner's evil spell was welcome. Even Epicureanism, with its rude denial of divine care for man, was from that point of view a boon. Better no divine care at all than such a grovelling care as the soothsayers ascribed to the gods. The Epicurean denial, with all its onesidedness, was a relative and beneficent truth, sweeping away an imposing falsehood, and preparing human hearts for receiving from another quarter an idea of Divine Providence possessing religious dignity and wholesome moral tendency. Thanks to Christianity, divination, speaking broadly, is a thing of the past. The fact helps us to realise that the world is actually advancing in religious faith and moral practice.

LECTURE VI

THE HEBREW PROPHETS

IN passing from the subject of Divination to that of Hebrew Prophecy and its characteristic doctrine of Providence, we do not escape from the world in which the spirit of soothsaying bore sway. That spirit exercised an evil dominion over the Semitic peoples not less than over the Greeks and Romans, from the most ancient times. And Hebrew prophecy stood to Semitic divination in a relation partly of development, but mainly of uncompromising antagonism. The prophet therefore will be all the better understood when he is placed in the light of a contrast with his Pagan kinsman. The picture of the diviner already hangs on the wall; let us place beside it that of the seer of Israel. And as the picture of the Stoic philosopher hangs immediately to the left of the picture of the diviner, it will make our comparative study complete if we allow our eye to wander to it also for an instant.

The resemblances and contrasts between the three types of men may be broadly stated thus. The

Hebrew prophet agreed with the diviner against the Stoic philosopher in attaching great, though not supreme, importance to outward prosperity. He agreed with the Stoic philosopher against the diviner in attaching sovereign value to virtue or righteousness. He differed from both in regarding outward good as dependent on, and attainable through and only through, righteousness.

As the Stoics came centuries later than the prophets, we do not expect to find in the pages of the latter any allusions to them and their tenets. But as the diviner was a contemporary, and by race a kinsman, of the prophet, we do expect to discover occasional references to him. We do find such, and they are so frequent and so emphatic that we are not only entitled but bound to have regard to them, and to use the class they so freely characterise as a foil to set off by contrast the thoughts and ways of the diviner's relentless critic.

The diviner and the prophet, or to describe them more antithetically, the old Pagan type of prophet and the new reformed type, are set in sharp antagonism to each other in the Book of Deuteronomy. The Hebrew legislator is represented, in one remarkable passage, as warning the people, conceived as about to enter the land of promise, against the abominations they will find prevailing there. Of these, two are selected for special mention : human sacrifice and the practice of divination. Some of the forms under which that practice was carried on are enumerated. The black list is as follows: 'There shall not be found among you any one ... that useth divination, or an observer of times, or an enchanter, or a witch, or a charmer, or a consulter with familiar spirits, or a wizard, or a necromancer.'[1] What arts are alluded to under these various terms it may be difficult precisely to determine;[2] but one cannot fail to be struck with the detailed enumeration, as indicative of wide baleful prevalence at the time when the Deuteronomic code took shape: that is to say, according to modern critics, in the seventh century B.C., when Josiah reigned in Judah, and Jeremiah exercised his prophetic functions. It was the dark hour of the diviner's power in the Pagan Semitic world; and that it was not confined to that world, but extended its malign influence within the pale of the chosen people, may be inferred from the anxious manner in which evil commerce with the unholy thing is interdicted. 'Thou shalt not learn to do after the abominations of those nations';[3] *i.e.* thou shalt neither practise divination thyself, nor consult the diviners that swarm among thy heathen neighbours. But what then? Is the Deuteronomic policy one of mere suppression? Is there to be no substitute

---

[1] Deuteronomy xviii. 10-15.
[2] *Vide* Driver's *Commentary on Deuteronomy, in loc.*
[3] Deuteronomy xviii. 9.

for the diviner, no one who shall in a happier and holier way satisfy the craving which gives the diviner his chance of power? Yes, a substitute is provided; the *Prophet* is his name, and his prototype is *Moses*. 'The Lord thy God will raise up unto thee a Prophet from the midst of thee, of thy brethren, like unto me; unto him ye shall hearken.'[1] Unto *him*, not unto those practisers of black arts who mislead to their hurt those who consult them, by their pretended knowledge of the future.

This sharp antithesis of itself suggests inferences as to the characteristics of the new type of *mantis*. He also will be able in his way to divine; that is, to make shrewd forecasts of the future. He will also use signs for this purpose. But the signs on which he will base his predictions will not be those of the heathen soothsayer. He will draw his significant tokens, not from the stars of heaven, or from the fowls of the air, or from the spirits of the dead, but from *human conduct*. 'Tell me how you live,' he will say to those who consult him, 'and I will tell you how you will thrive.' He will regard prosperity, not as a matter of luck, determinable beforehand by the skilful interpreta-

[1] Deuteronomy xviii. 15. 'Prophet' is to be taken here as referring to a class, not to one individual, *e.g.* Christ. The reference to Christ may be ultimately justifiable, but an exclusively Christian interpretation does away with the whole point of the statement, which consists in a contrast between two classes of men who profess ability to reveal God's will as to future fortune.

tion or manipulation of curious natural occurrences, but as a matter of reward for right behaviour, in accordance with a fixed moral order. Only when thus conceived does the new type of diviner, the prophet, present a radical contrast to the old one, such as justifies the hailing of his advent as a great reformation.

That our conjectural conception is correct, the reference to Moses proves. 'A prophet like unto me.' What sort of a prophet was Moses? The long discourse in the first eleven chapters of Deuteronomy, forming a hortatory introduction to the following body of laws, supplies the answer to this question. The burden of that discourse, put into the mouth of Moses, is: 'Do God's will and you will prosper.' The statutes of the Lord in general, and the Decalogue in particular, are the preacher's text. 'Keep these statutes, these Ten Words,' he says to his hearers, 'and it will go well with you throughout all generations.' 'It shall come to pass, if ye shall hearken diligently unto my commandments which I command you this day, to love the Lord your God, and to serve Him with all your heart and with all your soul, that I will give the rain of your land in its season, the former rain and the latter rain, that thou mayest gather in thy corn, and thy wine, and thine oil. And I will give grass in thy fields for thy cattle, and thou shalt eat and be full.'[1] Here is a

[1] Deuteronomy xi. 13-15.

very simple and definite programme: Do right and ye shall fare well. This is the doctrine of Moses as the Deuteronomist conceives him. Hence the prophet after the type of Moses, who is to supersede the diviner, must be one who teaches the same doctrine. He believes in a connection between conduct and lot, such that from conduct lot can be inferred. Therefore he tells all men that the one thing needful is to give heed to their ways, to be *righteous*. And it is obvious that if he be right the diviner's occupation is gone. The prophet after the manner of Moses will not only be a great improvement on the diviner; he will sweep the diviner and all his craft off the face of the earth. To what end consult the omens if all depends on conduct?

The occasional utterances of the prophets of Israel concerning the future fortune of their nation and its causes show how thoroughly they believed in the creed ascribed to Moses, and how utterly futile the practices of the soothsayer appeared in their sight. Exhaustive citation is unnecessary here; two examples will suffice, one taken from Jeremiah, the other from an older prophet, Micah. Jeremiah has before his mind the hard problem of Israel's duty and destiny in connection with the overshadowing power of Babylon. The diviners also, as the prophet knows, are busy with the problem, and they deal with it *suo more*. To king, princes, and all others consulting them they speak smooth words, saying in effect: 'The omens are favourable; no need to cringe to the great despot of the East, ye may defy him with impunity.' Jeremiah's counsel, on the contrary, is: 'Submit to the king of Babylon; submission is inevitable, it is the penalty of your sin; and it is your wisdom; you will fare worse if you obstinately resist his power.' 'Thus saith the Lord of hosts, the God of Israel; Let not your prophets that be in the midst of you, and your diviners, deceive you, neither hearken ye to your dreams which ye cause to be dreamed. For they prophesy falsely unto you in my name. I have not sent them, saith the Lord. For thus saith the Lord, After seventy years be accomplished for Babylon I will visit you, and perform my good word towards you, in causing you to return to this place.'[1] Micah, a contemporary of Amos, Hosea, and Isaiah, and representing their point of view, preaches a similar doctrine and with the same conscious antagonism to the diviners. Full of power by the spirit of the Lord, and of judgment and of might, he declares unto Israel her sin, and tells her that while she sins she must suffer, whatever diviners may say to the contrary. These false prophets he contemptuously describes as biting with their teeth, and crying peace; in other words, as selling predictions of good fortune for bread or money. As for him, all the signs in the world cannot make him believe that the ways of

[1] Jeremiah xxix. 8-10.

transgressors can conduct to any other end than disaster. To such as do evil his stern message is: 'Night shall be unto you, that ye shall not have a vision; and it shall be dark unto you, that ye shall not divine.'[1]

As to the other side of the doctrine connecting lot with conduct, the great prophets of Israel were equally well assured. They were firmly convinced that while their countrymen walked in God's ways, and in some considerable measure realised the ideal of a chosen people, no serious harm could come to them. Isaiah voiced the common prophetic sentiment when he said: 'Behold, I lay in Zion for a foundation a stone, a tried stone, a precious cornerstone, a sure foundation,'[2] having in his view not so much the actual material fortress, but 'the ideal Zion, built upon righteousness and justice.'[3] A nation doing righteousness had no occasion, according to the prophetic theory, to fear either Sennacheribs or soothsayers. The daughter of Zion might laugh the invader[4] to scorn, and as for the fortune-teller, his mercenary lying arts were utterly impotent. 'Surely there is no enchantment against Jacob, neither is there any divination against Israel.'[5] These words are put into the mouth of Balaam, the Aramæan prophet, as a confession of his inability to

---

[1] Micah iii. 6.   [2] Isaiah xxviii. 16.
[3] Renan, *Histoire du Peuple d'Israël*, vol. ii. p. 522.
[4] Isaiah xxxvii. 22.   [5] Numbers xxiii. 23.

182 THE MORAL ORDER OF THE WORLD

curse the chosen people. Critics may dispute their authenticity, and suggest that the oracles ascribed to Balaam in the Book of Numbers reflect not so much his thoughts as the self-consciousness of the people to whom they refer.[1] However this may be, one thing is certain, that the particular oracle quoted expresses an important article of the prophetic creed. The Hebrew prophet believed that blessing and cursing did not belong to diviners, but to the moral order of the world. 'Behold, I set before you this day a blessing and a curse; a blessing, if ye obey the commandments of the Lord your God; . . . a curse, if ye will not obey the commandments of the Lord your God.'[2]

The prophetic theory of Providence represents a great advance of religious thought when compared with that which underlies the practice of divination. Its supreme merit lies in its *profoundly ethical character*. It has its origin in an intense personal sense, on the part of the prophet, of the sovereign worth of righteousness, and its issue in a firm conviction that righteousness has not only subjective but objective value, is the law not only of the individual conscience but of the universe. The diviner, as such, shared neither the prophet's personal estimate of righteousness nor his conviction that justice and judgment are the habitation of God's throne. He assumed that to obtain good fortune was the chief

[1] Renan, *Histoire du Peuple d'Israël*, vol. ii. p. 45.
[2] Deuteronomy xi. 26, 27.

end of man, and that the end was attainable irrespective of character. The system of signs on which he founded his forecasts *had no inherent connection with the moral order.* It was a merely physical apparatus for determining the future; *skill*, not character, was required for its interpretation. And as the diviner's knowledge had no connection with personal morality, so the future which he professed to know had no connection with morality in the recipient of the predicted fortune. It was a matter of *luck*, not of character. It might even be obtained by immorality. The crown promised to Macbeth by the witches was gained by murder; and that is by no means the solitary instance in which the fortuneteller's predictions have found fulfilment through crime. If we were to regard the criminal as the dupe and victim of designing persons more culpable than himself, we should in many cases not be far from the truth. But without making the diviner responsible for the moral aberrations of his clients, we may at least assert that he predicts a future which, he cannot but know, may be associated with crime as its procuring cause. He is thus put on his defence, and we may conceive him making for himself an apology of this sort: 'If my prognostications should be fulfilled by crime I cannot help it. What I am responsible for is the matter of fact. My science enables me to foretell certain events that are to happen in a particular man's life, such as that he is to become a king or a very wealthy man. How the result is to be brought about I do not profess to know, nor, as a diviner, do I care. Murder, fraud, and other crimes may lie on the path that conducts to the goal. The way may not be desirable, but, observe, the end is reached, and my prescience is vindicated. The fact turns out to be as I predicted.'[1] It is a lame apology, but it is the utmost that can be said, and it is a virtual confession of the *non-moral*, if not of the immoral, character of divination.

In the light of this imaginary confession we can see clearly how impossible it is for any one to believe in divination who firmly grasps the truth that *morality has value for the divine Being*. It is not credible that a God who cares for righteousness would introduce into the frame of nature a system of signs, possessing significance irrespective of moral interests. Such a system, as has already been admitted, may be abstractly possible from a merely speculative point of view, but in a theory of the universe which makes the ethical supreme it can find no place. The moral order of the world crowds out the diviner's order. It is the abiding merit of the Hebrew prophets that they understood this and chose the better part. They saw that there was not room in the world for the two orders, and they preferred the order of universal righteousness to the

[1] *Vide* Lecture V.

order of omnipresent non-moral signs. Their vision was clear and their preference decided because their hearts were pure. The fundamental fact about these seers of Israel is that they were men in whose breasts burned the *passion for righteousness*. Out of this pure fountain sprang, in vigorous flow, the limpid stream of their religious faith. How easy for men, with that sacred passion burning in their souls, to believe in a God who loveth righteousness and hateth iniquity! And how natural for men believing in such a God to seek and find in human history traces of that divine love and hatred; to see in the good and ill of men's lot the reward and penalty of righteous and unrighteous conduct! And just because the prophet's creed was the natural outcome of his ethical spirit, it has a presumption of truth on its side. It is worthy to be true. The passion for righteousness needs no apologist. It is its own witness. It is the noblest thing in the world. Were it universal it would go far to rid the world of the many curses under which it groans. But this noble passion, which needs no apology, is the best apology for the creed which is congenial to it. It demands, and therefore justifies, faith in an ethical deity, and in a moral order revealing itself in the lives of men and nations.

But how stands the fact? Is the order of the world as moral as the prophetic theory requires? Are there not many things which seem to show that the lot of men is merely a matter of good or evil fortune, and that events happen either in accordance with a purely physical fate or by an utterly incalculable, inexplicable fortuity? And, if the order of the world be so non-moral in appearance, what guarantee is there that the universe is not presided over by a non-moral deity? The phenomena which raise such anxious questions did not escape prophetic observation. How could they? The phenomena are not new, a mere peculiarity of exceptional modern experience. They are as old as the world, and must always have been noticed by every person of ordinary discernment, not to speak of men of rare moral insight, like the prophets. Just because they intensely desired that the moral order should be perfect, the prophets would be keenly sensitive to everything that seemed to contradict their theory. It is, of course, a too common infirmity to shut the eyes to unwelcome facts, or to interpret them in harmony with theory. In the case before us that would mean reasoning back from lot to conduct, so inferring goodness from prosperity and wickedness from adversity. A pedantic theorist might do that, but hardly a Hebrew prophet. He was much more likely to feel acutely the pressure of the problem arising out of antagonism between theory and experience, and to be as one walking in darkness, simply trusting when he could not see. For a time, indeed, the problem might not exist in an acute form even for a prophet. The attention might be directed chiefly to broad aspects of providence confirmatory of theory, and facts of an opposite character might be simply overlooked, or there might not happen to be any such of a very arresting nature. But when once the problem had fairly announced itself, and become a subject of reflection, it would create a sense of ever-deepening perplexity, leaving the prophetic mind no rest till it had found some clue to the mystery. The faith of the earlier prophet might thus be comparatively confident and cheerful, while that of his brother belonging to a later generation might be overshadowed with doubt, and for a third seer of a still later time the darkness might pass into the dawn of a new light upon the very phenomena which had brought on the eclipse of faith.

Such differences in mood can be discerned in the prophetic writings; when we compare, *e.g.* Isaiah with Jeremiah, and with the unknown prophet of the Exile whose oracles form the later half of the canonical Book of Isaiah. In their respective views concerning the providential order these three prophets are related to each other somewhat after the manner of the three great tragic poets of Greece. Isaiah, like Æschylus, has an unclouded faith in the retributive justice of God; Jeremiah, like Sophocles, believes devoutly in the moral order, but not without a keen perception of the mysterious, inexplicable element in human life; the prophet of the Exile, like

Euripides, sees in the sufferings of the good, whereof Jeremiah had complained, not merely a dark fate, but an experience that is turned into a joy for the sufferer when he accepts it as incidental to a redemptive vocation.[1]

For the first of these prophets, the sphere within which divine justice displays itself is the nation as a whole. His firm conviction is that the nation which does God's will shall prosper, and that, on the contrary, the nation which fails to do God's will cannot prosper. His theory is formulated in the first chapter of the book which bears his name in these precise terms: 'If ye be willing and obedient, ye shall eat the good of the land; but if ye refuse and rebel, ye shall be devoured with the sword.'[2] The actual moral state of Israel when Isaiah uttered his prophecies was such as to demand insistence mainly on the latter of these alternatives; but the prophet had equal faith in the validity of the other, given the requisite moral conditions. When the spirit of righteousness was poured out upon the community, there would come a happy change in the social state comparable to the transformation of a wilderness into a fruitful field. 'The work of righteousness shall be peace; and the effect of righteousness quietness and assurance for ever. And my people shall dwell in a peaceable habitation, and in sure dwellings, and in quiet resting-places.'[3] Other prophets of the

[1] *Vide* Lecture III.   [2] Isaiah i. 19, 20.   [3] *Ibid.* xxxii. 17, 18.

THE HEBREW PROPHETS 189

same period say the same thing. The message of Amos to his countrymen is, 'Seek ye the Lord, and ye shall live,' or alternatively, 'Seek good, and not evil, that ye may live,'[1] the life promised including all that makes for national wellbeing. Hosea reveals his faith in the certainty of the connection between conduct and lot in national experience by employing the figure of sowing and reaping to convey his thought. 'They have sown the wind, and they shall reap the whirlwind.'[2] 'Sow to yourselves in righteousness, reap in mercy.'[3]

A hundred years later an altered tone is observable. The prophetic temper has become less buoyant and hopeful, more sombre and dubitating. The change may have been in part an effect of the sore discouragement inflicted on the loyal worshippers of Jehovah during the long, sinister reign of Manasseh, by whom all the interests dear to the heart of his father Hezekiah were treated with ungodly and unfilial contempt. The very length of that reign, as compared with the duration of the one preceding, was of itself a trial of faith in Providence. The godly father reigns only twenty-nine years, dying at the early age of fifty-four; the unworthy philopagan son wears his crown for the exceptionally long period of fifty-five years. What a blow to the sacred interests of religion and morality, and how

[1] Amos v. 6, 14. [2] Hosea viii. 7. [3] *Ibid.* x. 12.

hard to explain on the hypothesis that Jehovah cares for the right. That dreary half-century of misrule was an evil time for the faithful in the land. For them there was nothing but the cold shade of neglect or the fire of persecution, the royal favour being reserved for those who obsequiously followed a bad example. The *anavim*, the poor afflicted ones of those dismal years, would be forced by their own experience to meditate on a comparatively new problem, the reality of a Providence in the *individual life*. That the divine care for the right should show itself there also, as well as in the nation at large, was a very natural thought. Still more natural was it to expect that the divine care should show itself there at least, when it was not apparent anywhere else. Hence we are not surprised to find that in the pages of Jeremiah the fortunes of the individual righteous man have become a prominent subject of reflection. These fortunes, in the case of Jeremiah himself, not less than in the case of the like-minded of a previous generation, were of a distressing character; hence the urgency with which he asks the question, 'Wherefore doth the way of the wicked prosper?'[1] It is a question which he cannot answer. He is simply astonished that prosperity should so often be on the wrong side; bad men faring as if God loved them, good men faring as if God hated, or at least cared not, for them.

[1] Jeremiah xii. 1.

THE HEBREW PROPHETS

The matter could not end there. Deep thought on so vital a theme must issue in one or other of two results. Either the theory of a righteous Providence must be abandoned as untenable, or the sufferings of righteous men must be discovered to serve some good purpose in harmony with the supposed aim of Providence. In the golden oracles of the unknown prophet of the Exile we find the dialectic process coming to rest in the latter of these alternatives. The fifty-third chapter of the Book of Isaiah is the classic formulation of the new doctrine. A question vividly expressing the marvellous nature of the statement about to be made forms an appropriate prelude. 'Who hath believed our report?' asks the prophet, not by way of complaint that no one believes, for no one but himself yet knows what he is going to say, but by way of hinting that what he is about to declare is of so unheard-of a character that surprise and incredulity on first hearing will be very excusable. 'Who can credit what I am going to tell? it is a great wonder; listen!' And what then is the wonder? Is it that the righteous servant of Jehovah is a great sufferer? No! that for a good while, ever since the evil days of King Manasseh, has been a familiar commonplace, known to all men through the unwritten tradition of the sorrow of pious forefathers, and through the outspoken complaints of Jeremiah. Not that the servant of Jehovah suffers is the marvel, but that through suffering he passes into world-wide renown.[1] The glory that is to follow the suffering, not the suffering in itself, is the main theme of the prophecy. It is true, indeed, that the picture of the man of sorrow, exhibiting in sombre colours the tragic details of his woful experience, is what chiefly catches the eye of the reader. But the prophetic artist spends his strength here not merely to elicit the sympathetic exclamation, How great a sufferer! but to communicate insight into the source and the issue of the suffering. Three things he desires to teach those who can understand: that the suffering of the righteous one is due to the sin of the unrighteous; that there shall be a great reversal of fortune for the sufferer, humiliation passing into exaltation; and that those who made him suffer will participate in the honour and felicity awaiting him. 'He was wounded for our transgressions, he was bruised for our iniquities'; 'Jehovah hath laid on him the iniquity of us all'[2]—there is the first lesson. 'Therefore will I divide him a portion with the great, and he shall divide the spoil with the strong'[3]—there is the second. 'He bare the sin of many, and made intercession for the transgressors'[4]—there is the third. When these three truths are taken together, light dawns on the connection between the suffering and the subsequent glory, the humiliation and the

---

[1] *Vide* B. Duhm, *Das Buch Iesaia*, p. 367. Duhm thinks that the *servant of Jehovah* prophecies, including Isaiah lii. 13–liii. 12 are postexilian.

[2] Isaiah liii. 5.   [3] *Ibid.* liii. 12.   [4] *Ibid.* liii. 12.

exaltation. It is seen to be a connection not merely of sequence but of causality, the exaltation having its root in the humiliation. For what is the state of humiliation? Viewed from the outside, it is simply the state of one very miserable: despised of men, stricken, abandoned, cursed by God. But from the prophet's point of view it is the state of one who suffers unjustly through the sin of the very men who despise him, and who is all the while, in spite of appearances to the contrary, not the accursed, but the beloved servant of Jehovah. It is only a question of time when the prophetic view will be accepted as the true one. And when that time arrives the great reversal shall have begun. The new view of the old fact, embodied in the confession, 'surely he hath borne *our* griefs,'[1] will bring about the grand transformation: the despised one taking his place among the great, and winning divine favour even for the unworthy.

Such, in meagre outline, is the import of this unique oracle concerning the redemptive virtue of the sufferings of the good. The use made of it by Christian theologians, following apostolic example, to express the significance of Christ's death, is well known. That use has its own *rationale*, but it does not concern us here. We have to take this sublime utterance of an unknown Hebrew prophet, not as a miraculous anticipation of the theological theory

[1] Isaiah liii. 4.

of atonement, but as a vital part of the prophetic doctrine of Providence. It is an attempt at a solution of the problem: How are the sufferings of the righteous to be explained and justified, so that they may no longer be a stumbling-block to faith in a righteous providential order? As such it must be understood as of universal application. It is the announcement of a general law, not the explanation of one exceptional case coming under no general law of the moral world. Whether the prophet had a dim vision of One in whose unique experience should be absolutely realised his ideal picture of the Man of Sorrow is a question which cannot be authoritatively answered. In any case, it may safely be assumed that there were phenomena belonging to his own age to which he deemed the language of this oracle applicable: a suffering servant of Jehovah, collective or individual, whose strange tragic experience could be made intelligible and even acceptable to a believer in a Divine Providence by investing it with redemptive virtue. It may further be assumed that he would have used the same key to unlock the mystery of righteousness suffering, in whatever time or place it might make its appearance. Every instance of the kind demanded explanation, in his judgment, because on the face of it it seemed, of all the dark facts of human life, the one most incompatible with earnest faith in the righteousness of God. It is such faith, deep-rooted in his soul, that has set his mind to brood on the facts which seem to give it the lie, as he sits in sad exile by the rivers of Babylon. And here at last is the solution which brings rest and joy to his spirit: To every suffering servant of God are appointed ample compensations; not merely a happy change of outward personal fortune, as in the case of Job, but the power of bringing blessing to a world unworthy of him, whose ignorance and perversity have been the cause of all his woes.

This great thought is a splendid illustration of the power of strong faith in a providential order to give birth to new fruitful ideas. It is not a solitary example of its fertility. The whole group of prophetic oracles usually designated 'Messianic' may be regarded as a fruitage springing out of that faith as its seed. To this class belong those pictures of a better national future which abound in the pages of Isaiah, predicting a time when, under a king reigning in righteousness, the people will also be righteous and therefore happy.[1] These bright pictures of a time when God's providential action will take the form of blessing the good have all to be relegated to the future, because the present is prevalently bad, and affords scope mainly for the punitive display of divine righteousness. That there will ever be such a happy time is a matter of faith for the prophet. But it is an essential part

[1] Isaiah xi. and xxxii.

of his creed. For he cannot but feel that a divine Ruler who never does anything but punish is a very unsatisfactory object of worship. The theory of a righteous government of God in the world can command acceptance only when there is a supply of illustrations on both sides. If there are no beneficent exemplifications in the present or the past, they must be forthcoming in the future. In the future accordingly they are placed by the believing imagination of the prophet. In the future of this present world, for that, not a world to come beyond the grave, was the object of the Hebrew prophet's hope. He believed that there would come a time in the history of the people of Israel when it would be possible for God to show Himself on a grand scale as the rewarder of righteousness by inaugurating a state of general felicity.

This good time coming might, for a while, appear an object of reasonable expectation even in the ordinary course of things. Why should there not come a day when an instructed people like Israel should begin with one heart to seek the Lord and to do His will, and so at length obtain the long-deferred blessing? Times did vary for better as well as for worse; why should there not arrive a time of general and signal goodness, when it might be said without much exaggeration that all the people were righteous? But when generation after generation had passed without the golden age making its appearance, when what at first promised to fulfil hope had turned out a chilling disappointment, when the lapse of one hundred and fifty years, from the time when Isaiah uttered his oracles of the mountain of the Lord's house, and the rod out of the stem of Jesse, had brought, not a millennium but a Babylonian captivity, then men might begin to reason to an opposite intent and say: Since the good time has been so long in coming, what ground is there for thinking it will ever come at all? Such seems to have been the mood of Jeremiah when he uttered the famous oracle of the *New Covenant*. Only that oracle is not the expression of doubt pure and simple, but of faith victorious over doubt, arguing in this wise: 'There is indeed no hope of the good time coming in the natural course of things. One might indeed expect the captives to return from Babylon taught wisdom effectually by a severe lesson; but there is too much reason to fear that the exiles will come back only to repeat the follies of their fathers, possibly in a new and worse form. Yet God's purpose in Israel's election cannot fail; there must be a people on the earth keeping His commandments and reaping the appropriate reward. How can this be? Only on the footing of a *new* Covenant. The law must be written on the *heart*, not merely on tables of stone, so that men shall not only know their duty but be disposed and enabled to do it. Yea, and the law shall be written on the heart! The time will come when that greater boon, eclipsing the achievement at Sinai, shall be bestowed.'

Here was a great, bold, romantic idea born of faith tried by doubt, a new hope springing out of despair. Even if it were only a sweet dream, as the prophet's own description of the thoughts which filled his mind at that season might suggest,[1] yet it would be worthy to be regarded with reverence as one of the noblest dreams that ever visited the mind of man. It was a dream possible only for one who, with all his heart and soul, desired God's will to be done, and believed that will to have for its supreme object righteousness. It was a dream inevitable for one cherishing such a desire and such a faith. For if there be truth in the Hebrew idea of God as, before all, an ethical being, righteousness must be forthcoming in this world somehow. God cannot be conceived as cherishing an impotent desire for a thing supremely good in itself, but beyond His reach. Either He does not care for the right, or the right will enter into the world of reality. If one means of bringing it about does not suffice, another must be tried. Let Sinai, with its stone tablets, if you will, be the first experiment, but if it fail, then we must have the new Covenant with its law written on the heart. You may, with some,

[1] Jeremiah xxxi. 26: 'Upon this I awaked, and beheld; and my sleep was sweet unto me.'

call that idea of Jeremiah's, and the whole apparatus of Messianic prophecy, *extra belief, Aberglaube*, or, in plain terms, superstition. For naturalistic agnosticism it can be nothing else. But the prophets raise a clear issue, and we must face the alternatives. If God's chief end in this world be the reign of righteousness, then a Messianic King and a Messianic Kingdom, and the law written on the heart as a means towards its realisation, are natural corollaries. If these things are mere unrealisable ideals, then the prophetic idea of God and of Providence was a great, though a creditable, mistake. There is no God who cares for righteousness, no Providence having for its supreme aim the establishment of a kingdom of the good.

There are some who do not hesitate to affirm that the prophetic idea of God and of Providence was a mistake. I cannot accept this view. In saying this, however, I do not mean to assert that the prophetic theory of Providence was without defects. The prophet had the defects of his qualities, among which three may be specified.

1. The first of these defects was a tendency to assert in an extreme or crude form the connection between the physical order and the moral order of the world. That a close connection exists between these two orders must be held by all who believe in Divine Providence. This faith postulates that physical facts and laws shall serve moral ends. But

in the application of that general principle we must be on our guard against setting up arbitrary relations, by attaching every event in the physical world to some particular action or habit in the moral world as its reward or penalty. The moral government of God, as Butler long ago pointed out, does not consist of a number of single, unconnected acts of distributive justice and goodness, but is a vast connected scheme which can only be imperfectly comprehended, and ought therefore to be cautiously interpreted. No one duly mindful of this truth would feel warranted in regarding seasonable rains and good crops as sure marks of divine favour towards a virtuous community, and disastrous storms as the unquestionable sign and punishment of prevalent misconduct. It cannot justly be affirmed that the Hebrew prophets indulged in such superficial logic. They reasoned, indeed, with confidence, from conduct to lot, present or prospective, but they did not reason with equal confidence from lot to conduct. They were kept from doing so, partly through the keenness of their moral perceptions, partly through well-balanced views of the character of God. They did not need outward events to tell them who were good men, and who bad; they could discern between the righteous and the wicked by direct spiritual insight. And they were forced to acknowledge that those whom they perceived to be good did not always fare well, and that those whom they perceived to be evil did not always fare ill. Long life, *e.g.* a highly valued blessing, was not, they could see, a monopoly of the godly. The godly Hezekiah did not live much more than half his days, while his godless son, Manasseh, reached a comparatively old age. Then well-instructed conceptions of the divine character also preserved the prophet from adopting blindly the precarious logic of events. They knew that God was patient as well as righteous, and that He dealt with no man after his sins. In view of that truth prosperity could not be certainly interpreted as a sign of goodness; it might only mean that, in any particular instance, God was 'slow to anger, and plenteous in mercy.'

Nevertheless, it may be admitted that there was a tendency in the prophetic mind to assert with excessive emphasis the connection between conduct and lot, as if the two categories covered each other, and the character of either might be inferred from that of the other. Moses, as represented by the Deuteronomist, confidently promises to Israel hearkening diligently to God's commandments, 'the first rain and the latter rain,'[1] and when a dearth happens Jeremiah appears to take for granted that it is a divine visitation for sin.[2] Without seeming to disparage the prophets, we may acknowledge frankly that they did not grasp firmly, and apply consistently, the truth proclaimed by Jesus in the

[1] Deuteronomy xi. 14. [2] Jeremiah xiv.

Sermon on the Mount that God 'maketh His sun to rise on the evil and on the good, and sendeth rain on the just and on the unjust.'[1] In that respect the great ones of the Old Testament come far behind the greater Teacher who speaks to us in the New.

2. A second characteristic defect of the prophets was a tendency to lay a onesided emphasis on the punitive action of divine providence. They placed judgment above mercy. The 'day of Jehovah' in the prophetic dialect meant chiefly a day of judgment. This was not due to any ignoble vice of temper; it was rather an infirmity arising out of the passion for righteousness. The prophet loved right so intensely that he could not bear the sight of evil. 'Away with it!' he exclaimed impatiently, 'let the stormy wind of divine judgment sweep it off the face of the earth.' Then unhappily evil was usually more plentiful than good. What the prophet longed to see, justice and mercy, was too often conspicuous by its absence. Can we wonder if, weary to death of the monotonous dominion of bad custom, the devotee of righteousness gave utterance in grim tones to the sentiment, 'Let the sinners be consumed out of the earth, and let the wicked be no more.'[1] Then it has to be remembered that the theatre of divine justice for the prophet was this present world. He did not relegate the guerdons of good and evil to a life beyond the grave, and take

[1] Matthew v. 45.   [2] Psalm civ. 35.

philosophically the prevalence of any amount of moral confusion in the present life. He desired to see divine justice and goodness now, in the land of the living. And when he did not see them, when especially justice tarried long, and wickedness flourished like a green bay tree, he was wroth, and demanded a judgment day in terms fierce and peremptory, sounding possibly to our delicate modern ears savage and brutal. This was partly his merit, partly also his weakness. It was the infirmity of John the Baptist, who could not imagine the Christ coming without the axe of judgment to cut down barren fruit-trees. John was great in his holy rage against sin, but also little; the least in the Kingdom of Heaven was greater than he.

3. One other defect of the prophets remains to be mentioned. It is the tendency to attach too much value to outward good and ill as the reward and penalty of conduct. Herein they went to the opposite extreme from the Stoics. The Stoics reckoned outward good and ill matters of indifference; to the Hebrew prophet, on the other hand, these things appeared almost the *summum bonum* and the *summum malum*. Such a view reveals moral crudity, for the thoroughly instructed conscience cannot possibly attach so high a value to anything external. It also creates difficulty for one who desires earnestly to believe in a providential order. For character and outward lot are not so

uniformly correspondent as theory requires. The theory that God loves the righteous and hates the wicked breaks down unless marks of divine favour and disfavour can be found elsewhere than in external experience. That it is ever well with the good man can be maintained only when felicity is placed within, and made to consist in what a man is, not in what he has. At this point the doctrine of Jesus shows a great advance as compared with that of Hebrew prophecy. In the Gospels the method of outwardness gives place to the method of inwardness, and goodness becomes its own reward. Outward good has still some value. But it is secondary, not primary; a means to an end, not an end in itself. And outward ill can serve spiritual ends as well as outward good, nay, even in a higher degree. A man may have cause to rejoice in tribulation more than in wealth, or health, or length of days.

To this purer vision Hebrew prophets did not attain, though some came near to it, *e.g.* Habakkuk, when he sang his triumphant song, 'Although the fig tree shall not blossom.'[1] But though they fell short, their very limitations rendered service to the higher faith. They did the utmost possible for their own theory, and prepared the way for a better by making it manifest that, on their view of the connection between lot and conduct, the problem of Providence was insoluble.

[1] Habakkuk iii. 17-19.

While frankly acknowledging these defects, we must not permit them to blind our minds to the inestimable service rendered by the prophets to the higher interests of humanity. Their characteristic passion for righteousness was a virtue of such transcendent worth that of itself it might cover a multitude of infirmities. Their idea of God as an ethical being is worthy of all acceptation, and intrinsically fit to survive all other conceptions. They might be mistaken as to the precise mode and measure in which divine righteousness reveals itself in the world, but their imperishable merit is to have seen clearly that the only Divinity worthy of homage is one who careth for the right, and who can be acceptably served only by doing justly and loving mercy. Their broad assertion of the reign of retributive law in this present world, if too unqualified, was and will continue to be a much-needed moral tonic for the conscience of men. Let us not complain of them because they had so little to say about a future life and its compensations. It is possible to make a bad use of these; to be too meekly resigned to iniquity on earth because all things will be put right in the great Hereafter. The prophets were not guilty of this sin. They said: If divine justice be a reality, let it show itself here and now. It will be a bad day for the social and moral wellbeing of communities when their emphatic utterances to this effect come to be treated as antiquated delusions. They were not, as has been sometimes asserted, 'socialists,' but they strenuously insisted on social well-being as a thing to be earnestly promoted by all, according to their power; and they were never weary of advocating the claims of the poor. 'Do justly and love mercy' was the burden of their prophesying. Lastly, we owe a debt of gratitude to the great seers of the Hebrew race for so strongly affirming a connection between conduct and lot in the history of nations. Their declarations are, if you will, over-peremptory, onesided, extreme. That is the way of prophets. All things considered, this prophetic onesidedness is a very excusable fault. The truth they proclaimed is habitually overlooked by many, and neglected truths need vehement, monotonously reiterated, assertion to win for them an open ear. And what they thus asserted, though much disregarded, *is* true. It is a fact that righteousness makes for the well-being of a people, and that prevalent unrighteousness is not only disgraceful but ruinous. Let him that hath an ear hear!

LECTURE VII

THE BOOK OF JOB

No account of the history of human thought on the subject of Providence, however slight and sketchy, could omit the remarkable contribution made by that book in the Hebrew canonical literature which bears the name of *Job*. By its intrinsic merits it takes a foremost place, not only in that literature, but in the whole religious literature of the world. Mr. Froude does not exaggerate when he speaks of it as a book 'unequalled of its kind, which will one day, perhaps, when it is allowed to stand on its own merits, be seen towering up alone, far away above all the poetry of the world.'[1] As a discussion of the question as to the reality of a Providential order it is unique. There is nothing like it either in the Hebrew Bible or outside of it; nothing so thorough, so searching, or so bold. Surprise has been expressed that a work so audacious and free-spoken should have obtained a place in the Hebrew Canon, under the vigilant

[1] *Short Studies on Great Subjects*, vol. i. p. 187.

supervision of the scribes.[1] But there is much more in the Canon with which collectors and editors belonging to that class would find it hard to sympathise, *e.g.* many of the prophetic utterances. The prophets paved the way for Job. They inaugurated the type of doubting thought, and they cast the shield of their prestige over an author who went much further in the path of doubt than any of them had ventured. If a prophet might be allowed to ask: 'Wherefore lookest thou upon them that deal treacherously, and holdest thy peace when the wicked swalloweth up the man that is more righteous than he?'[2] why should not another earnest student of God's mysterious ways be permitted to make such an apparently irreverent question the theme of a daring, elaborate discussion?

If it entered into the plan of the compilers of the Canon to let the perplexities of thoughtful men on the subject of divine Providence find adequate expression, no book could have a better claim to recognition than the Book of Job. This is its very *raison d'être*: to give free rein to sincere, serious doubt; to probe the problem of the moral order to the bottom by discussing the test question, Do good men suffer, and why? Its method lends itself to ample exhaustive treatment. The author does not speak in his own name; he makes others speak, introducing as many interlocutors as are necessary

[1] Froude, *Short Studies*, vol. i. p. 187. [2] Habakkuk i. 13.

to represent all shades of opinion. He is not himself a dogmatist or theorist; he is much more concerned to show how the matter strikes other men than to offer himself as one in possession of a new, satisfactory, solution. He deals with his theme after the manner of a sage rather than after the manner of a prophet. The prophet spoke oracularly, delivering his belief in divine Justice as an inspired message, prefaced with a 'Thus saith the Lord.' The author of Job has no message from God to offer. His mental burden rather is that God does not speak, that He maintains an ominous, oppressive silence as to the meaning of His doings, leaving men to grope their way in the dark as best they can. What he gives us is an animated picture of these gropings, with an occasional illuminating word thrown in here and there to mitigate the gloom of night for such as understand.

As to the date of this priceless product of Hebrew wisdom critics are far from agreement. Opinion, ancient and modern, ranges from the time of *Moses*—the author according to the tradition of the synagogue—to the fourth century B.C., and even later still. The topic cannot be discussed here. Let it suffice to say that such a book, in the natural course of things, could only be produced when the question of Providence *in the individual life* had become acute. That did not happen in Israel, so far as we know, till the time of Jeremiah.

It is probable, therefore, that our book was written after that famous prophet had delivered his oracles and expressed his doubts about the righteousness of divine government. The reputation of the prophet for borrowing has indeed led some to assign to the author of Job the position of predecessor, both Jeremiah and Job cursing their birth-day in very much the same style. The similarity, however, may be accidental, or, if borrowing took place, it may have been on the other side. Our best guide to the time of composition is a suitable situation. Men write such books in times of dire distress, when the iron of a pitiless destiny has entered into their soul. From this point of view the most congenial general date is that of the captivity in Babylon. The unknown writer of the book of Job may have been a contemporary and companion in tribulation of the unknown prophet to whom we owe the second half of the book of Isaiah.

Coming to the book itself, we find it consists of a prologue and epilogue, both in plain prose, and lying between a long series of very impassioned speeches in poetic dialect arranged in the form of a dialogue, in which the speakers are the hero of the book, three of his friends, another person called Elihu, and finally Jehovah. The prologue quaintly tells the story of a man in the land of Uz, who was at once very good and, for a while, very prosperous, till, by a series of calamities, he was denuded of his prosperity and reduced to a pitiful state of misery. It further lets us into the secret of this change of state. In a gathering of the 'Sons of God' an accuser called Satan appears before the Lord, and insinuates a doubt whether Job would cultivate goodness if his righteousness and piety were to be dissociated from the well-being with which they had hitherto been accompanied.[1] There was only one way in which this sinister insinuation could be effectually disposed of, viz., by experiment. Job must be deprived of everything that entered into his cup of happiness—health, wealth, family—to see how he would behave. This happens accordingly, as we are shown in a succession of tragic scenes.[2] The epilogue briefly relates how the sufferer, after enduring patiently his trial, was rewarded by a prosperity exceeding that of which he had been temporarily bereft.[3]

The question has been raised, in what relation the author of Job stood to these opening and closing sections of the book. A not improbable suggestion is that he took these portions from a people's book previously in circulation relating the eventful story of the man of Uz, and inserted between them the long dialogue which forms his personal contribution to the discussion of the problem as to the connection between character and lot. Whether the whole of

[1] Job i. 6-12. [2] *Ibid.* i. 13–ii. 10. [3] *Ibid.* xlii. 10-17.

the intercalated material, forming the main body of the work, came from his pen is a point much disputed. Many critics think that the speeches of Elihu and Jehovah mar the unity of the book, and must have proceeded from another hand. This question does not greatly concern us. What we are chiefly interested to note is that the speeches of Elihu, whoever wrote them, contain a distinct view of the question in debate. They are on that account deserving of some notice in an attempt to estimate the amount of light thrown by the book of Job as it stands on the mysteries of providence. Besides, it has been maintained that, apart altogether from Elihu's utterances, the theory broached therein can be shown to be that which the author of the book meant to teach.[1] When we come to consider the didactic value of the book this opinion will have to be reckoned with.

The part of the work about whose genuineness there is, on the whole, least room for doubt is that in which Job and his three condoling friends hold debate. It is by far the most important as well as the most certainly authentic, and it will repay us to make ourselves somewhat closely acquainted with its contents by a detailed analysis.

Job begins the war of words by a soliloquy in which he curses not God, but his day. Leprosy has been long enough upon him to affect his

[1] *Vide* Karl Budde, *Das Buch Hiob*, Einleitung, pp. xxi.-xxxix.

temper, and he indulges his melancholy humour in fantastic imprecations on the day on which he was born, in passionate longing for the advent of death the great leveller, and for the sweet rest of the tomb; and in expressions of surprise at the continued existence of men so miserable as himself.[1]

This unrestrained outburst opens the mouth of friends who for seven days have sat in respectful silence in presence of suffering. They have their preconceived ideas about the cause of such sufferings, but they might have kept these to themselves had they not been provoked to speak. Now that Job had spoken so plainly, they may speak with equal plainness. They use their privilege to the full. Eliphaz the Temanite, Bildad the Shuhite, and Zophar the Naamathite, deliver their sentiments, if not with remarkable wisdom, at least with extraordinary fluency, copiousness, and emphasis.

The long discussion between Job and his companions divides itself into three cycles. The plan of the debate is that each of the three friends speaks in turn; Eliphaz first, Bildad second, Zophar third, Job replying to each in succession. The first encounter is described in Chapters iv.-xiv., the second occupies Chapters xv.-xxi., and the third Chapters xxii.-xxxi. In the third cycle Zophar does not speak.[2]

[1] Job iii.
[2] Some critics think that chap. xxvii. 8-10, 12-23, containing sentiments unsuitable in the mouth of Job, are really a part of Zophar's third speech which has strayed from its place.

214 THE MORAL ORDER OF THE WORLD

In the first cycle the combatants take up their ground and reveal their idiosyncrasies. Eliphaz, the oldest, wisest, and most considerate of the three visitors, states at the outset the position held in common by them. With perfect confidence that his theory of Providence is correct beyond question, he presents it for Job's consideration in these terms: 'Remember, I pray thee, who ever perished being innocent? or where were the righteous cut off? Even as I have seen, they that plough iniquity, and sow wickedness, reap the same.'[1] This amounts to an assertion that there is a perfect moral government of God in the world rendering to every man according to his deserts here and now. The problem of the book, Do good men suffer, and why? is thus solved by being voted out of existence. There is no such thing as a really good man suffering such calamities as have overtaken Job. The man who so suffers, if not absolutely bad, must at least have been guilty of some very heinous special sins whereof his sufferings are the just penalty. Job is accordingly invited by each of the three friends in succession to regard his afflictions as a call to *repentance* in hope of recovering thereby lost prosperity. 'Behold,' exclaims Eliphaz, 'happy is the man whom God correcteth: therefore despise not thou the chastening of the Almighty.'[2] 'If,' chimes in Bildad, 'thou wouldest seek unto God betimes, and make

[1] Job iv. 7, 8.   [2] *Ibid.* v. 17.

thy supplication unto the Almighty, surely now He would watch over thee and make thy righteous habitation secure, and thy beginning should be small (in comparison) and thy latter end should greatly increase.'[1]

While all holding the same general view, each of the three advocates of this naïvely simple theory supports the common thesis in his own way. Eliphaz bases his belief on observation, and also and very specially on a revelation made to him in a vision, which he introduces into his first speech with an imposing solemnity, whose effect is marred by theatricality in the style and exaggeration in the sentiment. Startled by the night-vision, and with hair standing on end, he hears this oracle uttered by the voice of an invisible speaker: 'Behold, God putteth no trust in His servants, and His angels He chargeth with folly. How much more them that dwell in houses of clay, whose foundation is in the dust?'[2] There may have been a time when such courtly, obsequious sentiments could pass for sound theology, but no one whose idea of God is Christian can accept them as bearing the stamp of a veritable divine revelation.

Bildad's stronghold is not special revelation, but the voice of *antiquity*. Setting little value on the opinion of such short-lived mortals as himself, he falls back for proof of his theory on the traditions

[1] Job viii. 5, 6.   [2] *Ibid.* iv. 12-19.

of the fathers. 'Inquire of the former age, and apply thyself to that which their fathers have searched out (for we are but of yesterday and know nothing, because our days upon earth are a shadow).'[1] And what is the testimony of bygone generations? That any prosperity which falls to the lot of the wicked is unstable; his good fortune is like the frail reed, or the delicate web of the spider.[2]

Zophar has neither divine vision nor old saw to enforce his argument. He finds in his own private judgment sufficient evidence of the truth of his views. He is a feeble, barren dogmatist, who makes up for want of thought by bold assertion, and covers the poverty of his imagination by violent language. He speaks to Job more harshly than either of his brethren. Eliphaz softens the charge of guilt by merging the individual case in the general sinfulness of humanity: 'Man (for his sins) is born unto trouble as the sparks fly upward.'[3] Bildad merely insinuates that Job may be insincere in his piety, by describing the end of a hypocrite.[4] But Zophar calls Job to his face a babbler, a liar, and a fool, and tells him that his sufferings are less than his iniquity deserves. The only thing with any pretensions to originality in his speech is a brief, impotently inadequate eulogium on the unsearchableness of divine wisdom. 'Canst thou,' he insolently asks Job,

[1] Job viii. 8. [2] *Ibid*. viii. 11-13.
[3] *Ibid*. v. 7. [4] *Ibid*. viii. 13.

'by searching find out God?'[1] as if it were Job, and not rather he and his friends who virtually claimed to have fathomed the depths and scaled the heights of the Almighty's mind and way!

Each of Job's replies to these opening speeches of his opponents is divisible into two parts. First, he answers his human adversary; then, forgetting men, he lifts up his soul to God and speaks to Him concerning his afflictions. To get a clear idea of his state of mind, it will be convenient to consider the replies to men and the addresses to God separately, not forgetting, however, that these addresses to the Deity are supposed to be heard by the friends, and to have an argumentative bearing on their position.

As against his human opponents, Job makes a good defence. He brings a preliminary charge of heartlessness against them all. Had they but sympathetically realised the extent of his affliction, he would have been spared the sermon which the Temanite had preached at him. 'Oh that my grief were thoroughly weighed, and that my sufferings were laid with it in the balances!'[2] 'Doth the wild ass bray when he hath grass? or loweth the ox over his fodder?'[3] That is to say: 'Do you imagine I have cursed my day without reason?' To justify that passionate outburst of impatience, he repeats the wish that his miserable life might forthwith

[1] Job xi. 7. [2] *Ibid.* vi. 2. [3] *Ibid.* vi. 5.

end.[1] Then turning on his friends, he reproaches them with lack of sympathy, comparing them to streams in the south which, rolling in full, turbid torrent in winter, dry up and disappear in the scorching heat of summer, just when they are most needed, to the grievous disappointment of travellers passing in caravans through the desert.[2]

While keenly hurt by his brethren's unkindness, Job is utterly unimpressed by their arguments. In replying to Eliphaz, he contents himself with flatly denying the position he had laid down. 'My sin,' he says in effect, 'is not the cause of my sufferings, whatever the cause may be.' He knows this from his own moral consciousness, whose testimony he trusts implicitly as he trusts his palate for the taste of food. 'Now therefore,' he says to Eliphaz with irresistible directness, 'be so good as to look upon me, look straight at me. I shall surely not lie to your face. Return, I pray you; don't be unfair. Return, I say again; my righteousness is at stake. Is there iniquity in my tongue? cannot my palate discern what is wrong?'[3] Do you think, that is to say, I don't know the difference between good and evil?

In his answer to Bildad the Traditionalist Job repeats his denial of the current theory in the form of an ironical admission. Bildad had concluded his speech with the words: 'Behold, God will not cast

[1] Job vi. 9. [2] *Ibid.* vi. 15-20. [3] *Ibid.* vi. 28-30.

away a *perfect* man, neither will he help the evil doer.'[1] To this Job replies: 'No doubt! I know it is so of a truth.'[2] That this is ironically meant appears from the fact that the speaker proceeds immediately to state that no one can be just before God, not because man is sinful and God holy, but because man is *weak* and God *mighty*. Frail mortals have no chance with One who is wise in heart and great in strength, who can uproot mountains, shake the solid earth, obscure the sun, seal up the stars, tread on the waves, and rejoice in the storm.[3] With such a powerful Being he, Job, would rather not contend. He would not care to appear with Him in court, either as pursuer or as defender. Even if he were innocent he would not reply to His charges, but would make supplication to his assailant. Though he might deem himself wronged, he would not call the Almighty One's doings in question, lest he should bring on himself more bitter plagues.[4]

Such sentiments imply that a regard to equity is not *apparent* in God's dealings with men. Not *right* but *might* seems to rule the world. Job accordingly openly, fiercely declares this to be his opinion. 'I am guiltless; I value not my life, I despise existence. It is all one, therefore I will out with it; guiltless and guilty He destroys alike.

[1] Job viii. 20.
[2] *Ibid*. ix. 2.
[3] *Ibid*. ix. 4-8.
[4] *Ibid*. ix. 14-20.

When the scourge slays suddenly, He mocks at the distress of the righteous. Earth is given by Him into the hand of the wicked. He covereth the faces of the judges thereof (so that their judgments are unjust or erroneous). If not He, who then is it? The fact at least is undeniable.'[1]

In replying to Zophar, Job becomes contemptuous. 'No doubt,' he exclaims, levelling the remark at all the three friends, but aiming especially at Zophar; 'no doubt but ye are the people, and wisdom shall die with you. But I have understanding as well as you; I am not inferior to you: yea, who knoweth not such things as these?'[2]—such platitudes, *i.e.* as Zophar had just uttered concerning Divine Might and Wisdom. He takes it as an insult to have such things said to him as if relevant to his case. They are not against him, they rather make a point in his favour; for the mysteriousness of God's ways was just the truth which his experience exemplified. Far from denying that truth, therefore, he enlarges on it, eloquently descanting on the wisdom and power of God as manifested in the works of creation and providence, and showing Zophar how far he can excel him even in his own line. This eulogium is one of the choice passages in the book.[3]

Facts proving that God is wise and mighty abound in the world. But what have they to do with the question at issue? Does God's sovereign power

[1] Job ix. 22-24. [2] *Ibid.* xii. 2, 3. [3] *Ibid.* xii. 13-25.

prove that he, Job, is now suffering on account of special sin? If Zophar had no better argument than that, he would have done well to remain silent. So to argue was to play the part of a sycophant towards God, maintaining that all He does must be right because He is almighty. This odious *rôle* Job without hesitation ascribes to his friends. He calls them *special pleaders* for God; charges them with speaking wrong in God's behalf, talking deceitfully for Him, accepting His person, taking His side because it is *safe*, saying in effect, 'The Almighty is of course right, and you are not to be listened to. He has grievously afflicted you, and that settles the matter; you are a wicked man.'[1] He warns them that God will not thank them for this service. For God *is* righteous, though His righteousness does not manifest itself as they imagine, and He will be angry at them for telling lies in His interest, and throwing a poor mortal beneath the wheel of His omnipotence, exclaiming, 'It is right that he should be crushed; it is the chariot of the Almighty that rolls over him!'

In his addresses to God the attitude of Job is more questionable. He utters in these some sentiments of an unbecoming character which, if deliberately entertained, would be blasphemous. In the Authorised Version Job's sayings to and about God do not appear so bad as they really are. The translators, having apparently been unable to conceive the

[1] Job xiii. 6-8.

possibility of any one pretending to piety addressing to the Deity such audacious language as Job actually uses, have toned down or whitewashed some of his utterances, so as to give to them an aspect of devoutness which does not belong to them. This is to be regretted, as one great religious use of the book is thereby partially frustrated, that, viz., of letting a suffering saint say the worst things about God which can enter into the minds of good men in their hours of temptation and darkness. There need be no hesitation, therefore, in making the afflicted patriarch appear as profane and irreverent as he is in the Hebrew original.

In his first address,[1] after a sad lament over the hard lot of man on earth, followed up by a piteous appeal to the Divine Taskmaster to remember the brevity of human life, fleeting as the wind, dissolving into nothing like a cloud, the sufferer resolves to indulge in unrestrained complaining. So he asks God, 'Am I a sea, or a sea monster, that Thou settest a watch upon me?'[2] (as if afraid of me). He ascribes to God the *rôle* of a gaoler, and tells Him that it is not worth His while to trouble Himself about so insignificant a creature as man. It is making too much of a man to visit him every morning and try him every moment. Why not look away and leave the poor sufferer alone to swallow his spittle? Granting said sufferer was a sinner, was it worth

---
[1] Chapter vii.   [2] Job vii. 12.

THE BOOK OF JOB

God's while to play the gaoler over him? Better forgive his sin and so relieve Himself of the burden of keeping guard over His criminal, all the more that ere long the criminal will have gone the way of all the earth, and his jealous Watcher will not have the opportunity of pardoning him even if He should wish.[1]

In his second address[2] Job waxes still more audacious. He declares that God has made up His mind to hold him, the sufferer, guilty, irrespective of the merits of his case. 'I know that Thou wilt not hold me innocent. I *have* to be guilty (right or wrong); why then labour I in vain? If I should wash myself with snow-water, and make my hands ever so clean, yet shalt Thou plunge me in the ditch, and mine own clothes shall abhor me.'[3] He calls God an oppressor: 'Is it good unto Thee that Thou shouldest oppress, to reject the work of Thine hands and shine upon the counsel of the wicked?'[4] Again: 'If I sin, then Thou markest me, and Thou wilt not acquit me from mine iniquity. If I be wicked, woe unto me; and if I be righteous yet will I not lift up mine head—Thou wouldest hunt me as a fierce lion, redouble thine indignation against me, marshal host on host against me.'[5]

In the third address[6] the tone becomes more subdued. Still we hear defiant notes, as when,

---

[1] Job vii. 17-21.   [2] *Ibid.*, chapter x.   [3] *Ibid.* ix. 28.
[4] *Ibid.* x. 3.   [5] *Ibid.* x. 14-17.   [6] *Ibid.* xiii.

according to the true translation, the sufferer says: 'He may slay me, I expect nothing else, yet I will maintain mine own ways before Him.'[1] But Job's charge against God now is, not that He afflicts without cause, but that, assuming the penal nature of his sufferings, they are out of proportion to his sins. He asks: 'How many are mine iniquities that thou writest bitter things against me, and makest me inherit the sins of my youth?'[2] He is conscious of faults committed in bygone years, but he wonders that God should remember them so long, if it be indeed for them he is suffering.

Finally, Job abandons the tone of an accuser altogether, and ends his third address and the first cycle of debate with an elegiac strain of lamentation over the sinful, sorrowful, fleeting character of human life, whose subdued pathos is fitted to touch the heart both of God and of man. Who can read unmoved the chapter which begins: 'Man born of woman is of few days and full of trouble'?[3]

Can we say that in all these speeches to and about God, Job sinned not with his lips? We cannot. Must we then admit that Satan has gained the wager, and that Job has been brought so far as to curse God? By no means. For the point at issue was not what Job, under the maddening influence of disease, would *say* about God, but whether he would continue to value virtue and a

---

[1] Job xiii. 15. [2] *Ibid.* xiii. 23, 26. [3] *Ibid.*, chapter xiv.

good conscience even after they had ceased to be profitable. Now that he did so continue, his very irreverences of speech conclusively demonstrate. Righteousness is of such unspeakable value to him that in defence of it he will put his back to the wall against the whole universe, even against God Himself. He will rather die, he will rather pronounce the government of the world an iniquity, than belie his good conscience, and say that he is wicked, because he is unhappy. He is not *self-righteous*. He is aware that he has done wrong, but he is also sure that he is not what is meant by a wicked man. He loves right, and he will not, to please God, or to make all His ways appear righteous, or to gratify men by homologating their theories, pretend that he does not. And in all this he unconsciously glorifies the great Being whom he seems to blaspheme, by showing himself to be the man God had represented him to be in the assembly of the sons of God, one, viz., to whom righteousness was the dearest thing in all the world.

But this is not all. There is an aspect of Job's bearing towards God which has not yet been looked at. In the very addresses in which we have found some very irreverent sentiments, Job expresses himself in a way which shows that in the depths of his soul he still trusts the God of whom he complains. He is divided against himself, and, corresponding to this war within his soul, there is a dualism in his representation of God. God is set against God, the God of *appearance* against the God of *reality*, the God of the *present* against the God of the *future*. This comes out even in the speeches of the first cycle, and it becomes more apparent as the debate goes on. Thus in his reply to Zophar he tells the friends that God will punish them for playing the part of special pleaders, even though it was in the divine interest. How could he more strongly express his belief that, in spite of appearances, God was just and would yet show Himself to be just in his cause? In the same speech he declares: 'Even He (God) shall be my salvation; for an hypocrite shall not come before Him.'[1]

Having analysed with some minuteness the first cycle in the great debate, the other two need not occupy us long. Little new matter appears in the speeches of the friends. They repeat themselves as dogmatists are wont to do. There are the same exaggerated sentiments about God putting no trust in His servants, and about the heavens not being clean in His sight; the same appeals to antiquity in support of the theory advocated; the same laboured descriptions of the downfall of the wicked. The three friends have but one or two ideas in their head, on which they tiresomely ring the changes. They have theoretic blinders on, that prevent them from seeing all round. Job, on the

[1] Job xiii. 16.

THE BOOK OF JOB

other hand, having no blinders on, sees in all directions, never repeats himself, as the debate advances becomes ever more fertile in ideas; not an uncommon experience in the case of all who keep their minds open, and do not imagine they have got to the bottom of everything.

Another contrast reveals itself in these later discussions. The three visibly lose their temper, while the afflicted man, though fighting against odds, as if conscious that he is having the best of it, grows more and more calm and dignified in his tone. A slight ruffling of temper is manifest in the speeches of the friends in the second cycle, but it is avowed only by Zophar, who is the type of those hot-headed zealots who fight fiercely for the cause of truth, ostensibly, but whose zeal is largely the product of wounded vanity. He gratifies his irritated feelings by drawing a frightful picture of the awful end of the ungodly man, the hypocrite, by whom he means Job, which is effectively replied to by another picture in more life-like colours of wicked men prospering in all their ways, living to great age, spending their days in wealth, and going down to the grave without lingering disease, in a moment; men whose whole life said to God: 'Depart from us, for we desire not the knowledge of Thy ways.'[1]

In the third cycle even Eliphaz loses command of himself, and in his anger at Job's obstinacy goes

[1] Job xxi. 7-15.

the length of charging him with horrible crimes without a particle of evidence, simply because the exigencies of theory required him. 'Thou hast taken a pledge from thy brother for nought, and stripped the naked of their clothing. Thou hast not given water to the weary to drink, and thou hast withholden bread from the hungry.'[1] When he began the debate, Eliphaz did not think so ill of his friend as to imagine him capable of these inhumanities. What will men not think and say of each other when they have got fairly involved in a religious controversy!

In Job's later speeches two things are specially noticeable: the sentiments he here utters concerning God, and his grand, triumphant, concluding oration.

There is discoverable progress in Job's theology. His sky is still stormy, but through the cloud-rack bright stars glimmer. The dealings of Providence with himself and with the world in general are still very incomprehensible to him. He cannot understand why God runs upon him like a giant, while there is no injustice in his hands and his prayer is pure,[2] and he asks why the Almighty does not appoint legal terms for trying causes, so that good men may be encouraged with the prospect of judgment on sinners, but allows the ungodly to do as they please with impunity—to remove landmarks, rob the poor, commit murder and adultery; in short,

[1] Job xxii. 6, 7.   [2] *Ibid.* xvi. 14-17.

THE BOOK OF JOB

to break every commandment in the Decalogue.[1] But while the God of appearances continues mysterious to him, his deep-seated faith in the God of reality grows in strength and clearness. He believes that *somewhere* in the universe there must be One who can understand and sympathise with him. He has been utterly disappointed in his friends. Despairing of getting justice from men, he is driven, as a last resource, to the very Being who has smitten him, and to the upright light arises out of the very darkness. 'O earth,' he exclaims with unspeakable pathos, 'cover not thou my blood, and let my cry have no place. Also now, behold, my witness is in heaven, and my record is on high. My friends scorn me, but mine eye poureth out tears unto *God*.'[2] Then he gives utterance to a very bold paradoxical thought, viz., that God will plead for the afflicted one *even against Himself*, as one man might intercede for another. The real idea escapes in the Authorised Version, which runs: 'O that one might plead for a man with God, as a man pleadeth for his neighbour.'[3] What Job really says is: 'Mine eye weeps to God that he would decide for the man (himself) against God.' The thought recurs a little further on: 'Lay down now (a price), be surety for me with Thyself, for who else will do me this service?' Not the friends certainly, 'for,' he adds, 'Thou hast hid their heart from understanding.'[4]

[1] Job xxiv. 1. [2] *Ibid.* xvi. 18-20. [3] *Ibid.* xvi. 21. [4] *Ibid.* xvii. 3.

The next bright star shining through the gloom of night is the famous passage: 'I know that my *goël* liveth.'[1] According to the traditional interpretation Job expresses in explicit terms his faith in One who, many centuries after, came to redeem men from sin, and in the resurrection of the dead. Recent expositors of all schools doubt whether such a Christian meaning can fairly be extracted from the words. The general import is clear enough. The *goël*, or redeemer, is God, and Job expects Him to appear for his vindication at some future time. The point on which opinion chiefly differs is whether the expected vindication is to be in this present life, or in a life beyond. That faith in a future existence should here make its appearance is not incredible. It would be another instance of a new hope springing out of despair. But we should be justified in imputing this new hope to Job only in case his words admitted of no other sense. This does not seem to be the fact. According to recent interpreters, the text can be translated with due regard to Hebrew idiom so as to eliminate all reference to a future life. The resulting sense is this: 'I know that my vindicator liveth, and that he shall stand as afterman (*i.e.* as one having the last word, pronouncing final verdict) upon the earth: and from behind my skin, out of (*i.e.* still in) the flesh, shall I see God. Whom I shall see favourable to me,

[1] *Ibid.* xix. 25-27.

THE BOOK OF JOB

mine eyes shall see, and not as a stranger—my reins in my body sigh for it.'[1] Job waits for God as they that wait for the dawn. The winter night may be long, cold, dreary, but the dawn, he is sure, will come; come while he lives in his mortal body; come, bringing the divine word: 'Yes! Job My faithful servant *is* righteous.'

Now we pass to the grand final charge with which our hard-pressed Hero, fighting single-handed, wins his Waterloo. Job's last speech is very long, filling six chapters.[2] First he replies to the last word of his friends spoken by Bildad, consisting in a feeble repetition in a few sentences of the now trite commonplace: 'God is mighty; who can contend with Him? God is holy, even the stars are not pure in His sight: how much less man the worm!'[3] Job ironically compliments Bildad on the profundity and comprehensiveness of his speech, then launches forth into the praise of divine power and wisdom in a style far above Bildad's capacity, then announces to him and his two companions his fixed determinaation not to abandon his position: 'God forbid that I should justify you: till I die I will not remove mine integrity from me.'[4] Then follows a magnificent eulogium on Wisdom, as more difficult to be found, and more worthy to be sought after, than the

---

[1] *Vide* Budde's Commentary. The text of the passage is regarded by scholars as very corrupt. *Vide* Cheyne, *Job and Solomon*, p. 33.
[2] Chapters xxvi.-xxxi.   [3] Chapter xxv.   [4] Chapter xxvii. 5.

precious metals men dig for in the earth, ending with the solemn announcement that this incomparably precious thing consists in fearing God and departing from evil;[1] an announcement conclusively showing that in spite of his sufferings and his utter perplexity as to their cause, Job has no thought of bidding good-bye to piety, is indeed incapable of such a thought.

Then finally comes a sublime monologue in three parts: the first describing the lost felicity;[2] the second vividly picturing present misery:[3] sitting on a dunghill, wasting into dust, the sport of gipsy vagabonds whose fathers he would have disdained to set with the dogs of his flock; the third solemnly protesting innocence of any crime that could possibly account for such unparalleled woe, and depicting in minute detail the character of the bygone life in happier years.[4]

This self-depiction is of importance as a commentary on the brief characterisation at the beginning of the book: a man perfect and upright, that feared God and eschewed evil. Job, as described by himself, justifies this encomium. His righteousness is not pharisaical, but like that commended by Jesus in the Sermon on the Mount. He is chaste, not only in outward act but even in look and thought. He is just even to his slaves, remembering that in God's

[1] Chapter xxviii. [2] Chapter xxix.
[3] Chapter xxx.   [4] Chapter xxxi.

sight master and servant are on a level. He is
merciful as well as just. He eats not his morsel
alone, but gives the fatherless a share. The loins of
the unclad poor bless the man who covered them
with cloth made from the fleece of his sheep. He is
no purse-proud, grasping mammon-worshipper, no
idolator of gold as the *summum bonum*; still less an
idolator in the common sense of the word. He has
never cast a superstitious look at the sun by day, or
at the full moon walking in brightness through the
sky by night. He is not vindictive; he has never
rejoiced at the fall of an enemy, or wished a curse
upon his sons. He has attended to the duties of
hospitality, never allowing the stranger to lodge in
the street, ever opening his door to the traveller.
He keeps open table, so that it seems a proverb:
'Who has not been satisfied with his flesh?' Finally,
he has not been a secret sinner, keeping up a fair
appearance before men, from fear of the multitude and
the contempt of families, and indulging private vices.
At home and in the market he is the same man.

What, now, is the didactic significance of this
solemn debate on Providence? Renan remarks
that the genius of the poem lies in the indecision
of the author on a subject where indecision is the
truth.[1] The observation is to a certain extent
just. The writer is as far as possible from being

[1] *Histoire du Peuple d'Israel*, vol. iii. p. 82.

a dogmatist, or from imagining that he has at last found the key that will open the mystery. Still, he is something more than a merely neutral listener to a discussion in which other men air their opinions. He has his bias. His sympathies, it is safe to say, are decidedly with Job. The transcendent power of Job's speeches, as compared with those of the other interlocutors, reveals not only the high-water mark of his poetic talent, but the secret source of his inspiration in passionate personal conviction. He indorses emphatically Job's position, and his main interest in writing his book probably was to establish it once for all. What, then, was that position? It was negative in form, but very important in import. Job dared to maintain that the theory so confidently contended for by the friends was unfounded. Relying on his moral sense, he is perfectly sure that a good man may suffer as he is suffering, and that any theory which denies this is false. Why such a man suffers he does not profess to know, but that he may suffer he regards as certain. As the proof of his thesis is drawn from his own experience he naturally states it, not with didactic calmness, but with much heat and passion. Hence the imputation of injustice to God. It is a way of putting the theorists in a corner, saying in effect: You teach that only the wicked suffer. I suffer, and I am not wicked; therefore your view is mistaken. The accusation brought against God of being an unrighteous judge has mainly argumentative value. The same remark applies to the suggestion that God uses His power to crush the weak without regard to the merits of their cause. What Job really asserts is the brutality of men who put him down with a cut-and-dried theory. Their behaviour appears to him to amount to the worship of power, and to making might right. His own idea of God rises far above that which would degrade Him into an almighty arbitrary despot. It finds its clearest expression in the great word: 'I know that my *goël* liveth,' which amounts to a declaration of belief that God would eventually indorse the self-estimate of the sufferer, and say that he was not wicked. That is all he expects from God: not restoration of prosperity, simply a verdict in his favour. The man who expects this believes that he already enjoys the divine approval, his calamities notwithstanding. And with this approval and that of his own conscience he is content. It is not indispensable to him to recover good fortune, however much he may appreciate it. He could, if need be, live and die a leper.[1] Continuance of misery will not shake his faith, or imperil his moral integrity. He can and does serve God for nought.

---

[1] Budde maintains that an unhappy ending of his heroic life is for the author of Job impossible, and he characterises the opposite view as a Stoicism of which there is no trace in the Old Testament in general, or in the book of Job in particular. *Vide* his *Das Buch Hiob*, Einleitung, p. xxxvi.

236 THE MORAL ORDER OF THE WORLD

For the fear of God, wisdom, character, uprightness, is more in his esteem than any amount of material good. It is the *summum bonum*. It is of priceless, incomparable worth; 'it cannot be valued with the gold of Ophir, with the priceless onyx, or the sapphire.'[1]

This is a great advance on the time-honoured theory of Eliphaz and his brethren. It brings us to the borders of the New Testament. It may indeed seem as if the epilogue of the book of Job stood in the way of our ascribing to its author so enlightened a view. It is there stated that 'the Lord blessed the latter end of Job more than his beginning.' If the writer thought that necessary, was his theoretical position not essentially that of Job's friends? If he regarded the return of prosperity simply as an accidental fact vouched for by tradition, ought he not to have passed it over in silence, that there might be no doubt as to his attitude towards the theory of the Temanite? Or did he give to the tragic story of the man of Uz this pleasant ending simply as a good-natured concession to popular ideas, trusting that wise readers would take it for what it was worth? Or, finally, is the epilogue an editorial appendix for which the writer is not responsible, his last words being: 'The Lord also accepted Job'?[2] This is the critical problem of the epilogue, with possible solutions.

[1] Job xxviii. 16. [2] *Ibid.* xlii. 9.

Good men, then, may suffer long, manifoldly, tragically—that is a settled matter for the author. But *why* do they suffer? What is the rationale of their affliction? That question stands over. Three kinds of answer are possible. First that there is no rationale, that the sufferings of men through such calamities as befell Job have no special significance, that they belong to the chances of life which overtake indifferently good and evil men alike. This view is hinted at by Job when he says: 'He destroyeth the perfect and the wicked.'[1] Next, it may be held that the sufferings of good men have a meaning, and that the meaning is to be found in their effect upon themselves by way of moral discipline or purification. This is the view advocated by Elihu.[2] This interlocutor differs from his three friends in his judgment of the sufferer. He regards Job as a sincere, pious, but faulty man, and his sufferings he views as a chastisement sent by a gracious God for his spiritual improvement. Finally, it may be held that the sufferings of good men have a meaning, and that their highest meaning is to be found in their bearing on others. What if, *e.g.* the rationale of such suffering should be to satisfy a sceptical world that there is such a thing as disinterested goodness? This is the view suggested in the prologue.

Such thoughts as these do occur in Job, whatever

[1] Job ix. 22.
[2] *Vide* his speeches in chapters xxxii.-xxxvii.

the relation of the author to them may be, and they are to be taken for what they are worth. But the question may legitimately be asked, To what extent does the writer make himself responsible for these views, what value does he set upon them? Perhaps the answer which comes nearest the truth is, that he regarded them all as worth stating, but accepted none of them as a complete or ultimate solution. He offers them simply as guesses at truth on a dark subject. The position of a preferred theory is claimed by some for the view propounded by Elihu.[1] If, however, the honour of being spokesman for the author belongs to him, then it must be said that the author's grasp of the problem at issue is not so deep or so comprehensive as the power and boldness displayed in his work would lead us to expect. The theme is: the sufferings of the righteous, their reality and their rationale, and the supposed thesis: the righteous may suffer, even grievously; but they suffer because, *though* righteous, they *sin*, and their suffering is the divinely appointed means of their purification. This view is true so far as it goes, but it does not go to the root of the matter or cover the

---

[1] This is the view of Budde. Kautzsch, on the other hand, thinks that the Elihu speeches are utterly opposed to the aim of all the rest of the book. He finds the key to solution of the riddle in the Jehovah speeches, holding it to be so clear and simple there that no one who does not shut his eyes can miss it, a very confidently expressed opinion but very slightly founded. Vide *Outline of the History of the Literature of the Old Testament* (Williams and Norgate).

whole ground of the inquiry, To what extent and why do the righteous suffer? It says: A man may suffer *though* righteous, because while righteous on the whole he is still sinful. But is there not such a thing as suffering *for* righteousness; the more righteous the more suffering, the perfectly righteous one presumably the greatest sufferer of all? Think of the tribulations of a Jeremiah, for example. If, as is probable, these were known to our author, it is not credible that he could offer as the final word on the subject at issue: *discipline, purification*. It is altogether too partial and shallow a solution.

The theory of the prologue goes much deeper. It contemplates the case of a man suffering *for* righteousness, not merely though righteous. The more righteous the man, the more urgent the demand for a testing experience. A sceptical Satan (or world) says: 'Yes, here are phenomenal piety and goodness; but see how prosperous is the state of this saint! Deprive him of his enviable fortune, and will not even he break down?' It is the signal character of the virtue that makes the experiment worth trying. And it takes place, not for the sufferer's moral improvement, which is not much needed, but to silence doubt as to the reality of goodness.

The author of Job, it may be assumed, recognised in the representation of the prologue at least one point of view from which the sufferings of the righteous might be contemplated. If he did, he could not have intended to offer Elihu's contribution as an exhaustive solution, or indeed as indicating anything higher than a secondary, subordinate use of affliction. The pregnant hint of the prologue directs attention to a service of much greater importance to the moral order, for which there is ever a need in this world. There are always plenty of people ready to play Satan's part, and to ask the sneering question: 'Doth Job fear God for nought?' The ruling spirit of the world is selfishness, and the majority are sceptical as to the possibility of any man aiming at a higher end than personal advantage. How can this plausible lie be met? For the good of mankind, for the sake of all the higher interests of society, it is indispensable that it be conclusively refuted. How can this be done? Only by the noble-minded, who believe in something loftier than mere happiness, enduring suffering for their convictions. Persecutions must come. When they do come the sceptical, base-minded, self-seeking world is struck dumb. The accuser of the brethren is silenced and confounded when he sees how the white-robed army of martyrs scorn fear and face torture and death. 'They overcame him by the blood of the Lamb, and by the word of their testimony; *and they loved not their lives unto the death.*'[1]

It is to be noted that the sufferings which in the

[1] Revelation xii. 11.

prologue are reported to have overtaken Job are not of the nature of persecutions. They are of an outward, accidental character, not such as arise directly out of the doing of righteousness, as in the case of Jeremiah, who was persecuted for the faithful fulfilment of his prophetic vocation. The afflictions of the prophet did not consist in the accidental loss of property, family, and health, but in misunderstanding, derision, illwill, the immediate inevitable effect of his moral fidelity. It is only in such a case as his that the idea of suffering *for* righteousness reaches full realisation. It is not to be hastily supposed that the conception of this type of suffering had not risen above our author's mental horizon, even if we regard the prologue, not as a datum lying ready to his hand, but as a composition of his own. The afflictions of his hero are skilfully adapted to the simple conditions of life in ancient times, and to popular capacities in all times. An experience like that of Jeremiah could hardly occur in a patriarchal age, and if it did, its lessons could not easily be made generally intelligible. But there is more than this to be said. The sufferings of Job correspond to the theory which it is the object of the book bearing his name to criticise. The theory assumed that piety and prosperity must go together. The criticism consists in showing that piety and prosperity must sometimes be dissociated, if it were only to let piety have an opportunity for evincing its

242 THE MORAL ORDER OF THE WORLD

sincerity.[1] An experience like that of Job could alone serve that purpose. Jeremiah's experience could be turned to higher account. The fifty-third chapter of Isaiah reads its peculiar lesson.

Is there any trace of that lesson in the book of Job? There is, and, strange to say, it is found in the last speech of Eliphaz, where, speaking of the good Job might do by his repentance, he says: ' He (Job) shall deliver the not-innocent ' (that is, the guilty); 'he (the guilty) shall be delivered by the pureness of thine hands.'[2] Eliphaz seems to ascribe a vicarious merit to the righteousness of a saint purified from sin by the fires of affliction. It is remarkable that at the close of the book this stray thought of the Temanite finds actual fulfilment. The function and influence of an intercessor are assigned to the much-tried man of God, and Eliphaz himself gets the benefit of Job's mediation. Here again is an anticipation of Christian thought. The book of Job, for as dark as it seems, and in many respects is, yet touches the New Testament here and there in sudden flashes of insight, and surprisingly adventurous turns of thought.

---

[1] The history of the patriarchs in Genesis presents an actual example of piety tested by loss. Abraham must give up Isaac to show that he really fears God (Gen. xxii. 12).

[2] Job xxii. 30. *Vide* the Revised Version.

LECTURE VIII

CHRIST'S TEACHING CONCERNING DIVINE
PROVIDENCE

IN passing from the pages of the prophets and of Job to the Gospels, we are conscious of a great change in the 'psychological climate.' The change is all the more remarkable that it takes place in the same spiritual territory. In the words of Jesus there is the same intense faith in the moral order, the same passion for righteousness, the same faith in the blessedness of the righteous that we have become familiar with as the outstanding characteristics of the Hebrew seers. There is also the same conviction that the experience of the righteous man is by no means one of uniform happiness, which finds pungent expression in some burning utterances of the later prophets, and reaches white heat in the book of Job. But the prophetic ideals of righteousness and its rewards have undergone transformation. The querulousness of Jeremiah and the bitterness of the man of Uz have utterly disappeared. The storm is changed into a calm, and the accents of complaint have been replaced by a spirit of imperturbable serenity.

Our statement of Christ's doctrine of Providence may conveniently begin with an expansion of this brief comparison between His thoughts and the thoughts of those who in a very real sense were preparers of His way.

The prophetic ideal was a righteous nation enjoying prosperity; an ideal far from being realised in Israel in any present time known to any particular prophet; but which, when it did arrive, would be a veritable Kingdom of God: God's will done, and the doing of it rewarded with general well-being by the Divine Governor, the happy people having for its creed: 'The Lord is our Judge, the Lord is our Lawgiver, the Lord is our King; He will save us.'[1] When Jesus came, He too proclaimed a Divine Kingdom. The burden of His Galilean gospel was: 'The Kingdom of God is at hand.'[2] But the Kingdom of Hebrew prophecy and the Kingdom of the Evangel, while the same in name, were different in essential characteristics. The Messianic Kingdom of the prophets, especially of the earlier prophets, was national and political; the Kingdom whose advent was heralded by Jesus is spiritual and universal. The immediate subject of God's reign in this new Kingdom is the individual man, not a whole people, and the seat of dominion is the

---

[1] Isaiah xxxiii. 22.   [2] Mark i. 15.

human heart. All may become citizens who possess the receptivity of faith, Gentiles as well as Jews, the worst not less than the best. The heart is the seat of the blessedness of this kingdom, as well as of its rule. The reward of righteousness is within, not, as of old, without. And because it is within it is certain, subject to none of the chances of all outward felicity. 'Blessed are they which do hunger and thirst after righteousness: for they *shall* be filled,'[1] not merely *may be*. And none but they who hunger shall be filled. It cannot by any chance happen that the satisfactions proper to the righteous shall fall to the lot of the unrighteous. 'Wickedness is never rewarded, and righteousness is never punished. It is no reward to lose one's life; it is no punishment to save one's life.'[2]

This programme of a moral order, spiritual and inward in its rewards not less than in its requirements, leaves room for any amount of troublous experience in the outward lot. The citizen of this kingdom may suffer, not only in spite but on account of citizenship. Blessed ones may be, on a secular estimate, miserable. The Beatitudes of the Teaching on the Hill are a series of paradoxes, which seem to say: Blessed are the unblessed. Speaking generally, the doctrine of Jesus concerning outward good and evil is startling. It may be

[1] Matthew v. 6.
[2] Watson, *Christianity and Idealism*, p. 86.

summed up, in so far as it is peculiar, in three propositions: (1) that external good and evil are to a large extent common to men irrespective of character; (2) that there are sufferings which inevitably overtake all who devote themselves to the highest interests of human life; (3) that those who so suffer are not to be pitied, either by themselves or by others; that, on the contrary, they have good cause, as also capacity, for joy.

The classic text for the first of these positions is that in which it is taught that the Divine Father 'maketh His sun to rise on the evil and on the good, and sendeth rain on the just and on the unjust.'[1] A companion text, setting forth the dark aspect of the same general truth, may be found in the words: 'Suppose ye that these Galilæans were sinners above all the Galilæans, because they suffered such things? I tell you, Nay: but, except ye repent, ye shall all likewise perish. Or those eighteen, upon whom the tower in Siloam fell, and slew them, think ye that they were sinners above all men that dwelt in Jerusalem? I tell you, Nay: but, except ye repent, ye shall all likewise perish.'[2] These statements sound commonplace now, but they were by no means commonplaces, as coming from the mouth of a Jewish teacher nineteen centuries ago; they were rather startling novelties. To perceive the truth of this assertion in reference to the saying about the

[1] Matthew v. 45.   [2] Luke xiii. 2-5.

CHRIST'S TEACHING ON PROVIDENCE

sun and the rain you have only to compare it with the text in Deuteronomy wherein the first rain and the latter rain necessary for a good harvest are guaranteed to those who keep God's commandments.[1] The other saying concerning disasters which befell certain men of Galilee and Jerusalem is seen to be equally novel in tone when we remember how customary it was with prophets and sages of Israel, in ancient times, to regard signal calamities as the punishment of special sins. In the case of the men of Galilee and Jerusalem the calamities were signal enough, but, in opposition to popular opinion inherited from past ages, it is expressly denied that there was necessarily any corresponding speciality in sin. That is to say, it is denied that the disasters in question were of the nature of judgments on sin. It is implied, though not said, that they might have overtaken men remarkable for goodness rather than for wickedness, that among the men on whom the tower in Siloam fell might have been some of the best people in Jerusalem.

The two sayings just commented on do not signify that sunshine and shower, and disastrous casualties visiting good and evil alike, are entirely destitute of moral significance. On the lips of Jesus, they only meant that in such matters Divine Providence does not proceed according to the law of retributive

[1] Deuteronomy xi. 14.

justice. Though the justice of God is not apparent in them, some other attribute may be revealed. In the case of the saying concerning sun and rain, we are not left to guess what the attribute may be. In the universal and indiscriminate bestowal of these vitally important boons, Jesus read divine *magnanimity*. He saw in the fact proof that God is something more and higher than a Moral Governor, that to a very large extent He deals not with men after their sins, that 'the Lord is good to all, and His tender mercies are over all His works.' In the accidents named in the other saying Jesus saw not a judgment on the dead, but a warning to the living. He said to His hearers in effect: 'You have listened to these reports with superstitious awe, and have wondered what heinous crimes the miserable victims have been guilty of. Think not of them, but of yourselves. They may or may not have been sinners exceedingly, but there is no doubt how it stands with you, the men of this generation. You are in a bad way; a judgment day is coming on Israel for her sins, and if you *will* moralise on the recent events in Galilee and Jerusalem, I advise you to see in them emblems of approaching horrors on a larger scale, whose connection with sin is unquestionable.'

The second thesis in Christ's doctrine of suffering is contained in the saying: 'If any man will come after Me, let him deny himself, and take up his cross, and follow Me.'[1] The cross stands for the most ignominious and cruel form of penalty for crime, as inflicted by the Romans, and the general lesson is that the criminal's lot may overtake the devoted servants of the loftiest moral ideal; that notable suffering, exciting horror or pity in the beholder, may befall those who of all men least deserve it. Not only *may* but *shall*; it happens not by accident but by law; not necessarily, of course, literal crucifixion, or the maximum of possible suffering in every case, but acute, soul-wringing anguish, from which sensitive nature shrinks, in some form: loss of home, brethren, lands, love, reputation, life. This is the hard lot appointed to those who are the sons of God indeed, to those who let their light shine when the temptation is to hide it, to the moral pioneers of humanity, the path-finders, and their early disciples.

The third article in the doctrine of suffering as taught by Jesus, viz., that the sufferers for righteousness are not proper subjects of pity, is set forth in one of the Beatitudes in these glowing terms: 'Blessed are they which are persecuted for righteousness' sake: for theirs is the kingdom of heaven. Blessed are ye, when men shall revile you, and persecute you, and shall say all manner of evil against you falsely, for My sake. Rejoice, and be exceeding glad: for great is your reward in heaven:

[1] Matthew xvi. 24.

for so persecuted they the prophets which were before you.'[1] The blessedness of the persecuted is not, in Christ's view, merely prospective, a share in the future beatitude of heaven compensating for present trouble. It may be enjoyed now. It comes, in the first place, through an exceptional capacity for joy. 'Rejoice,' says the Master to His disciples. The exhortation means: 'Give full play to the sunny, light-hearted temper with which you are favoured.' For it is a fact that the spirit of the persecuted is irrepressibly buoyant. It knows nothing of habitual depression; it can mount up on wings like an eagle; it has the nimble feet of the hind; it can walk, and even leap, on rugged, rocky high places like the chamois.[2] That is the hero's primary consolation for the hardships of his life. But there are other consolations. He knows, *e.g.* that he is in good company. 'So persecuted they the prophets.' It is a privilege to be associated with earth's noblest ones even in tribulation. The thought brings a sustaining sense of dignity not to be confounded with vainglory, which is but its caricature. Then, since the Christian era began, it has been an open secret that the persecuted suffer not in vain. They may have to die for the cause to which they are devoted, but their lives are not thrown away. The sacrifice

[1] Matthew v. 10-12. Christ's words may have undergone expansion in this passage, but the Beatitude as it stands is true to the spirit of His teaching.
[2] Habakkuk iii. 19.

CHRIST'S TEACHING ON PROVIDENCE

has redemptive virtue. So Jesus taught in reference to His own case, thereby revealing through the supreme instance a universal law. 'Greatness,' He said to disciples ambitious to be first, 'comes by service; service in its highest form means self-sacrifice; but a life laid down in such sacred ministry is not lost: it is a ransom for many.'[1]

It is obvious that these new, inspiring thoughts of conduct and lot, and the cheerfulness with which they are uttered, presuppose a *new idea of God*. There is a bright light on the morning landscape, which, when we turn our eyes to the east, is seen to mean that the sun has risen. The sun of Divine Fatherhood rose on the world when Jesus began to teach. God is no longer the mere Moral Governor rendering to every man according to his works, but a God of inexhaustible patience, not prone to 'mark iniquities,' and reward accordingly, but removing transgression from men as far as east is from west.[2] Grace reigns instead of retributive justice, which has not indeed become obsolete, but retires into the background as a partial truth absorbed into a larger whole. *Benignancy* is the conspicuous attribute of Providence in the doctrine of Jesus. This will become apparent when we consider attentively the relative sayings.

Jesus taught that the Father in heaven exercises a beneficent Providence over *all* His creatures:

[1] Matthew xx. 28. [2] Psalm ciii. 8-13.

plants, birds, men, evil men as well as good men; and over all the interests of all men. He clothes the grass of the field with beauty,[1] such as we see on a summer day in a meadow enamelled with buttercups and daisies. He feeds the fowls of the air.[2] He cares both for the valueless sparrow devoid of beauty and of song, and for the propagators of a new, precious faith. A sparrow, struck dead it may be by a stone thrown by a schoolboy, falls not to the ground without His notice; and as for the apostle, the very hairs of his head are all numbered.[3] But not he alone, the consecrated missionary of a religion destined to bless the world, is the object of providential care. The Divine Father regards all men as His children, and by means of sun and rain confers on them in every clime food and raiment—all things needful for temporal well-being.[4] Nor does He provide for their bodily life alone; He remembers that they are men made in His image, and that their spiritual nature needs food convenient. He does not overlook even the moral outcasts; them also He invites to the spiritual feast.[5] He despises not the ignorant; He reveals the things of the Kingdom unto 'babes.'[6] He welcomes the return of the prodigal to the forsaken paternal home.[7] The

---

[1] Matthew vi. 30. [2] *Ibid.* vi. 26. [3] *Ibid.* x. 29-31.
[4] *Ibid.* v. 45. [5] Luke xiv. 21.
[6] Matthew xi. 25. [7] Luke xv. 11-24.

CHRIST'S TEACHING ON PROVIDENCE 253

God of Jesus will have all men saved: 'yet there is room.'[1] He is the Father, not of the few but of the many, not of the privileged cultured class, but of the uncultured, unsanctified mass of mankind; and it is His desire that in even the most unpromising members of the human race all the moral possibilities of man's nature may be realised. 'Go to the lost sheep of the house of Israel.'[2]

The spiritual welfare of man is, of course, in the view of Jesus, the most needful and worthy object of God's care. But it reveals the considerateness of His conception of Divine Goodness that He makes it embrace the lower interests of life. Outward good is not, in His view, beneath the notice of Providence. It is second; the Kingdom of heaven and its concerns are first and supreme; yet food and raiment have their place.[3] Note here the soundness and sanity of Christ's doctrine, as compared with the onesided extravagance of ideal Stoicism, for which outward good was a matter of indifference. Jesus avoids the falsehood of extremes. He places the Kingdom first; but temporalities are not overlooked. 'These things shall be added.'[4] 'Your heavenly Father knoweth that ye have need of all these things.'[5] They may be prayed for. 'Give us this day our daily bread.'[6] Thus the providence of the Father is very homely and

[1] Luke xiv. 22.　　[2] Matthew x. 6.　　[3] *Ibid.* vi. 33.
[4] *Ibid.* vi. 33.　　[5] *Ibid.* vi. 32.　　[6] *Ibid.* vi. 11.

254 THE MORAL ORDER OF THE WORLD

kindly, and concerns itself about the humble wants of the ordinary man, not merely about the sublime aspirations of the wise man.

Christ's doctrine of Providence is thus, in the first place, eminently *genial*. But it is also distinguished by *reasonableness*, judged even by a modern scientific standard. Providence accomplishes its purposes through what we call the course of nature. The providential order and the natural order are not mutually exclusive spheres; they are the same thing under different aspects. 'Those things'—food and raiment — shall be added: how? Through the ordinary action of sun and rain, by whose beneficent influence bread-stuffs are reared and the raw material, out of which cloth is manufactured, is produced. God does for all what no man by any amount of care could do for himself: adds, viz., a cubit (and more) to the stature of every one who has reached maturity.[1] How does He accomplish that apparently impossible feat? By the slow, insensible, noiseless process of growth, whereby we pass unawares from the stature of infancy to that of manhood. That is the work of a beneficent Providence, in the view of Jesus. But it is not the miraculous product of immediate divine activity; it is throughout the effect of physiological law, and if you are so minded you can exclude Providence altogether and make it throughout an affair of vital mechanics. It is just

[1] Matthew vi. 27.

CHRIST'S TEACHING ON PROVIDENCE 255

the same in the higher region of the spirit. God gives the Kingdom, the first object of desire, to His servants, as He gives to them food and raiment, and increase of bodily stature. How? Again by the operation of natural law. 'So is the kingdom of God, as if a man should cast seed into the ground; and should sleep and rise, night and day, and the seed should spring and grow up, he knoweth not how. For the earth bringeth forth fruit of herself; first the blade, then the ear, after that the full corn in the ear.'[1] The coming of the Kingdom in the individual and in the community is a matter of growth, just like the coming of bread, gradual growth passing through well-marked stages, like the growth of grain under the influence of sun and shower—first blade, then ear, then ripe corn. The whole process is so natural that one who thinks of divine action as occasional, transcendent, arresting, will be apt to inquire: Where is the hand of God, where is His spirit?

Christ's doctrine of Providence is manifestly of an *optimistic* character. His conception of God is optimistic. God is a Father, and His spirit is benign. His idea of the world is not less optimistic. The course of nature lends itself as a pliant instrument for the working out of the Divine Father's beneficent purposes.

But is this optimistic view of Providence not con-

[1] Mark iv. 26-28.

tradicted by facts? It seems to be, and Jesus was not ignorant of this; nor did He pass over in discreet silence whatever appeared irreconcilable with His sunny faith. The dark side of nature, indeed, He did not discourse on; but He boldly faced the discouraging phases of human experience. In our study on Job we had occasion to note a distinction made in the utterances of the afflicted man between the God of appearance and the God of reality. I now remark that Christ was fully alive to the necessity of making this distinction. He has made it with a vividness and impressiveness which leave the impassioned words of Job far behind. The parables of the *Selfish Neighbour* and the *Unjust Judge*[1] depict God as He appears in Providence to faith sorely tried by the delayed fulfilment of desires. The didactic drift of both is: Pray on, delay notwithstanding; you shall ultimately prevail. In both, the power of persistence to obtain benefit sought is most felicitously illustrated. The man in bed can be compelled by 'shameless' knocking to give what is asked, were it only to be rid of a disturbance which would be fatal to sleep. It is, of course, very rude, unmannerly, even indecent, to continue knocking in the circumstances. Any one would desist who had the smallest regard to propriety. But the man outside the door has no regard to propriety. He is desperate, and without compunction goes on

[1] Luke xi. 5-8; xviii. 1-7.

using his power of annoyance till he gains his end,—a supply of loaves to meet the emergency. Similarly in the case of the unjust judge. He neither fears God nor regards man, as he confesses with cynical frankness; but he has a very pronounced regard to his own comfort. He hates bother, and as the widow in her frantic determination to get justice seems likely to give him plenty of it, he decides the cause in her favour to get quit of her.

The relevancy of these parabolic narratives to the moral they are designed to point requires us to regard the two unlovable characters depicted as representing God as He appears in Providence to tried faith. In the weary time of delayed fulfilment He seems as unfriendly as the man in bed, as indifferent to right as the unprincipled judge. No more unfavourable view of the divine character could be suggested. But in the case of Jesus such dark thoughts of God have their source, not in personal doubt, as in the case of Job, but in acute sympathy with perplexed souls.

In both the parables, which have for their common aim to inculcate perseverance in prayer, the chief object of desire is supposed to be the interests of the divine kingdom. It is therefore important to notice that delay in the fulfilment of desire is regarded by Christ as a likely experience even in this region. Men have to wait even here. They cannot obtain moral benefit, spiritual good, for themselves or for others, off-hand. Jesus regards that as a certain fact, and He makes no complaint. It is God's way in the moral order of the world, and it is right —such is His fixed, unalterable conviction. Comparatively few thoroughly realise the fact; fewer still are completely reconciled to it as fitting and reasonable. Why, men are inclined to ask, should the kingdom of God not come *per saltum*? Why should the realisation of the moral ideal in the individual, or in the race, be a matter of slow process during which hope deferred makes the heart sick? Could the process not be accelerated, or even resolved into an instantaneous consummation, by sufficiently earnest desire? Christ says, No: though you break your heart it will be a slow movement, a gradual growth from seed to fruit. Growth is the law of the natural world; it is also the law of the spiritual world. This great truth Jesus taught in the most explicit manner and with exquisite felicity in the parable of the Blade, the Ear, and the full Corn. No more significant statement of it is to be found in the Bible, or indeed anywhere else. By the utterance of this word Jesus showed himself more philosophic than some modern philosophers, who, while recognising the universal sway of the law of growth or evolution, maintain that process in the moral sphere is inadmissible on theistic principles. A God infinite in goodness and might must make the moral world perfect at once.[1] From the parable just referred to, as well as from the two parables inculcating perseverance in prayer, it is clear that Christ felt no such difficulty. He accepted process as the law of the moral world, and He saw in it no reflection on divine goodness and power. The paternal love of God appeared to Him to be sufficiently vindicated by the result. Eventual fulfilment of aspiration supplied an adequate theodicy. The Father in heaven, whose character undergoes eclipse for weak faith during the period of waiting, is shown to be in reality worthy of His name if, after years in the case of the individual, or after centuries in the case of a community, spiritual desire be at length satisfied. If Jesus Christ had lived in our time, and had heard Mr. John Fiske bring his indictment against the theistic creed on the ground that the moral progress of society is a matter of slow secular growth, He would have administered to him the gentle rebuke: Man, where is thy faith?

The faith of Jesus in the benignity of Providence was absolute. While fully acknowledging all the facts on which the pessimist might construct his dismal creed of a non-moral or malignant Deity, He claimed for the Divine Father implicit trust. 'Take no thought for the morrow,'[2] He said to His disciples on the hill. The counsel implies cheerful confidence

---

[1] Vide *The Providential Order of the World*—my first course of Gifford Lectures—p. 137. [2] Matthew vi. 34.

260 THE MORAL ORDER OF THE WORLD

in the future, assurance that under the Providence of the Father all will go well. Not that the possibility of evil on the morrow is denied. It is recognised that each future day may have its own trouble.[1] But the Master's advice to disciples is: Wait till it comes; do not anticipate evil. And He means, though He does not say, When the day comes its evil will be transmuted into good; the things that beforehand seem to be against you will, on their arrival, be found to be in your favour. Leave your times in God's hands.

Jesus lived His own philosophy; witness that sublime devotional utterance: 'I thank thee, O Father'![2] For what does He give thanks? For the boon of a few illiterate disciples who lovingly follow Him while the scholars and religionists of Israel treat Him with disdain. Their unbelief is the evil of the day, and in view of it the prayer of Jesus looks like an act of resignation under defeat. But it is more than that. Jesus speaks, not under depression, but in buoyant hopefulness. In the adhesion of the 'babes' He sees the promise and potency of a great future for His cause. Hence the note of triumph: 'All things have been delivered unto Me of My Father,' which means, 'The future is Mine; the faith I preach shall become the faith of the world. Scornful Rabbis and haughty Pharisees

---

[1] κακία: physical, not moral evil.
[2] Matthew xi. 25-30; Luke x. 21, 22.

will pass away, and these little ones will grow into a great community of men in every land who shall worship the Father in spirit and in truth.' What spiritual insight is here! What power to estimate the relative force of contemporary currents of thought, to discern in the belief of babes a more potent factor than the unbelief of influential religious leaders, the representatives and strenuous upholders of a venerable but decadent tradition! What faith in the law of growth: calm conviction that the little one shall become a thousand, the small one a strong nation, the handful of corn scattered on the mountain top a mighty harvest waving in the wind of autumn! How impossible depression for one possessing such insight, such unlimited reliance on the action of moral laws, such sunny trust in the goodwill of the Father!

Such trust, habitually practised by Jesus under extreme difficulties, is possible for all, and worth cultivating. It banishes from the heart care and fear. Where it is, the diviner's occupation is gone. What chance is there for the fortune-teller with one who does not want to know what the future will bring? He does not want to know in detail, because he knows already in general that all will be well. The childlike trust in a paternal Providence inculcated by Christ is one of the forces by which the Christian religion is raising the world above Paganism. Paganism has three characteristics: (1)

It cherishes low ideals; material good is its *summum bonum*: 'after all these things do the Gentiles seek.'[1] (2) It is not a religion of trust: it is not sure that God cares for man. (3) It seeks after diviners to reveal a future which is dark, and whose uncertainty appeals at once to hope and to fear. Christ's teaching cuts the roots of all three defects. It lifts the heart up to higher things than food and raiment. It tells us that God is a Father who loves and cares for men as His children. It promises good, whatever betide, to those who live for the highest.

About the loftiness of Christ's ideal of life there will be no dispute. It may, however, be questioned whether it be not too high and one-sided, treating the Kingdom of heaven not merely as supreme, but as everything, and all else—the world of nature, the present life, secular interests and callings, social well-being—as nothing. To this question it might be enough to reply that such a way of contemplating the universe is more Aryan than Semitic, more Indian than Hebrew. The Hebrew, as we see him in the Old Testament, took a firm hold of the present material world, and a very slight hold of the world to come. The life beyond, indeed, at least in the earlier period, seems to have had a very small place in his mind. But the lapse of time brought considerable modifications in Hebrew thought. Gentile ideas gradually obtained an entrance

[1] Matthew vi. 32.

CHRIST'S TEACHING ON PROVIDENCE 263

into the Jewish creed, and faith in immortality assumed an importance in the post-captivity period which it did not possess in ancient ages. This faith Jesus espoused and preached with emphasis, and it is not inconceivable that the dazzling light of the eternal world might extinguish for His eye the feeble starlight of time. But we have ample evidence that nature, time, sense, the transient and the temporal, counted for something in His esteem. In the first place, the physical world could not be a nullity for one who found in it, everywhere, God. That world, in the view of Jesus, was the habitation of God—a theatre in which God's power and beneficence were displayed. God does all that happens therein: clothes the lily with beauty, feeds the birds, sends sunshine and rain in their season, makes the child grow from the tiny dimensions of infancy to the full stature of manhood. Then all in nature that appeals to the senses was for Jesus a source of intense æsthetic enjoyment. 'Solomon in all his glory was not arrayed like one of these.'[1] What a keen sense of the beautiful, in its simplest form, as seen even in the wayside wild-flowers, is revealed in that reflection! It could not have been uttered by any man of ascetic habit and morbid fanatical mood. A man of this type would not notice the charm of the lily, or the sweet song and graceful movement of the

[1] Matthew vi. 29.

lark, or the music of a mountain stream. Even the sublimity of the thunder-storm, so eloquently depicted in the epilogue of the Sermon on the Mount, would scarcely succeed in arresting his attention. 'Descended the rain, came the floods, blew the winds'—it was not a weary-of-the-world hermit who drew that picture. The world of nature had a value for Jesus such as it has for a poet or a painter.

Human life also, with its ordinary occupations, had substantial meaning for the Galilæan Teacher. This appears from realistic descriptions of scenes from common every-day life contained in several of the parables, *e.g.* the housewife leavening the dough or searching for a lost coin, the shepherd going after the straying sheep, the farmer taking life leisurely between the seed-time and the harvest. It may be said, indeed, that these are simply incidental references in parabolic narratives wherein the natural is utilised to emblem the spiritual. But the point to be noted is that the spiritual use presupposes lively, sympathetic interest in the natural. The scenes introduced into the parables would not have occurred to the mind of one who had not a genuine love for the common ways and work of men, as these might be seen in and around Nazareth; still less would they have been so felicitously depicted. In His parabolic teaching Jesus is shown not merely as a sage, but as a man with a poet's eye, and with a kindly human heart. Impossible for Him to say: What boots all that daily toil from dawn to sunset? It is vanity and vexation of spirit; the Kingdom of heaven and the life beyond alone deserve a thought.

The healing ministry of Jesus has much significance as an indication of a rational interest in the physical well-being of man. This department of Christ's activity has been a battle-ground of naturalistic critics and supernaturalistic apologists, the former concerned to eliminate it from an otherwise attractive story, the latter bent on utilising it as a miraculous attestation of the evangelic doctrine. The relation of the healing acts to physical law has monopolised attention. It is time to turn away from that comparatively barren debate, and to consider more carefully the healing ministry as a *revelation of the spirit of the worker*. When thought is concentrated on this topic, the curative phase of Christ's public life ceases to repel as a thaumaturgic display which one would gladly forget, and is seen to possess permanent didactic value. Duly to estimate that value we must begin by accepting the healing ministry as an emphatic reality. It is a simple fact that Jesus healed disease extensively, one might say systematically; a fact all the more remarkable that activity of that kind on a great scale was a new thing in the history of the religious teachers of Israel. The bare fact, altogether apart from the apparently preternatural character of some of the cures, is full of significance. Suppose there was nothing unusual in any of them, and that Jesus simply did what ordinary physicians were doing every day, still it would be worthy of remark that He too did such things. He, the herald of the Kingdom of God, the original, inspired Teacher of lofty, spiritual thought, did not disdain to play the physician's part. The human body was not beneath His notice. Physical health interested Him. He was the sworn foe of disease. He wanted all men to enjoy life while it lasted, to have the full use of their eyes and ears and hands and feet, to be sound and sane in body and in soul. The humanity of all this is, of course, apparent, but the thing to be specially noted in the present connection is the evidence supplied by the healing ministry that the healer was free from all morbid, one-sided spiritualism which despises the body and thinks it does not matter in what condition the earthly tabernacle may be during the short time the immortal soul occupies it as a tenant. This healer throws Himself into this humble part of His work with the enthusiasm which a less many-sided man would have reserved for the higher function of teaching. He regards this work as in accordance with God's will, nay, as God's own work. He claims to cast out devils 'by the finger of God.'[1] The cure of the maniac of Gadara is, through Him, an act of divine

---

[1] Luke xi. 20.

Providence. Whatever makes for health has the sanction and blessing of the Father in heaven. And the presumption is that the world that Father has made is amply stored with the means of health, that a remedy for every disease is hidden somewhere in nature, that the day will come when there will be no malady under which man suffers which medical skill will not know how to conquer. That Jesus cherished this hopeful creed is a fair inference from the well-attested fact that, as He went about from place to place, He never failed to lay a healing hand on the bodies of the sick.

Christ's doctrine of man supplies good ground for the faith that social well-being falls within the scope of Divine Providence. It does not teach or imply that social health is the chief end for God. That prerogative it assigns to the Kingdom of God, which in the first place means an order in which right relations are established between man and God. But the doctrine involves that social health will be a secondary result of the chief end being realised. Jesus taught generally that man as such, in virtue of his human attributes, is inherently superior to the beasts. 'Are ye not much better than they?'[1]—*i.e.* than the birds. 'How much is a man better than a sheep?'[2] The fact is stated in the first case as justifying the assertion that man is an object of special care to God, in the second as supporting a

[1] Matthew vi. 26.   [2] *Ibid.* xii. 12.

claim on behalf of every man to benevolent treatment by his fellow-men. Jesus taught further, and more specifically, that man as such stands indefeasibly in the relation of a son to God. All men indiscriminately are God's sons, the only difference being that some by divine grace, and in virtue of their spirit and life, are worthy to be called sons, while others are not worthy of the honourable appellation. God treats all as sons, performing a father's part towards them according to the requirements of each case. Hence arise for all men certain obligations. The first and fundamental obligation is to realise the *dignity* of man. It is the duty of all to respect themselves and to respect each other, as men. It is incumbent on every man to remember that he is by nature better than a beast, and to be in life superior to the lower animals. It is incumbent on every man to treat his fellow-men as better than a sheep or an ox, or a horse. The next duty arising out of Christ's doctrine of man is to cherish and give practical effect to the sense of a common brotherhood. Sons of God, therefore brethren. All sons of God, therefore all brethren, whether regenerate or unregenerate, religious or irreligious, Christian or heathen. Finally, there is the obligation to acquiesce in no cleavage between man and man as absolute and insurmountable. Chasms must be bridged, partition-walls broken down, common humanity asserted against all that divides and alienates. Wherever this obligation is virtually denied, the Christian faith, though formally confessed, is renounced in spirit.

Christ loyally worked out the logical implications of His own teaching. He treated the lowest and worst of men as still a man, and therefore a potential son of God. He despised no man; He despaired of no man. He maintained fraternal, comrade-like relations with men whom one might be strongly tempted to despise and despair of. He entered into friendly relations with classes which on political, moral, or religious grounds were shunned as social outcasts. If there was anything settled in current Jewish opinion, it was that a publican was to be treated as an unclean Pagan. Jesus dared to disregard this deep-rooted prejudice, and met and ate with publicans.[1] By so doing He implicitly proclaimed a great principle, admitting of manifold applications; this, viz., that no class of men may, on any account, be allowed to fall into or remain in the position of persons having no claims on their fellow-men to human relationship, fair treatment, and friendly offices. The working out of this principle would of itself go a long way towards bringing social health to a community. When it is considered how many class distinctions still exist which are, or tend to become, inhuman, and how extensively the spirit of class interest and class

[1] Matthew ix. 9-13.

pride still prevails, it will be seen that there is plenty of scope for the application of the principle. Its thorough-going application would not necessarily mean the abolition of distinctions. There might still be rich and poor, high-born and low-born, employers and employed. Distinctions essentially inhuman, or powerfully gravitating towards inhumanity and barbarism, the principle, taken in dead earnest, would sweep away. Hence the disappearance in European civilisation of slavery, which at length became intolerable to the Christian spirit. There are distinctions which cannot be abolished, *e.g.* that based on colour. No amount of Christianity can make the skin of a black man white. But a Christianity worthy of the name ought to be able to humanise the relations between black men and white men. It is a hard problem for a community where the two races co-exist; but not harder than the problems with which the apostolic Church had to deal—those arising out of the distinctions between Jews and Gentiles, and between freemen and bondsmen, successfully solved by the union of both classes in one faith and fellowship.

Reviewing all that has been said on the range of providential action as conceived by Jesus, we find it to be very comprehensive. God's providence embraces all men and all human interests, and its aim is to make the life of man full of righteousness, peace, and pure hallowed joy. It is the enemy of

CHRIST'S TEACHING ON PROVIDENCE 271

all evil; of moral evil first, of physical evil in the second place. Its goal is the redemption of man from all evil.

But how is there evil at all in a world presided over by so beneficent a Being? Is He subject to some fatal limitation of power? Not so thought Jesus. He conceived of the Divine Father as Lord of heaven and earth, *i.e.* of the whole universe. How evil came into the world He does not in any of His recorded words explain. He deals with evil as a fact. He sees it all around, in the heart and in the life, in the individual and in the community, among the religious not less than among the irreligious; and He makes it His business to fight it wherever He sees it. But He does not seem to have theorised about the origin of evil. In particular, there is no trace of theoretic dualism in the Gospels. There is indeed a malign being who flits like a ghost over the evangelic pages. He is mentioned a few times in later books of the Old Testament, and during the period between the close of the Hebrew Canon and the beginning of the Christian era he seems to have attained increasing definiteness of shape and width of function in popular Jewish theology. His name is Satan, *alias* Beelzebub. He is represented as working mischief in two ways: killing souls by tempting to moral unfaithfulness,[1] taking baleful possession of men's

[1] Matthew x. 28; xvi. 23.

bodies in connection with diseases which present to the eye the appearance of subjection to a foreign power—such as insanity, epilepsy, rheumatism.[1]

This conception appeals to the religious imagination, giving to evil the aspect of an awful mystery, and it makes it possible to think of man as a victim rather than as the sole or prime agent in sin. Some are of opinion that Satan was not more than a convenient pictorial thought for the mind of Jesus. That He used current ideas with a measure of freedom is evident from His identifying the Elijah that was expected to appear with John the Baptist. In any case, there is nothing to show that He regarded the idea as offering an adequate explanation of the evil that is in man and in the world. He did not assign to Satan the place of antigod, but only that of an adversary who can be controlled and subdued. As a tempter he can be foiled, not only by the Father in heaven, but by any son of man on earth who with pure, firm will says to him, 'Get thee behind me, Satan.'[2] As a tyrant, in person or by deputy, over men's bodies through disease, he can be cast out of his victims by the finger or spirit of God, as lightning is ejected from the clouds in a thunder-storm.[3]

---

[1] Matthew viii. 28-34; xvii. 14-18; Luke xiii. 10-13. Beelzebub possesses men through the devils of which he is prince. The Scribes seem to have thought Jesus an incarnation of Beelzebub. They said, 'He *hath* Beelzebub' (Mark iii. 22).

[2] Matthew iv. 10; xvi. 23.   [3] Luke x. 18.

CHRIST'S TEACHING ON PROVIDENCE 273

Some forms of evil are ascribed directly to divine agency in the teaching of Christ; such, viz., as can be viewed as the penalty of moral transgression. To this category belonged the spiritual blindness of the Scribes. God sent it upon them as the punishment of their self-complacency and self-righteousness. 'Thou hast hid these things from the wise and prudent.'[1] To the same category belonged the fearful ruin which, a generation later, overtook the Jewish nation, the natural result of the judicial blindness of its religious leaders. That ruin also Jesus regarded as the work of the Father in heaven. 'What shall therefore the lord of the vineyard do? He will come and destroy the husbandmen, and will give the vineyard unto others.'[2] The impending judgment of Israel He foretold as certain and acquiesced in as right. It is at this point that Jesus comes into closest contact with the Hebrew prophets. They were largely prophets of judgment. He, too, was a prophet of judgment, though not principally or by preference. In the exercise of this function He was severe. But severity was tempered by tender pathos, as in the piteous lament, 'O Jerusalem, Jerusalem!'[3] In that lament He protested that He had tried to save the holy city and the people it represented. It was no vain boast. Jesus had not only tried to save Israel, but He would have succeeded had that infatuated people laid to

[1] Matthew xi. 25.   [2] Mark xii. 9.   [3] Matthew xxiii. 37.

heart His words. He had sought to save His countrymen by exposing the delusions and vices of their religious guides, and by emancipating their minds from the idolatry of legal tradition and from the spell of a spurious Messianic hope. If they had listened to Him, they would have been saved. If they had accepted Him as their Messiah, instead of clinging to the vain expectation of a Christ who would restore Israel to political independence, they would have become a regenerate people at peace with God and safe under the yoke of Rome. But they 'would not.' They rejected and crucified the true Christ, cherished their fond Messianic dream, fought for it with the obstinacy which only religious fanaticism can inspire, and perished in the unequal struggle. What a tragedy it was we know from contemporary historians. With the clear eye of a prophet Jesus foresaw it all, not without tears, but without rebellion against the will of Providence. In the judgment of Israel He saw the righteous moral order of the world asserting itself. He bowed His head, and said in effect: 'Even so, Father, for so it seemed good in Thy sight.'

We thus see that Christ's doctrine of Divine Providence had its stern side. It was not an insipid optimism. It could look awful facts in the face. It presented to faith a genial, winsome idea of God as Father, in which grace or benignity had the dominant place. But retributive justice is not

CHRIST'S TEACHING ON PROVIDENCE 275

excluded or slurred over. The Father will have all men saved, and spares no pains to bring sinners to repentance; but they who being often reproved harden their neck must at last be destroyed. So it is in the world of fact, so it is also in Christ's world of theory. He does not impose on facts a theoretic conception with which they cannot be made to square. He simply reads the world with enlightened eyes, and frames His idea of God to correspond. He finds in the world national catastrophes like that of Israel, and He recognises these as the work of God acting as Ruler through the eternal laws of the moral order. But this dark aspect of Providence does not blind His mind to the paternal benignancy of God which He makes it His main business to proclaim. A benign God is His gospel. The Lord God is for Him not mainly a *Storm*-God, but above all a sun and a shield. Jesus preferred to think so of God. He believed also that the facts of history justified Him in so thinking.

The methods by which Providence works out its beneficent designs—election, solidarity, and sacrifice[1]—find distinct, if not copious, recognition in the teaching of Jesus. He was conscious of being Himself an Elect Man, one charged with a mission, 'sent unto the lost sheep of the house of Israel.' He

---

[1] Vide *The Providential Order of the World*, Lectures X., XI., XII.

acted on the principle of election in the execution of His own plans. 'He ordained twelve that they should be with Him, and that He might send them forth to preach.'[1] He explained by apt emblems the nature or aim of election, as a destination, not to exceptional privilege, but to a beneficent function for the benefit of others. 'Ye are the salt of the earth,' 'ye are the light of the world,'[2] He said to chosen disciples. He acknowledged the principle of *solidarity* when He gave to these disciples the direction, 'Let your light so shine before men, that they may see your good works.' This rule may be violated in two ways: by hiding the light in fear of trouble, or by removing it too far away from the eye of the beholder. The former is the mistake chiefly in view, but both may be held to be covered by the prescription of the Master. He would have His disciples, in the performance of their duty as the propagators of a new religion, show respect for the law of solidarity in a twofold form: first, by not shrinking from the personal discomfort resulting from the conservative reaction of the social mass against new ideas; second, by taking care to present their message in a form at once luminous, sympathetic, and self-commending. Thought is to be uttered, not buried in the breast, and it is to be uttered, not to show how far the thinker is in advance of his time, but that it may

[1] Mark iii. 14. [2] Matthew v. 13, 14.

find lodgment in other minds. The parable of the leaven is another tribute to the law of solidarity. The leaven is placed in the mass of dough that it may leaven the whole lump. Finally, the law of sacrifice is conspicuously recognised as a condition of moral power. It is he who lays down his life as a ransom that becomes the great one. How death in the form of self-sacrifice may issue in multiplied life is felicitously illustrated by a saying recorded in the Fourth Gospel, in which Jesus likened Himself, as about to suffer on the cross, to a corn of wheat falling into the ground and through death bringing forth much fruit. The analogy does not explain how self-sacrifice becomes spiritually fruitful, but it shows that it *may*—an important service when the truth taught appears an incredible paradox.

Christ's doctrine of Providence is acceptable in every point of view. It satisfies the demands alike of heart, conscience, and reason. It satisfies the heart by offering to faith a God whose nature is paternal, and whose providential action has for its supreme characteristic benignancy. It satisfies the conscience by ignoring no dark facts in the world's history; by looking moral evil straight in the face; and by recognising frankly the punitive action of the moral order. It satisfies the reason by avoiding abstract antitheses between providential action and natural law, by viewing that action as immanent and constant rather than transcendent and occasional—pervading the course of nature and working through it, rather than interrupting it by supernatural incursions. Its rationality is further revealed by its unreserved acceptance of growth, progress, as the law of the spiritual, not less than of the natural, world. In this respect modern evolutionary philosophy, far from superseding the teaching of Christ, only tends to illustrate its wisdom, and helps us to a better understanding of its meaning.

LECTURE IX

MODERN OPTIMISM: BROWNING

WE now make a sudden great leap over eighteen hundred years—from the beginning of the Christian era to our own time. My apology must be that our limits are narrow, and that, whatever is to be omitted under pressure of controlling conditions, we cannot afford to pass over in silence the outstanding features of contemporary thought on our chosen theme. And, great as is the interval between the Founder of the Christian religion and the present age, one is not conscious, in making the transition, of passing into an entirely different thought-world. On the contrary, we are sensible rather of close affinity, as if the leading thinkers of our time had come to their task fresh from the study of the Gospels, and had derived their main inspiration from Jesus of Nazareth. Therefore, while, for the full comprehension of any system of ideas current at a particular period, exhaustive knowledge of the history of opinion on the subject to which they relate may be necessary, it would seem as if we might, without serious loss of insight, proceed from the study of the teaching of Christ on Divine Providence to a brief consideration of the kindred wisdom of the nineteenth century.

In a previous course of lectures I had occasion to advert to a prevalent pessimistic temper as one of the evil influences which make faith in a providential order difficult for the men of this generation. I do not regret that I pointedly directed attention to the portentous phenomenon called modern pessimism. But it is comforting to reflect that that type of thought, so anti-Christian in temper, is not in undisputed possession of the field. There is a vigorous, exhilarating *modern optimism* as well as a baleful, blighting modern pessimism. It is a river of faith in God as 'our refuge and strength,' which makes glad the city of God and all its citizens. Of this river of life, 'clear as crystal,' and making 'sweet music with the enamell'd stones,' I propose now to speak.

The optimism of the century now approaching its close is of a much weightier and worthier type than that of the century preceding. The optimist of the eighteenth century gained his victory over evil, physical and moral, far too easily. He underestimated greatly the strength of the antagonist. In physical evil, even death, he saw good in disguise, and in moral evil—sin, crime—only infirmity. Of the tragic element in human life he had no adequate conception; as far as possible he shut his eyes to it, and in so far as he was aware of its existence, he fathomed neither its source nor its rationale. The *summum bonum*, for him, consisted in happiness rather than in goodness, and his theory of the universe provided for its realisation by conceiving of God as a Being with one predominant attribute, benevolence, and of the world as a complicated apparatus for supplying sentient creatures with pleasant sensations. There were no clouds in his sky, save such as relieved and beautified the blue.

Widely different in tone and tendency is the more recent optimism as expounded by its best representatives. Echoes of the eighteenth century type can indeed be heard in some nineteenth century utterances. When, *e.g.*, Theodore Parker declares that there must be another world—a heaven—for the sparrow as for man, and that all mankind must be eternally saved as a mere matter of justice from the Creator to the creature, and shall be, in spite of the small oscillations of human freedom within the bounds of beneficent omnipotent predestination,[1] we have not only deism revived but deism out-deismed, if we take a Rousseau as its spokesman. Of Emerson also, though a wiser, calmer, and more discriminating man, it may be said with a measure of truth that his optimism is 'a plunge into the pure blue and away from facts.'[2] 'I own,' he writes in one of his charming essays, 'I am gladdened by

[1] *Works*, vol. xi. pp. 115-119.   [2] Professor Jones, *Browning*, p. 78.

seeing the predominance of the saccharine principle throughout vegetable nature, and not less by beholding in morals that unrestrained inundation of the principle of good into every chink and hole that selfishness has left open, yea, into selfishness and sin itself; so that no evil is pure, nor hell itself without its extreme satisfactions.'[1] A still more recent American author, the well-known poet, Walt Whitman, outdoes both his fellow-countrymen in optimistic audacity; witness these lines:—

> 'Omnes! Omnes! let others ignore what they may,
> I make the poem of evil also, I commemorate that part also.
> I am myself just as much evil as good, and my nation is—
>   and I say there is in fact no evil
> (Or if there is, I say it is just as important to you, to the
>   land or to me, as anything else).'[2]

Witness also the poem entitled 'Chanting the Square Deific,' which turns the Trinity into a Quaternity, and represents the Holy Spirit as including all life on earth, touching, including God, including Saviour and Satan.

Such extravagances as these are not to be found in any important English expounder of optimism, least of all in *Browning*, the greatest modern apostle of that buoyant, hope-inspiring creed. Browning's optimism is sober as well as bold, circumspect as well as uncompromising. It is not a matter of genial temperament and robust health, but the well-considered faith of one who has thought earnestly

[1] *Essays*, No. x.   [2] *Starting from Paumanok*.

and long, and who understands and accepts the philosophic implications of his creed. It is not an eclectic system, but a belief resolutely maintained in view of all relevant facts, and aiming at a complete vindication of God's ways. It asserts its position with earnest purpose not to compromise moral interests, with ample knowledge of the evil that is in man, and with fearlessness in looking into its darkest depths, as revealed, *e.g.* in the character of a Guido.[1] When a man of whose intellectual and moral attitude all this can be said, announces as his conviction that love is the divinest thing in the universe, and the key to all mysteries ; that, though manifested in its true nature only at a late stage in the evolution of the world it explains all that went before ; that it is the light of the present and the hope of the future ; that there are seeds of goodness in even the most depraved characters ; that by conflict with evil good is reached ; that not otherwise can it be attained ; that evil is here, not to be tolerated but to be overcome, and that it is not invincible ; that the conflict is going on more or less strenuously in all, and that it will continue beyond the grave with good hope, if not with absolute certainty, of universal ultimate victory, we are bound to give him a respectful, candid hearing. It is not blameworthy to hold and try to establish such a bright creed. The attempt

[1] Vide *The Ring and the Book*, v.

may fail, but it is legitimate and even noble. Success in the endeavour would be fraught with much moral advantage. It would cure the paralysis resulting from doubt whether God be a Being of infinitely good will, and whether the victory of good over evil be possible :—

> 'So might we safely mock at what unnerves
> Faith now, be spared the sapping fear's increase
> That haply evil's strife with good shall cease
> Never on earth.'[1]

Debatable questions apart, this creed of Browning's, in its general spirit and tendency, is Christian and, I may add, Biblical. For an optimistic strain runs through the whole sacred literature of the Hebrews: through Psalms, Prophets, Gospels, and Epistles. 'The earth is full of the goodness of the Lord';[2] 'Thou hast made summer and winter';[3] 'Make a joyful noise unto the Lord, all ye lands . . . for the Lord is good, His mercy is everlasting; and His truth endureth to all generations':[4] thus cheerily sing the lyric poets of Israel. Messianic prophecy, with its Utopian pictures of the good time coming, is the outcome and triumphant expression of Hebrew optimism. Jesus, with His inspiring doctrine of a Father-God who careth for all, and His invincible hope for the redemption of the worst of men, was emphatically optimist. Even Paul, sombre

---

[1] Vide *Parleyings*: 'Bernard de Mandeville.'
[2] Psalm xxxiii. 5.   [3] Psalm lxxiv. 17.   [4] Psalm c.

though his theology in some aspects seems, was, in His general religious tone, in sympathy with the Master. He believed that if sin abounded grace abounded more, that all things work together for good to them that love God, and that God's mercy is over all. The most orthodox and devout adherents of the Christian faith may, therefore, open their ears to the teaching of the fervent apostle of modern optimism, without timidity or distrust, assured that they listen to a friend, not to a foe.

Let us consider in detail the salient features in Browning's creed.

Foremost stands his doctrine of God. It is, in brief, that *God is love and love is God.* In Browning's view love is the greatest, mightiest, most all-pervasive thing in the world. Where it is, even in the smallest measure, and in the meanest guise, there is something divine; where it is not, were the lack even in God Himself, there is no divinity. Man, nay even the lowliest worm, loving were greater than God not loving.

> 'For the loving worm within its clod
> Were diviner than a loveless God
> Amid His worlds, I will dare to say.'[1]

'Do I find love so full in my nature, God's ultimate gift,
That I doubt His own love can compete with it? Here the parts shift?
Here, the creature surpass the Creator—the end, what Began?'[2]

[1] *Christmas Eve.*   [2] *Saul.*

286 THE MORAL ORDER OF THE WORLD

But the poet cherishes no such doubt. God, in his view, is the fountain of all love.

> 'I believe it! 'Tis thou, God, that givest, 'tis I who receive:
> In the first is the last, in Thy will is my power to believe.
> All's one gift.'[1]

God is the perfect exemplar of love. Whatever man can do in the way of heroic love, God can do still more:—

> 'Would I suffer for him that I love? So wouldst Thou
> —so wilt Thou!
> So shall crown Thee, the topmost, ineffablest, uttermost crown—
> And Thy love fill infinitude wholly, nor leave up nor down
> One spot for the creature to stand in!'[2]

No other attribute of God, however august, is allowed to eclipse his love. The 'All-Great' is also the 'All-Loving';[3] the Almighty and Omniscient One the infinitely good:—

> 'So, gazing up, in my youth, at love
> As seen through power, ever above
> All modes which make it manifest,
> My soul brought all to a single test;
> That He, the Eternal First and Last,
> Who, in His power, had so surpassed
> All man conceives of what is might—
> Whose wisdom, too, shewed infinite—
> Would prove as infinitely good;
> Would never (my soul understood),
> With power to work all love desires,
> Bestow e'en less than man requires.'[4]

---

[1] *Saul.* [2] *Ibid.*
[3] *An Epistle containing the Strange Medical Experience of Karshish.*
[4] *Christmas Eve.*

God's love is revealed in the universe not less clearly than His power and His wisdom. It is immanent in the constitution of the world and manifested through the laws of nature :—

> 'I have gone the whole round of creation : I saw and I spoke ;
> I, a work of God's hand for that purpose, received in my brain
> And pronounced on the rest of His handiwork—returned Him again
> His creation's approval or censure : I spoke as I saw.
> I report, as a man may of God's work—all's love, yet all's law.'[1]

God's love, finally, is immanent and operative in human life, in its sin and sorrow, transporting, transforming aspiring souls from worst to best ; there ever really, though not always plainly :—

> 'I have faith such end shall be :
> From the first, Power was—I knew.
>   Life has made clear to me
> That, strive but for closer view,
>   Love were as plain to see.'[2]

Browning's doctrine of *man* is in full sympathy with his genial idea of God. He accepts the view, confirmed by modern science, of man's place in the universe as the crown of the creative process; and in man's history he sees the continuation of the

[1] *Saul*. [2] *Asolando*: 'Reverie.

288 THE MORAL ORDER OF THE WORLD

evolutionary movement, carrying him upwards ever nearer to the moral ideal:

> 'All tended to mankind.
> And, man produced, all has its end thus far :
> But in completed man begins anew
> A tendency to God.'[1]

The Godward tendency is admitted to be faint enough in many instances, but it is not believed to be in any case altogether wanting. Our poet would subscribe to the sentiment of Emerson: 'That pure malignity can exist is the extreme proposition of unbelief. It is not to be entertained by a rational agent; it is atheism; it is the last profanation.'[2] To character as well as to lot he would apply the words he puts into the mouth of the Persian sage Ferishtah:

> 'Of absolute and irretrievable
> And all-subduing black—black's soul of black,
> Beyond white's power to disintensify,
> Of that I saw no sample.'[3]

He finds dim traces of good in most unexpected quarters, in a Fifine at the Fair, e.g. the gipsy trull who traffics in 'just what we most pique us that we keep'; in her freedom from pretence, her kindness to parents, her capacity of devotion, common to her sex, and notable when compared to that of men: 'women rush into you, and there remain absorbed';[4]

---

[1] *Paracelsus.*   [2] *Representative Men*: 'Swedenborg.'
[3] *Ferishtah's Fancies*: 'A Bean-Stripe.'   [4] *Fifine at the Fair*, lxxi.

'women grow you, while men depend on you at best.'[1] Even in her case he believes

> 'That through the outward sign, the inward grace allures,
> And sparks from heaven transpierce earth's coarsest covertures.'[2]

With reference to all beings, animate and inanimate—grains of sand or strolling play-actors—his confident persuasion is that

> 'No creature's made so mean
> But that, some way, it boasts, could we investigate,
> Its supreme worth : fulfils, by ordinance of fate,
> Its momentary task, gets glory all its own,
> Tastes triumph in the world, pre-eminent, alone.'[3]

Not merely *alongside* of evil, but even *in* evil itself, our poet can descry good, or the promise and potency of good; in its *energy*, for example. He admires above all things earnest purpose, vigorous will, and demands these qualities of all men, whatever their aims. Indifference, lukewarmness, half-heartedness, is for him the unpardonable sin :

> 'Let a man contend to the uttermost,
> For his life's set prize, be it what it will.'[4]

Does a man leap from a tower to test his faith, he holds his act rational, though it ends in death :

> 'Hold a belief, you only half-believe,
> With all-momentous issues either way,
> And I advise you imitate this leap,
> Put faith to proof, be cured or killed at once.'[5]

It will be evident that one holding such views as

[1] *Fifine at the Fair*, lxxi.   [2] *Ibid.*, xxvii.   [3] *Ibid.*, xxix.
[4] *The Statue and the Bust.*   [5] *Red Cotton Night-Cap Country*, iv.

to the presence of good even in characters to all appearance desperately evil, can recognise no hard-and-fast line of demarcation between good men and bad men, saints and sinners, sages and fools. Character becomes fluid, dividing-lines melt away, a little of the saint is found in every sinner, and not a little of the sinner in every saint. In view of accepted theological classifications, this may seem a dangerous doctrine, but it is little more than was said long ago by so good a Christian as Richard Baxter. In a comparative estimate of his religious experience in youth and age, he sets down this shrewd observation: 'I now see more good and more evil in all men than heretofore I did. I see that good men are not so good as I once thought they were, and find that few men are so bad as their enemies imagine.'[1] Baxter lived before the days of evolutionary philosophy, and had only an open eye and a candid mind to guide him. Besides these, Browning had the benefit of a theory of development which, applied to the moral sphere, means that at no time can you say of any man that he altogether is free, rational, good, or the reverse, but only that he is becoming such to a greater or less extent. The one valid distinction between men is one of tendency and momentum.

It goes without saying that a benevolent estimate of human character and conduct which discovers a

[1] *Reliquiæ Baxterianæ.*

soul of goodness in things evil, will have no difficulty in assigning value not only to the victories and successes, but even to the defeats and failures of the good. Human life even at the best is full of such experiences: of wishes that have not ripened into purposes, of purposes that have remained half executed, of ideas unrealised, of aspirations that have not got beyond impotent longing. It is the consciousness of this that so often clouds the evening sky with sadness. Browning would fain remove this shadow from the mind of the aged. By the mouth of a wise Rabbi he bids them be of good cheer, and preaches to them this comfortable doctrine:

> ' Not on the vulgar mass
> Called " work," must sentence pass,
> Things done, that took the eye and had the price;
> O'er which, from level stand,
> The low world laid its hand,
> Found straightway to its mind, could value in a trice:
>
> But all the world's coarse thumb
> And finger failed to plumb,
> So passed in making up the main account:
> All instincts immature,
> All purposes unsure,
> That weighed not as his work, yet swelled the man's amount:
>
> Thoughts hardly to be packed
> Into a narrow act,
> Fancies that broke through language and escaped:
> All I could never be,
> All, men ignored in me,
> This, I was worth to God, whose wheel the pitcher shaped.'[1]

There is a truth here, though the teaching of Ben

[1] *Rabbi Ben Ezra.*

Ezra certainly goes counter to the adage: 'Hell is paved with good intentions'; and it is questionable whether one should be very ready to accept its consolation, even in old age, not to speak of youth, which assuredly should not be content to dream, but take heed that dreams pass into vows and vows into performances.

Browning's optimism reveals itself conspicuously in his *mode of dealing with the problem of evil.* That problem, in his view, lies chiefly in the phenomena of moral evil in the lives of individual men. He does not altogether overlook physical evil; characteristic utterances on that topic also are scattered up and down his pages. *Ferishtah's Fancies*, one of Browning's later works, supplies good samples. In one of these 'Fancies' a disciple of the sage, having got his thumb nipped by a scorpion while culling herbs, asks: 'Why needs a scorpion be?' nay, 'Wherefore should any evil hap to man?' assuming that 'God's all-mercy mates all-potency.' The answer in brief is:

> 'Put pain from out the world, what room were left
> For thanks to God, for love to Man?'

The connection between pain and sympathy is illustrated by supposing the case of the Shah wasting with an internal ulcer. As Shah, born to empire, he is nothing to his subjects; his very virtues are discounted as matters of course. But speak of the ulcer, and anon pity wells up:

> 'Say'st thou so?
> How should I guess? Alack, poor soul! But stay—
> Sure in the reach of art some remedy
> Must lie to hand?'

To the suggestion that it does not matter though the malady should end in death in the case of one 'Odious, in spite of every attribute commonly deemed loveworthy,' the disciple exclaims:

> 'Attributes?
> Faugh!—nay, Ferishtah, 'tis an ulcer, think?
> Attributes quotha? Here's poor flesh and blood,
> Like thine and mine and every man's, a prey
> To hell-fire! Hast thou lost thy wits for once?'[1]

In another 'Fancy' the question is propounded:

> 'A good thing or a bad thing—Life is which?'

The answer is given in a parable of beans representing the days of man's life, the question being which colour in a handful predominates—black or white. The disciple agrees with Buddha in thinking that black is the reigning colour. The master finds that no beans or days are absolutely black, and that the blackish and whitish qualify each other, yielding a prevailing grey. Joys are bettered by sorrow gone before, and 'sobered by the shadowy sense of sorrow which came after or might come.' Such has been his own experience; others, he knew, may not fare so well. What then? Why:

> 'God's care be God's! 'Tis mine—to boast no joy
> Unsobered by such sorrows of my kind
> As sully with their shade my life that shines.'[2]

---

[1] *Mihrab Shah.* [2] *A Bean-Stripe.*

This is not ambitious philosophy.

A different judgment may be supposed to be called for on the poet's solution of the problem of *moral* evil.

Browning's theory may be summed up in these six propositions :—

1. Morality, the realisation of the moral ideal, is the highest good.

2. Process, progress by conflict, is necessary to morality.

3. Evil is the foe with which man has to fight.

4. Evil is needed to make a struggle possible.

5. Ignorance of the true nature of evil is necessary to give strenuousness and even reality to the struggle.

6. The struggle will have a happy issue in all.

That the first of these theses has a place in the poet's scheme of thought needs no proof. The conviction that righteousness, goodness, is the *summum bonum* for God and for men, and that all else in human life is to be valued by its bearing thereon, is the underlying assumption of all he has written. The Moral development of the soul is, in his view, the one thing in human life of supreme interest: 'little else is worth study.' So he thought at an early period when he wrote *Sordello*;[1] so he continued to think nearly fifty years later when he published his *Parleyings with certain People*.[2] To

---

[1] Bearing date 1840: *vide* prefatory letter to the poem.
[2] Bearing date 1887.

evolutionists who look from above downwards seeking to explain man by the fiery cloud, he says by the mouth of Francis Furini:

> 'Have you done
> Descending? Here's ourself—man, known to-day,
> Duly evolved at last; so far, you say,
> The sum and seal of being's progress. Good!
> Thus much at least is clearly understood—
> Of power does Man possess no particle!
> Of knowledge—just so much as shows that still
> It ends in ignorance on every side:
> But righteousness—ah, man is deified
> Thereby, for compensation.'[1]

Righteousness is man's prerogative:

> 'Where began
> Righteousness, moral sense, except in man?'[2]

and the crown of creation is due to him on that account:

> 'Rather let it seek thy brows,
> Man, whom alone a righteousness endows
> Would cure the world's ailing! Who disputes
> Thy claim thereto?'[3]

But the crown is not one of moral perfection, but only of indefinite moral capability.

The moral ideal is a far-off goal, to be reached only by arduous effort. This is a very fundamental item in Browning's creed, affirmed and re-affirmed with unwearying iteration. Perfect goodness, he holds, is not attained *per saltum*; cannot be, would

[1] *Francis Furini*, ix. [2] *Ibid.*, ix. [3] *Ibid.*, ix.

not be worth having even if it could. Progress is 'man's distinctive mark':

> 'Not God's and not the beasts': God is, they are,
> Man partly is and wholly hopes to be.'[1]

He should not be sorry that the fact is so. He should rather

> 'Welcome each rebuff
> That turns earth's smoothness rough,
> Each sting that bids nor sit nor stand but go !
> Be our joy three-parts pain !
> Strive, and hold cheap the strain ;
> Learn, nor account the pang ; dare, never grudge the throe !'[2]

The smooth life of effortless virtue and unchequered joy—no want, no growth, no change, no hope, no fear, no better and no worse — were an utter weariness from which one would be glad to escape into a world where all these things were familiar facts of experience. The inhabitant of the star Rephan, the imagined scene of the smooth life, grows tired of its monotonous felicity, yearns for a 'difference in thing and thing' that might shock his sense 'with a want of worth in them all,' and so startle him up 'by an Infinite discovered above and below.' He would

> 'Strive, not rest,
> Burn and not smoulder, win by worth,
> Not rest content with a wealth that's dearth.'[3]

He is past Rephan ; his proper place is Earth.

---

[1] *A Death in the Desert.* [2] *Rabbi Ben Ezra.* [3] *Asolando* : 'Rephan.'

Earth is the scene of struggle, and it is the struggle with evil that gives zest, value, tragic significance, to life:

> 'When the fight begins within himself,
> A man's worth something. God stoops o'er his head,
> Satan looks up between his feet—both tug—
> He's left, himself, i' the middle: the soul wakes
> And grows. Prolong that battle through his life!
> Never leave growing till the life to come!'[1]

But does this not amount to saying that evil is in its own way good, or at least that it is a necessary means to good as its end, as supplying the stimulus to a heroic struggle without which life would lack moral interest? It does, and Browning does not shrink from this daring conception. He puts into the mouth of the bishop who gives such a graphic description of man's fight, with God and Satan for spectators, the bold expression: 'the blessed evil.' Evil is deemed blessed for various reasons. One is, because it helps to hide God:

> 'Some think, Creation's meant to show Him forth:
> I say it's meant to hide Him all it can,
> And that's what all the blessed evil's for.
> Its use in Time is to environ us,
> Our breath, our drop of dew, with shield enough
> Against that sight till we can bear its stress.'[2]

Another reason is because without power and temptation to do evil goodness would lose its value:

> 'Liberty of doing evil gave his doing good a grace.'[3]

Yet another reason is that for our poet the struggle

[1] *Bishop Blougram's Apology.*   [2] *Ibid.*   [3] *La Saisiaz.*

with evil is an end in itself, more important than the victory.

> 'Aspire, break bounds! I say,
> Endeavour to be good, and better still,
> And best! Success is nought, endeavour's all.'[1]

One who so worships 'endeavour' cannot be content with the bare liberty to do evil. There must be actual moral aberration to give zest to the struggle —to make it sublime, nay, even to make it real:

> 'Type needs antitype:
> As night needs day, as shine needs shade, so good
> Needs evil.'

This doctrine seems to come perilously near to confounding moral distinctions and making evil good in disguise, with equal rights to existence in the universe, as Spinoza contended. But Browning is no Spinozist, though he fails, as has been pointed out,[3] to grasp clearly the distinction between pantheistic optimism and that of which he himself is the champion. He regards evil not as a thing to be contemplated with philosophic complacency, but rather as a foe to be resolutely fought with; and that makes all the difference. And yet he is in the position of a man divided against himself. His robust moral sense constrains him to view moral evil as a great tremendous reality which might conceivably assert its power in the universe victoriously and permanently. On the other hand, his assured conviction that, under the reign of a God of love,

---

[1] *Red Cotton Night-Cap Country.*   [2] *Parleyings*: 'Francis Furini.'

[3] *Vide* Professor Jones, *Browning as a Philosophical and Religious Teacher*, p. 309.

this cannot be, tempts him to think of sin as part of the divine plan: no detail, not even the vice of a Fifine, but, in place allotted to it, 'prime and perfect.' How, then, does he get out of the dilemma? He takes refuge in *ignorance*, and asserts that it is impossible for us to know whether sin be a grim reality, or only a shadowy appearance. And he thinks that this ignorance is beneficent, that without it one could not be in earnest in the struggle against evil, that certainty either way would paralyse moral energy, or even make moral action impossible. This curious doctrine of ignorance and the use it serves occupies a prominent place in Browning's later poems, and the seeds of it are to be found even in the earlier. The need for ignorance as a spur to action is broadly asserted in these lines:

'Though wrong were right
Could we but know—still wrong must needs seem wrong
To do right's service, prove men weak or strong,
Choosers of evil or of good.'[1]

That uncertainty is necessary to give action moral quality is not less explicitly affirmed in this passage:

'Once lay down the law, with nature's simple : "Such effects succeed
Causes such, and heaven or hell depends upon man's earthly deed
Just as surely as depends the straight or else the crooked line
On his making point meet point or with or else without incline"—
Thenceforth neither good nor evil does man, doing what he must.'[2]

---

[1] *Parleyings*: 'Francis Furini.'   [2] *La Saisiaz.*

This doctrine is plausible but sophistical; one wonders how so robust and healthy a mind as Browning's could have anything to do with it. Certainty as to the deep radical distinction between good and evil is not paralysing to the moral energies; it is uncertainty that paralyses. Firm, unfaltering conviction as to the reality of moral distinctions is the foundation on which strong character is built, the most powerful aid to moral achievement, and one of the most conspicuous characteristics of all who have fought well the good fight. No man ever made a great figure in the moral world whose state of mind was that of Francis Furini—deeming it possible that wrong might be right, but adopting as a working hypothesis that wrong is wrong in order to a decided choice between good and evil. Decided choices cannot rest on make-believe. Decision in will demands decision in thought. Then, as for the supposed compulsory and therefore non-moral character of action arising out of belief in the certainty of the law connecting lot with conduct, it is a fallacious notion due to not distinguishing between physical and moral necessity. Man is under no brute-compulsion to do right because he is morally certain that wrong-doing will bring penalties. He may be ever so sure that his sin will find him out and yet commit sin; ever so sure that it shall be well with the righteous and yet take his place among the unrighteous. Faith in a moral order which acts with the certainty of the law of gravitation is a motive to well-doing which may be powerful, but is never irresistible. Its power is greatest over those who freely follow the dictates of reason, least over those who are the slaves of evil desire and habit. The citizens of the Kingdom of heaven have no doubt that those who hunger after righteousness shall be filled. Does that conviction annihilate their righteousness? On the whole, this doctrine of uncertainty has no proper place in a truly optimistic theory. Its metaphysical presupposition is an agnostic theory of knowledge; it introduces a dualism between thought and conduct which cannot fail to be a source of moral weakness; it suggests a view of the illusoriness of life whose true affinities are with pessimism.

The last article in Browning's theory for the solution of the problem of evil is that the struggle will in all cases have a happy issue. There will be no final irretrievable failure, not even in the case of those who can hardly be said to have struggled, because they have been through life the abject slaves of evil passion. There will be no failure even in the case of a Guido the reprobate, though in his case salvation should mean unmaking in order to remake his soul—a soul in which there is nothing good save the raw material as it came from the hands of the Creator. The trust in such a case cannot, of course, be in the will of man, but solely in the unchangeable gracious purpose of God, which is assumed to have for its aim the realisation in all human souls of all moral possibilities. That being the aim, failure to realise it in any instance would mean a soul made in vain, the divine purpose frustrated by its perdition, which, though the soul be that of a Guido, 'must not be.'[1]

The scene of the unmaking and remaking is the world beyond the grave. There, in general, the problem of evil finds its adequate solution, according to the firm conviction of our poet, who in this belief is true to the spirit of optimism. Not that all optimists believe in the future life. Some find it unnecessary to go outside the present life for support and vindication of their sunny creed. Emerson writes: 'Men ask concerning the immortality of the soul, the employments of heaven, the state of the sinner, and so forth. They even dream that Jesus has left replies to precisely those interrogatories. Never a moment did that sublime spirit speak in their *patois*. . . . It was left to His disciples to sever duration from the moral elements, and to teach the immortality of the soul as a doctrine, and maintain it by evidences. The moment the doctrine of immortality is separately

[1] *The Ring and the Book*: 'The Pope,' 2132.

taught man is already fallen. In the flowing of love, in the adoration of humility, there is no question of continuance. No inspired man ever asks this question, or condescends to those evidences. For the soul is true to itself, and the man in whom it is shed abroad cannot wander from the present, which is infinite, to a future which would be finite.'[1] Far otherwise thinks Browning, who sees in this life without a life beyond only a hopeless muddle.

> 'There is no reconciling wisdom with a world distraught,
> Goodness with triumphant evil, power with failure in the aim,
> If you bar me from assuming earth to be a pupil's place,
> And life, time—with all their chances, changes—just probation-space.'[2]

In the light of a life to come all the ills of this life seem easily bearable:

> 'Only grant a second life, I acquiesce
> In this present life as failure, count misfortune's worst assaults
> Triumph, not defeat, assured that loss so much the more exalts
> Gain about to be.'[3]

> 'Grant me (once again) assurance we shall each meet each some day,
> Walk—but with how bold a footstep! on a way—but what a way!
> —Worst were best, defeat were triumph, utter loss were utmost gain.'[4]

---

[1] Emerson: *Essays*: 'The Oversoul.'
[2] *La Saisiaz.*   [3] *Ibid.*   [4] *Ibid.*

These two great teachers of our century represent two different types of optimism. That of Emerson is so serene that the present satisfies, and leaves little room for wistful questionings regarding an unknown future. That of Browning is so painfully conscious of the abounding sin and sorrow of the present world as to be ready to exclaim with St. Paul, 'If in this life only we have hope, we are of all men most miserable.' Mood and theory in either case correspond, and both in mood and in theory the two representative men will always have their followers. Philosophers of tranquil didactic temper will teach that a solution of life's problem must be found here or nowhere, and that it *can* be found here; theologians brought more or less closely face to face with the dark side of life will tell you that without faith in immortality the moral conception of the universe is untenable. A momentous issue is thus raised, and those who worthily take part in the debate will not lack eager listeners. The minds of many are in a state of suspense. They know not what to think as to the life hereafter, either as to its reality or as to its nature. Old arguments for its reality have ceased to tell, and old conceptions as to its nature have ceased to interest. Nothing will win attention or produce faith but fresh, free, fearless, while reverent, discussion; and those who bring contributions of this character should be welcomed even when their reasonings conduct to conclusions we would rather not adopt. It is a hopeful sign of the times that such contributions are not wanting. I gladly recognise one in a work recently published, *Immortality and the New Theodicy*, by Dr. George Gordon of Boston.[1]

This book has something to say deserving a respectful hearing both as to the reality and as to the nature of the life to come. Dr. Gordon recognises three postulates of immortality, three positions on which faith in a hereafter depends, and from which it surely follows. These are: 'The moral perfection of the Creator, the reasonableness of the universe, and the worth of human life.'[2] On the first he remarks that 'the belief in the moral perfection of God is an assumption for which there is proof, but by no means complete proof. Its deepest justification is that it is the assumption without which human life cannot be understood; without which the ideals and the higher endeavours, the best character and hope of man, are unaccountable and insane.'[3] With reference to the second postulate, he observes that 'death as a finality is the demonstration of the delusion of belief in the universe as intelligible. For it is man's universe that in the

[1] This work reproduces in printed form a lecture delivered by the author as first Ingersoll Lecturer on 'The Immortality of Man' in Harvard University. It has been published in this country by James Clarke and Co., London.

[2] Page 46.   [3] Page 53.

first place is supposed to be intelligible, not the absolute universe, whatever that may mean. And a universe that defeats his best life, that contradicts his deepest thought, cannot be considered by man at least as the expression of Supreme Reason.'[1] The third postulate, the worth of human life, is held to be a corollary from the Christian idea of God as a Father. 'The worth of human life to such a God is beyond dispute. It must be of permanent value, not only in those solitary instances when it becomes the flowering of moral beauty and disinterested service, but also in our total humanity so long as the bare possibility of noble character continues.'[2]

According to the author of whose views I now give an account, the foregoing postulates compel faith not only in immortality but, and in order to that faith, revision of current opinions as to the nature and conditions of the immortal life. Illogical limitations of divine interest in mankind must, above all, be discarded. Of these Dr. Gordon specifies three: the Hebrew idea of the remnant, the Augustinian doctrine of election, and restriction of the opportunity of salvation to this life: character for eternity fixed in time. Setting aside all three, he holds that God's interest covers the whole of humanity, including prehistoric man, and that the future life will be no *Rephan*-like stagnation in a

[1] Page 57.   [2] Page 58.

character that has assumed final form, but a life subject to the law of evolution assumed to hold sway there not less than here. In maintaining these positions, he does not regard himself as an advocate of universalism, which has to do with matters of fact, and contends that, as a matter of fact, all men will be finally saved. What he is concerned with is God's relation to mankind, His disposition towards the human race, the scope of His moral purpose.[1]

The thesis of the theologian, broadly stated, is identical with that of our optimistic poet: A life to come, a life under conditions favourable to the culture of goodness, a life open to all, a life not of stagnation but of perpetual progress:

> 'Greet the unseen with a cheer!
> Bid him forward, breast and back as either should be,
> "Strive and thrive!" Cry "Speed—fight on, fare ever there as here."'[2]

What is to be said of it? That, regarded from the point of view of natural theology, and in connection with the general principles involved in the providential order as set forth in a former course of lectures, it possesses a considerable measure of probability. If man be, as has been steadfastly maintained, a chief end for God, a life after death is highly probable. There is no apparent reason *a priori* why the divine interest in man should be restricted either in the number of its objects or in

[1] Page 67.   [2] Browning, *Asolando*: 'Reverie.'

the aims it cherishes for their benefit. The presumption is that the beneficent Father in heaven seeks the good of all His children, in all possible ways and in all worlds; that He 'willeth that all men should be saved,' in the highest sense of the word, here and hereafter. Election, historically interpreted, is not incompatible with this view. As one of the methods by which Providence seeks to accomplish its beneficent purposes it does not imply partial interest or exclusive regard. It simply means the use of one—man or people—to bless the many. So far is it from involving a monopoly of favour for the elect that in the light of history we might rather be tempted to think that the lot of chosen vessels was to convey a cup of blessing to others, then to be dashed in pieces. In no case is benefit confined to them.[1] If this be the fact in the providential order, why should it be otherwise in the spiritual order, either in the divine intention or in actual result? It is true, indeed, that in the spiritual sphere we have become so accustomed to associate election with exclusive benefit to favoured individuals that it is difficult to dissociate the two ideas. Yet even here changes have taken place in the significance of phrases which ought to help us over the difficulty. The phrase 'elect infants dying in infancy'[2] does not now mean, whatever it may have meant origi-

---

[1] Vide *The Providential Order of the World*, Lecture x.
[2] *Westminster Confession*, chapter x. § 3.

nally, that some of the class denoted are chosen to salvation and others doomed to perdition. The term 'elect' is now taken as applying to the whole class. This extension of reference has been brought about, not by the exegesis of relative texts, but by the imperious logic of human feeling pronouncing infant damnation an intolerable thought. That logic is a formidable force to encounter, which may be expected to assert its power on a larger scale in connection with the whole subject of eschatology, and it will be well if the theology of the future shall be able to avoid a collision which may give rise to a disastrous eclipse of faith. Some say that this can be done simply by giving due heed to Bible texts which have been 'severely let alone as leading the mind in unorthodox directions,' and which, when taken in earnest, will 'create a literature more abundant and infinitely nobler than that which other sentences, isolated from them, and thus made to conflict with them, have generated.'[1] It does not suit my temper to speak oracularly. I am content to occupy the humble position of one who feels keenly the pressure of the question.

In the same spirit would I contemplate the other issue raised by recent discussions, viz., the extension of the principle of evolution into the future world. One who believes in evolution as a law of the universe in all stages of its history is bound to admit

[1] Gordon, *Immortality and the New Theodicy*, pp. 94-95.

that the presumption is in favour of its operation continuing in the state after death. As Bishop Butler said: 'There is in every case a probability that all things will continue as we experience they are, in all respects, except those in which we have some reason to think they will be altered.'[1] He applied the principle to the *continuance* of life after death, holding that there was no reason to regard death as a change sufficiently great to involve destruction of the living powers. But may we not apply the principle to the *quality* of the future life, and say, *a fortiori*, that there is no reason to regard death, great change though it be, as involving the abrogation of the great universal law of development according to which things become what it is in them to be, not *per saltum*, but by a slow, insensible process! Suppose that law obtains there as here, what will it mean? Judging from analogy of what goes on here, this: those who pass out of this world with some appreciable measure of goodness growing slowly better, moving steadily onwards towards, if never reaching, the moral ideal; those who die with only the barest rudiments of good in them finding opportunity for quickening those dormant seeds into life; and—for this also, I fear, must be contemplated as a possibility—those who in this life have gone on from bad to worse, evolving character in a downward direction, undergoing ever-deepening degene-

[1] *Analogy*, chapter i.

racy. That this bad possibility might be kept from becoming a realised fact by the action of divine love incessantly at work with redemptive intent is conceivable; but there it is, in the mysterious Beyond, an unwelcome alternative to be reckoned with by those who would cherish the larger hope. We may not lightly dispose of it by exaggerated notions of irresistible grace, which in effect cancel human freedom and responsibility, and degrade divine love into a physical force. Rather let the shadow remain, dark and awful though it be. Dark and awful it surely is. Degeneracy, or say even arrested growth, what a fate! It is Hell enough:

> 'However near I stand in His regard,
> So much the nearer had I stood by steps
> Offered the feet which rashly spurned their help.
> That I call Hell; why further punishment?'[1]

---

[1] *Ferishtah's Fancies*: 'A Camel-Driver.'

LECTURE X

MODERN DUALISM: SCIENTIFIC AND PHILOSOPHIC ASPECTS

MODERN DUALISM, under all its phases, is a totally different phenomenon from the Pessimism which we had occasion to consider in connection with our first course of Lectures. The pessimist sees in the universe nothing but evil. God is evil, man is evil, the world is evil, and there is no hope of improvement. The best thing were that whatever exists ceased to be, and that nothing remained but an infinite eternal void. Dualism, on the other hand, believes in good, above all in a good God. The very rationale of theistic dualism is zeal for the goodness of God, the wish to relieve the Divine Being of responsibility for whatever evil may be in the world. Various expedients may be resorted to for that end; but their common aim is to guard the moral purity of Deity against stain, and to maintain intact the creed that 'God is light and in Him is no darkness at all.' This is an attitude which all can honour, even when not convinced that the need for guarding the divine character is as great as the dualist supposes. Nor

MODERN DUALISM

can the opinion of those who think the need is urgent be treated lightly, when it is remembered that it has been entertained by some of the greatest religious and philosophic thinkers of the past, such as Zoroaster in Persia, and Plato among the Greeks. The Zoroastrian method of guarding the divine purity was to invent an antigod, an evil spirit supposed to be the ultimate author of all the evil in the world, the good being credited to the benign spirit, Ahuramazda. Plato's method was different. He conceived of matter as existing independently of God, a *datum* for the divine Architect of the cosmos, unalterable in its essential character, and presenting a certain intractableness to divine Power, so that, with the best intentions, God could not make the world absolutely good.[1] By comparison with this Greek idea the device of Zoroaster may appear crude, but even it commands our respect in virtue of its aim. And when, amid such diversity in the nature of the solutions, we find the great thinkers of both peoples agreed in the feeling that there was a problem to be solved, we must pause before waiving the question aside as not worthy of consideration.

[1] So in the *Timæus*, where we find such thoughts as these: 'God desired that all things should be good and nothing bad, in so far as this could be accomplished.' 'The creation is mixed, being made up of necessity and mind. Mind, the ruling power, persuaded necessity to bring the greater part of created things to perfection, and thus in the beginning, when the influence of reason got the better of necessity, the universe was created.'—Jowett's *Plato*, vol. iii. pp. 613, 630. For another view, from *The Laws*, *vide* the end of this Lecture.

The mental activity of our age has given birth not only to a theistic dualism kindred to that of ancient times, but to what may be characterised as an agnostic dualism, of which the chief representative is Mr. Huxley. This distinguished scientist took a pessimistic view of nature, seeing in its methods of pursuing its ends in the process of evolution a brutal indifference to morality, which, apart from all other grounds of doubt, made the hypothesis of a divine Creator hard of credence. Yet Mr. Huxley was not a pessimist out and out. What saved him from sinking to that level was, besides his English good sense, his robust manly faith in the supreme worth and imperious obligations of morality. He was a dualist after a fashion: the conflict in his theory of the universe being not between a good God and a bad God, as Zoroaster conceived, or between a good God and an intractable primitive matter, as Plato imagined, but between Evolution and Ethics, or between a physical nature entirely innocent of morality and man, in so far as earnestly-minded to realise an ethical ideal. Man ethically-minded is a gardener cultivating a small patch of ground wherein he seeks to rear the fruits and flowers of human virtue, striving heroically to keep out the weeds of the wilderness beyond the fence, that is to say the moral barbarism of Nature. In the value which it sets on moral endeavour this agnostic dualism is Christian, though in his temper its author and

MODERN DUALISM

advocate is a disciple of the Stoics rather than of Christ. The zeal for morality which it inculcates may well appear an alien phenomenon in a universe which is, so far as we know, without a good God or indeed a God of any kind, and is itself the product of a cosmic process that 'has no sort of relation to moral ends';[1] and one may very reasonably doubt whether such zeal can long survive the theistic creed of which it forms an integral part. But let us be thankful that it does still survive here and there in agnostic circles, and acknowledge those who, without the support of faith, manfully fight for the right as friends, not foes, to the great cause which all true theists have at heart.

With this passing reference to a type of thought which discovers no divine element in the world save in man, I pass to speak more at length of dualism in the proper sense of the term, that is to say, of the religious philosophy which, believing in a Deity, makes it its business to protect his character from being compromised by evil. The view of Nature entertained by the representatives of this philosophy is not so dark as that of Mr. Huxley. It discovers some good in the cosmic process whereon an argument may be founded for goodness as an attribute of the Great First Cause. But it discovers also so much that is not good that it professes itself unable to retain faith in the divine

[1] *Evolution and Ethics*, p. 83.

316 THE MORAL ORDER OF THE WORLD

goodness except on the hypothesis that its beneficent purpose has been thwarted by some counterworking power.

The rudiments of this dualistic theory may be discovered in Mr. John Stuart Mill's *Three Essays on Religion*. The author of these posthumous essays is indeed far from being a satisfactory representative of the theory. He is almost as pessimistic in his conception of Nature as Mr. Huxley, and he is at the best a very faint-hearted and hesitating theist. The indictment he brings against the physical system of the universe for the brutalities it daily perpetrates is tremendous, and his summing up of the net results of Natural Theology on the question of the divine attributes is very disenchanting. Here it is. 'A Being of great but limited power, how or by what limited we cannot even conjecture; of great, and perhaps unlimited intelligence, but perhaps, also, more narrowly limited than his power: who desires, and pays some regard to, the happiness of his creatures, but who seems to have other motives of action which he cares more for, and who can hardly be supposed to have created the universe for that purpose alone.'[1] The summation is not only meagre in its total, but it adds together attributes suggestive of incompatible conceptions. The phrase 'of great but limited power' fits into the hypothesis of a Being absolutely good

[1] *Three Essays*, p. 194.

in his intentions, but unable to do all he wishes—
the conception proper to dualism. On the other
hand, the formula in the last part of the statement
referring to the divine motives of action goes on
the assumption that the power of Deity is unlimited,
that he is therefore responsible for all that happens,
and that his moral character is to be judged
accordingly—an idea emphatically negatived by
the dualist.

The interest and value of Mr. Mill's views lies
not in their adequacy or in their consistency, but in
the fact that he was a man feeling his way. With
an open, unprejudiced eye, and without the blinders
of a philosophical or theological theory, he looked all
round on the world, trying to learn from the things
he observed what sort of a Being its Maker must
be, assuming that it has one, and then honestly
reported how it struck him. Every statement in
the report of such an observer is worth noting,
whether it agree with other statements or not.
Accordingly, I note with interest what I have called
the rudiments of a dualistic theory in the essay on
Nature. It is contained in this significant sentence:
'If we are not obliged to believe the animal creation
to be the work of a demon, it is because we need
not suppose it to have been made by a Being of
infinite power.'[1] The facts to which the suggestive
remark refers are those alluded to in the sentence

[1] *Three Essays*, p. 58.

preceding, which runs thus: 'If a tenth part of the pains which have been expended in finding benevolent adaptations in all nature had been employed in collecting evidence to blacken the character of the Creator, what scope for comment would not have been found in the entire existence of the lower animals, divided, with scarcely an exception, into devourers and devoured, and a prey to a thousand ills from which they are denied the faculties necessary for protecting themselves!'[1] It is implied that the blackening process might be carried the length of making out the Creator to be a very demon, and the suggested escape from that unwelcome conclusion is limitation of the Creator's power by what we may suppose to be the thwarting power of another demon. Malign influence is at work somewhere. If God be not the demon, then he must be discovered in an antigod of diabolic nature.

There is no evidence that Mr. Mill seriously entertained the project of reviving Persian dualism as the best possible solution of the problem raised by the conflicting phenomena of the universe. The notion of a demon counterworking the Good Spirit seems to have been a passing thought thrown out by an active mind fertile in suggestion.[2] But one

[1] *Three Essays*, p. 58.

[2] In the essay on 'The Utility of Religion' (second of the *Three Essays*), p. 116, Mr. Mill speaks with respect of dualism both in the Persian or Manichæan, and in the Platonic form, as the only theory

can never be sure that the stray hint of one thinker will not become the deliberate theory of another, especially in a time like the present, when men are extensively leaving the safe havens of traditional opinions and launching out on new voyages of discovery. At such a time long-extinct theories may be revived with the ardour and confidence inspired by fresh revelations, and crude notions propounded with all the gravity of scientific method. It is not the part of wisdom to treat such escapades of modern religious thought with contempt. They at least serve to show that there is some problem troubling men's minds which has not yet received a generally accepted solution, and when a sincere thinker frankly tells us that he is among the malcontents and has something better to offer, the least we can do is to listen respectfully. Ardent optimists may exclaim: 'After Browning who would have expected a recrudescence of dualism, not to speak of pessimism!' Yet dualists may make their appearance just because there are men amongst us who have learned the lesson of Browning too well, and who judge the world by the standard of an extravagant abstract optimism for which the great poet cannot be held responsible.

respecting the origin and government of the universe which stands wholly clear both of intellectual contradiction and of moral obliquity. But he pronounces the evidence for it as shadowy and unsubstantial, and mildly characterises its possible truth as a 'pleasing and encouraging thought.'

A really capable and well-reasoned defence of a dualism of the Persian type has recently been given to the world in a book entitled *Evil and Evolution*, by the author of *The Social Horizon*. Its sub-title is: 'An attempt to turn the light of modern science on to the ancient mystery of evil.' The author accepts without reserve the theory of evolution by the survival of the fittest, involving struggle and the destruction of the less fit, as true to the actual facts of this universe. But he does not regard the actual as the only possible, or the necessary, state of matters. Something, he holds, went wrong in the evolutionary process at a far-back stage, whence came in all the dark features which have perplexed theists and supplied writers like Mill with copious material for a Jeremiad against Nature. And who or what caused the wrong? The unhesitating answer of our author is: 'The devil.' As a man living in the nineteenth century, imbued with the scientific spirit, and aware that in the view of many the idea of a devil is finally and for ever exploded, he feels that an apology is due to his readers for reviving so antiquated a conception. His apology is that that conception renders the origin and nature of evil comparatively simple and intelligible, and that 'to eliminate Satan is to make the moral chaos around us more chaotic, the darkness more impenetrable, the great riddle of the universe more hopelessly

MODERN DUALISM

insoluble,' while retention of belief in his existence is 'the only condition upon which it is possible to believe in a beneficent God.'[1] For taking up this position he has received the thanks of reviewers in religious periodicals, not so much, apparently, because it offers a satisfactory solution of a vexed question, as because it is in one point a return to old-fashioned orthodoxy. But he himself professes no interest in orthodoxy as such. He rests his claim to consideration solely on the arguments by which he endeavours to show that the hypothesis of a devil or an antigod, bent on doing all the mischief he can, throws light on phenomena connected with the evolution of the universe not otherwise explicable, and irreconcilable with that goodness of God in which he firmly believes.

The author of *Evil and Evolution* is not so pessimistic in his view of Nature as Mr. Huxley or even Mr. Mill. He believes the good to be the stronger force in the world.[2] He is not inclined to exaggerate the physical evils of the animal world; he is rather disposed to believe that they are enormously less than they are often represented. The well-known phrase to which Tennyson gave currency: 'Nature red in tooth and claw,' conveys, he thinks, a very false impression. 'Nature on the whole,' he maintains, 'is nothing of the kind. Nature is all aglow with pleasure—dashed with pain just here

[1] *Evil and Evolution*, p. 7.   [2] *Ibid.*, p. 64.

and there. The rule everywhere is the prevalence of happiness. Evil is the comparatively trivial exception. It cannot reasonably be disputed that, taking the world all over, and all its phases of life, the laws of Nature are overwhelmingly productive of good, and that evil—though frightful enough in the aggregate regarded absolutely—is after all only what might be produced by a very slight disturbance of the perfect adjustment of things.'[1] He finds in the animal kingdom not merely voracity, but altruism, at work. It came in just at the point where it was needed, at that stage in the evolution of the animal world when it became possible for selfishness to be in any sense an evil.[2] He sees the evidence of the presence and power of the new principle of love in the predominance of parental affection over selfishness, in the case of animals with their young, and in the attachments which, apart from parental affection and sexual passion, animals are capable of towards one another.

On the whole, the world is so good that one cannot sufficiently wonder why it is not better. It cannot be the Creator's fault. The prevalence of happy life, and the inbringing of a beneficent principle counteractive of selfishness just at the proper point, reveal what the Creator aimed at. His benignant will is further shown in other instances in which, when a law of nature is in danger of becoming a

[1] *Evil and Evolution*, p. 98. [2] *Ibid.*, p. 158.

MODERN DUALISM 323

source of evil, its action is suspended by the action of another law. A case in point is: water contracting and becoming denser by cold down to a certain temperature, below which it begins to expand and grow lighter, having for result that ice floats on the surface instead of sinking to the bottom, to lie there for ever and go on accumulating till the sea became a solid mass and life impossible.[1] Such facts, it is argued, show what the world might have been, and would have been, had the Creator been able to carry out his intention: laws always modified or counteracted when in danger of becoming hurtful; love made so strong as to keep in due subjection the selfishness which has filled the animal world with internecine strife.

Whence the great miscarriage? From the interference of a being possessing 'the intellect and the power of a god and the malignity of a devil.'[2] He is to be conceived as looking out upon the work of creation, watching his chance of doing mischief on a great scale, and finding it at the point where, 'in the slow unfolding of life, love and selfishness first came into conflict.'[3] Not that that is supposed to be the time at which the Satanic monster began to exist, or even to act *suo more*. Both his existence and his malign activity are dated as far back as the 'day-dawn of creation, or shortly after.'[4] But his first

[1] *Evil and Evlution*, p. 74.
[2] *Ibid.*, p. 138.
[3] *Ibid.*, p. 158.
[4] *Ibid.*, p. 64.

serious stroke of business as a marrer of God's work
consisted in altering the relative strength of selfishness and love, so as, against the Creator's intention,
to secure for selfishness the predominance. If you
ask how that was done, the modern reviver of Persian
dualism cannot tell; he can only speak of the fell
achievement as a disturbance of the divinely ordered
adjustment by some inscrutable modification of law.
The Satanic method generally is to bring about
maladjustment. He is not a law-maker, or a worker
according to law, but a disturber of law. The good
Spirit, the Creator, works, we are told, 'by means of
law and only by means of law,' but his arch-enemy
works by the disturbance of law to the effect of producing 'flaws and failures' in the established order
of nature.[1]

This one disturbance of the divinely intended
balance between the principle of selfishness and
the counter-principle of love was momentous and
tragic enough. We have only to imagine what
evolution without this maladjustment might have
been, to realise in some degree the extent of the
mischief. In the unmarred world of God the
struggle for existence would have had no place.
In consequence of that, birds and beasts of prey
would not have been evolved.[2] Tigers and hyænas,
vultures and sharks, ferrets and polecats, wasps
and spiders, puff-adders and skunks, would have

[1] *Evil and Evolution*, p. 93.   [2] *Ibid.*, p. 142.

been as conspicuous by their absence as Neros and Buonapartes and millionaires.[1] For it is the struggle for existence that has produced birds and beasts of prey, and in all probability it is the malignity of the struggle that has produced the venom of so many reptiles.[2] Then, in a world in which there was no wholesale destruction there would be no need for the immense fertility that characterises many species of living creatures, which at once supplies food for foes and makes foes necessary to keep teeming life within bounds. The cod-fish would produce only as many young as are left after its predatory enemies have done their utmost to destroy its millions of progeny. For the fertility of the actual world is to be conceived as the result of the destruction that goes on, and the destruction in turn as the effect of the fertility. Destruction demands and produces superabundance, and superabundance destruction.[3]

Within the human sphere, in the world of divine intention, the state of things would have corresponded to that of the ideal animal world. War would have been unknown. Animals would not have been killed for food. The hunting and pastoral occupations of primitive society would have had no existence. Men would have been content to live on such fruits and vegetables as they could find till they learned the arts of agriculture. Vegetarianism would

[1] *Evil and Evolution*, p. 144. [2] *Ibid.*, p. 142. [3] *Ibid.*, p. 150.

have been the order of the day.[1] Verily a different world from the one we actually live in! And all the difference is due to the one act of interference whereby a malignant spirit secured for the selfish principle preponderant power in the universe.

How are we to conceive this malevolent being, and what precise place are we to assign him in the scale of being? At first view he appears mightier than God, possessed of skill and power to get and keep the reins of the universe in his hands. How he ever came to be is a question that will have to be looked at hereafter; meantime we wish to know what idea we are to form of his nature and endowments. Our guide here must be his achievements; and these suggest a being of very imposing attributes. The modern dualist, accordingly, while careful to place him beneath God, invests him with very godlike qualities. The Satan of most recent invention is a being after this fashion. He was in existence from the beginning of the world, and from the beginning was on evil bent, not, like Milton's Satan, a good angel at first, who subsequently fell.[2] He has a nature akin to that of God; is, like God, a spiritual power endowed with similar faculties combining the intellect and energy of God with the malignity of a devil.[3] He has godlike perception, enabling him to comprehend the

[1] *Evil and Evolution*, p. 157. [2] *Ibid.*, p. 64. [3] *Ibid.*, pp. 62, 138.

MODERN DUALISM

intricacies of the cosmic system, the possibilities latent in primordial matter, and the hidden nature of all physical forces such as that of gravitation.[1] He can impose his will on the elementary particles of matter, lay down laws, fit one law for modifying or balancing another, and disturb the adjustments made by the Creator.[2] He cannot wreck creation, but his power is equal to unsettling the balance and seriously disturbing the divine adjustment of things.[3] He has been engaged in this bad work during the millions of years that have elapsed since the world began, and, as we must suppose that the good Spirit would gladly have put an end to his evil influence long ago, if it had been possible, the inference is that the wicked Spirit is too potent to be readily subdued and overcome; that his power, indeed, approximates to that of the Supreme Being himself.[4] Yet this approximation must be taken *cum grano*. The supremacy of the Great First Cause must be guarded, and in order to that it must be held as an article of faith, in spite of all appearances to the contrary, that between the potency of the evil Spirit and that of the good Spirit there is 'an infinity of difference.'[5] Satan could neither create a world, nor prevent another from creating it; he could only mar a world already made.[6] And though he

---

[1] *Evil and Evolution*, p. 63.   [2] *Ibid.*, p. 63.   [3] *Ibid.*, p. 63.
[4] *Ibid.*, pp. 48, 62.   [5] *Ibid.*, p. 91.   [6] *Ibid.*, p. 92.

be so strong that the Maker of the Universe, however desirous, cannot destroy him and his influence offhand, yet his doom is eventual defeat and destruction. The time will come in the far future when the benignant Creator 'shall reign with a sway absolutely undisputed.'[1]

In proceeding to criticise this latest attempt at a dualistic theory of the universe, I frankly own at the outset that it deserves at least the praise of ingenuity. The modern Satan is skilfully constructed. The construction proceeds on the inductive method of modern science. First, all the good elements and beneficent aspects of the universe are picked out, and from these are formed the idea of the Being to whom is assigned the honourable position and name of the Creator. Then the remaining features, forming the dark side of nature, are collected and examined. From their wholly diverse character it is inferred, in the first place, that they must owe their existence to a Being whose spirit is absolutely antagonistic to that of the Creator. From the proportion which the evil element bears to the good, and from the relation in which the former stands to the latter, the status, attributes, and *modus operandi* of the evil Spirit are determined. The whole process bears a look of patient investigation which seems to justify the claim made for *Evil and Evolution* 'that it is an attempt to turn the light of modern science on to the ancient mystery of evil.'

[1] *Evil and Evolution*, p. 184. The words quoted above are the last in the book.

MODERN DUALISM

The attempt, however, is very open to criticism.

1. I remark in the first place, that the scheme of thought whereof an outline has been given has for its underlying postulate what may be characterised as an extravagant optimism of a peculiar type. There are at least three distinguishable forms of optimism. There is the type of which Browning is the best-known modern representative, which says: 'In the actual world there is much wrong, but all is in course of becoming right,' and thinks that enough to justify God and content reasonable men. Then there is the optimism of the pantheist, which says: 'The actual world as it is is right.' There is, finally, the optimism of the modern dualist, which differs from both the preceding types: from pantheistic optimism by maintaining that in the actual world there is much that is wrong, and from optimism of the Browning type by maintaining that the mere fact that the wrong is in course of being set right does not furnish a sufficient vindication of Providence. Faith in an absolutely good God it holds to be untenable on the hypothesis that God is responsible for the actual world, though all the evil that is in it be destined to be ultimately eliminated. Therefore it takes refuge in the ideal world, the world of *might-have-been*, and which would have been if God had got his own way. That world, as it lives in the dualistic imagination, might be described

as a paradise never lost, and therefore not needing to be regained. Pain practically unknown, predatory instincts non-existent, the wolf dwelling with the lamb, and the leopard lying down with the kid; man from the beginning 'a perfect creature in a perfect environment,'[1] thinking always right thoughts on questions of good and evil, showing no desire to do wrong; even primitive man utterly free from savagery, and innocent of hunting and warring propensities; development possible but ever normal and free from sin, and deriving its moral stimulus, not from pain and sorrow, but from pleasure and joy.[2] In that happy, harmless world death would not be unknown, but it would come merely as sleep after a long day's work, or like 'the fading of a flower, the dropping of fruit in the late autumn, the dying out of the light of day to the dreamy music of the birds and the babbling of the brooks.'[3] It would be as easy to die in such a world as 'in a world of perfect health, there is abundant reason to believe, it would be to be born.'[4] It would be such a delightful world, indeed, that merely to live in it for, say, a hundred years, would satisfy all legitimate cravings for existence; a hereafter would not be felt to be necessary.[5]

Such is the ideally best world of dualistic dreams.

[1] *Evil and Evolution*, p. 103.   [2] *Ibid.*, p. 33.
[3] *Ibid.*, p. 176.   [4] *Ibid.*, p. 177.   [5] *Ibid.*, p. 177.

It may be a very good world, so far as sentient happiness is concerned, but is it in any true sense a moral world? The demand of the theory is that in the lower animal creation there shall be little pain,[1] and in the human sphere not only little pain but no *sin*. It postulates not merely that there *may* be a world without sin, but that there *must* be, in so far as divine intention is concerned, if we are to believe that God is good. Such is the kind of world we should have had but for diabolic interference. The author of *Evil and Evolution* assumes that at this point he is in accord with the author of Genesis. He credits the book of Genesis with the view that God made man absolutely perfect, and that man would have continued such had not Satan seduced him into evil.[2] There is reason for thinking that, following the example of scholastic theologians, our author has read into the story of Adam a meaning which its statements will not bear. But there can be no doubt that the opinion he imputes to the sacred writer is at least his own. He believes that the primitive man, the outcome of a slow secular process of evolution, was in the strict sense morally perfect.

[1] The author of *Evil and Evolution* thinks that in the world which might have been, pain would have been comparatively infinitesimal in amount, that it would have had a self-evident cause and purpose, that it would have been remedied by nature, and that it would never have been caused by the direct operation of law. *Vide* p. 87.

[2] *Vide* pp. 23, 24.

This conception raises some hard questions. How did it come about that a morally perfect man was so easily tempted even by a tempter of diabolic skill? Ought not a morally perfect being to be temptation-proof? Then, if, as is supposed, the good God was able to conduct the evolution of the human creature, with entire success, up to that point, in spite of all Satanic attempts at marring the great work of making a morally perfect being, why should he encounter such fatal frustration after that consummation had been reached? Lastly, and above all, one is forced to ask: Is this notion of a moral subject made perfect and guaranteed against lapse by Divine power not destructive of morality? The reality of moral distinctions may be undermined in more than one way. One way is that of the pantheist who affirms that moral evil, so called, is in its own place good. But another way is that of the modern dualist, who in effect affirms that in a divinely ordered universe moral evil would be impossible. May one not venture to say that the actual universe, full though it be of wrong, is preferable to the imaginary universe from which wrong is excluded by divine omnipotence? Compulsory holiness is not holiness; it is simply the mechanical service of a tool.

2. The exemption of the good Spirit from responsibility for the misery and sin of the actual world is purchased at a great price. That price is

MODERN DUALISM

not merely, or even chiefly, the sacrifice of divine omnipotence; it is rather the reluctant acceptance of the repulsive, hideous conception of an absolutely bad, unmitigatedly malignant antigod. One's whole soul rises in rebellion against this revolting notion. Is it possible to believe that such a being, evil from the beginning, can exist? How could he ever come to be? The author of *Evil and Evolution* declines to look at this question, but it cannot be evaded by any radical advocate of dualism. There are just two alternatives: either the evil Spirit, like the good Spirit, is unoriginated, eternal;[1] or he owes his being, like all other creatures, to the good Spirit. The former alternative amounts to this, that good and evil are both alike divine; a position which involves at once the cancelling of moral distinctions and the destruction of Deity. If good and evil be both alike divine, then there is no ground for preferring good to evil save personal liking. If there be two gods with equal rights, though radically opposed to each other, then there is no god. Two rival gods, like two rival popes, destroy each other, and leave the universe without a divine head.

With the other alternative—Satan the creature of the good Spirit—we are in an equally hopeless predicament. What is gained by relieving God of

[1] The author of *Evil and Evolution* seems to incline to this view. He says: 'I can no more undertake to say how such a being as Satan came into existence than I can account for the existence of the Deity' (p. 8).

responsibility for all other evil in the world, if we end by making him responsible for the existence of the malign being by whom all the mischief has been wrought? Is not the presence in the universe of such an absolutely wicked spirit an infinitely greater evil than all the other evils put together? Better make God the Creator of evil under mitigated forms than the Creator of a hideous being who is an unmitigated evil, and through whose diabolic agency He becomes indirectly the cause of all the evil that happens. There is, doubtless, one door by which the Deity may seem to escape responsibility for the badness of Satan and his work, viz., by the hypothesis that Satan was created good and afterwards lapsed into evil. But it is observable that our author does not avail himself of this way of escape. He could not, consistently with his view of God's relation to moral agents as that of one able and willing to guard a moral world conceived as good against the intrusion of evil. If Satan was once good, why did not God keep him from falling?

3. The dualistic scheme under review, while making pretensions to scientific method, is unscientific, in so far as it destroys the unity of the universe. The universe ceases to be the homogeneous result of a uniform process of evolution, and becomes the heterogeneous effect of two processes counterworking each other. And the two processes are not

only opposite in tendency, but discrepant also in their method of working. The Creator works only by law, his antagonist works by occasional disturbance of law. The Creator's action is natural, that of his antagonist is unnatural, and in a sense supernatural or miraculous. The Creator is immanent in the world, and works in it from within through its inherent laws and forces. His antagonist is transcendent, and works upon the world from without as a disturbing influence. The whole conception implies a separation between the evil and the good in nature which has no existence. The two in reality are closely interwoven, and are to be regarded as complementary effects of the same causes. Such is the judgment of Mr. John Stuart Mill, who, while not committing himself to the dualistic hypothesis, has, more than any other scientific man of modern times, expressed himself favourably regarding it. Discussing the attributes which observation of nature justifies us in ascribing to God, he thus writes: 'The indications of design point strongly in one direction—the preservation of the creatures in whose structure the indications are found. Along with the preserving agencies there are destroying agencies, which we might be tempted to ascribe to the will of a different Creator; but there are rarely appearances of the recondite contrivance of means of destruction, except when the destruction of one creature is the means of preservation to others. Nor can it be supposed that the preserving agencies are wielded by one Being, the destroying agencies by another. The destroying agencies are a necessary part of the preserving agencies: the chemical compositions by which life is carried on could not take place without a parallel series of decompositions. The great agent of decay in both organic and inorganic substances is oxidation, and it is only by oxidation that life is continued for even the length of a minute.'[1] The conclusion to be drawn from such facts is expressed by Mr. Mill in these terms: 'There is no ground in Natural Theology for attributing intelligence or personality to the obstacles which partially thwart what seem the purposes of the Creator.'[2]

4. The advocates of dualism may justly be charged with morbid views of the evil that is in the world. They look on some things as evil that are not, they exaggerate the evils that do exist, and they largely overlook the fact that evil is good in the making, or a possible good not understood. The author of *Evil and Evolution* regards vegetarianism as a necessary feature in the world as it ought to be. Is that dictum to be accepted as final? He reckons birds and beasts of prey as creatures of the evil Spirit. Have they not some useful functions in the world—the vulture, *e.g.*, as one of Nature's

[1] *Three Essays*, p. 185.   [2] *Ibid.*, p. 186.

scavengers? Of the exaggerative habit we have an interesting instance in Mr. Mill's remarks on childbirth, which are as follows: 'In the clumsy provision which she (Nature) has made for that perpetual renewal of animal life, rendered necessary by the prompt termination she puts to it in every individual instance, no human being ever comes into the world but another human being is literally stretched on the rack for hours or days, not unfrequently issuing in death.'[1] Compare with this the saying of Jesus: 'A woman when she is in travail hath sorrow, because her hour is come: but as soon as she is delivered of the child, she remembereth no more the anguish, for joy that a man is born into the world.'[2] Which of these two utterances is the healthier in sentiment and the truer to the feelings of the sufferers concerned?

It might help to cure the dualistic mood if those who suffer from it would make a study of the good that is in evil. They might take a course of lessons from Emerson, and con well such a passage as this: 'Wars, fires, plagues, break up immovable routine, clear the ground of rotten races and dens of distemper, and open a fair field to new men. There is a tendency in things to right themselves, and the war or revolution or bankruptcy that shatters a rotten system allows things to take a new and natural order. The sharpest evils are bent into

[1] *Three Essays*, p. 30.   [2] John xvi. 21.

that periodicity which makes the errors of planets and the fevers and distempers of men self-limiting. Nature is upheld by antagonism. Passions, resistance, dangers, are educators. We acquire the strength we have overcome. Without war, no soldier! without enemies, no hero! The sun were insipid if the universe were not opaque. And the glory of character is in affronting the horrors of depravity to draw thence new nobility of power. . . . And evermore in the world is this marvellous balance of beauty and disgust, magnificence and rats. Not Antoninus, but a poor washerwoman, said, "The more trouble the more lion; that's my principle."[1]

From the same master the dualist might learn how many so-called evils are evil only relatively to man's ignorance. The world for the savage is full of devils which become good angels for the man who knows their use. Water, air, steam, fire, electricity, have all been devils in their time. 'Steam,' writes Emerson, 'was, till the other day, the devil which we dreaded. Every pot made by any human potter or brazier had a hole in its cover to let off the enemy, lest he should lift pot and roof and carry the house away. But the Marquis of Worcester, Watt, and Fulton bethought themselves that where was power was not devil, but was God; that it must be availed of, and not by any means let off and

[1] *Works*, vol. ii. p. 417 ('The Conduct of Life,' Essay VII.).

MODERN DUALISM

wasted.'[1] This is wholesome teaching, though it come from one whose optimism may be deemed extreme. I had rather think with Emerson than with Huxley and Mill concerning Nature. Of Huxley one has said that 'he is as positive, and, one might add, as enthusiastic, in his faith that all things work together for evil to those who love, as Plato and Paul were that all things work together for good.'[2] It is easy to see on which side the superior sanity of thought lies.

But at this point we may be reminded that there was a dualistic element both in the Platonic and in the Pauline system; and the fact may be pointed to in proof that even with the utmost desire to take an optimistic view of things strenuous and candid thinkers find dualism in some form unavoidable. Plato believed in an intractable matter, Paul in a Satan; not identical, indeed, in all respects with the Satan of modern invention, still occupying a somewhat similar position in the universe as the malignant marrer of God's work.

The statement cannot be denied, and it certainly suffices to show that to carry out the programme of absolute optimism is difficult if not impossible. The intractable matter of the Greek philosopher and the Satan of the Christian apostle testify to the presence in the physical and moral universe of

[1] *Works*, vol. ii. p. 322 ('The Conduct of Life,' Essay I.).
[2] Gordon, *Immortality and the New Theodicy*, p. 23.

a perplexing mystery which speculative reason finds it hard to clear up. Whether either of the solutions does more than confess the mystery and call it by a peculiar name is another question. We may, if we choose, consider which of the two names is to be preferred. The impersonal abstraction of Plato is more in accordance with Western habits of thought, while the embodiment of evil in a malignant personality commended itself to the realistic Semitic mind. Then the suggestion that the imperfection of the world is due to the unmanageableness of the raw material out of which it was built, is free from the moral repulsiveness attaching to the conception of an intelligent agent absolutely devoted to the bad vocation of doing all the mischief in the world he can. But the more important question is, Whether our minds can find final rest in either of the suggested solutions of the problem? The intractableness of matter—why intractable? Because matter is independent of God, and with its inherent properties pre-exists as a ready-made *datum* for the divine Architect who proposes as far as may be to turn it into a *cosmos*. Can reason rest in this view of God's relation to the world? How much more satisfactory to think of the physical universe, whether eternal or not, as having its origin in God, as existing through spirit and for spirit, and thoroughly plastic in the hands of its divine Maker? On this view the intractableness vanishes; there is nothing

MODERN DUALISM

in matter which God has not put there, and which He cannot use for His purposes.[1]

Turn now to the Semitic conception of a personal obstructer, which may or may not have come into Jewish theology from Persia, and consider how far it offers a final resting-place for thought wrestling with the problem of evil. We note first, with satisfaction, that the Biblical Satan has a much more restricted range of action than the Satan of modern dualism. The latter begins to meddle almost at creation's dawn, and becomes specially active at the point where the principle of altruism first makes its appearance in the animal world—that is to say, ages before the evolution of life culminated in man. The Satan of Scripture, on the other hand, becomes active, for the first time, in the human sphere, his one concern being to wreck the moral world whose possibility was provided for by the advent of man. The writer of Genesis conceives of the creation up to that point as good, no fault to be found in the inanimate or lower animate world; herein differing both from Plato, who imagined that even the primitive *hyle* was not free from fault, and from the author of *Evil and Evolution*, who places Satanic activity

[1] In his latest work, *The Laws*, Plato seems to teach that mind was before matter, soul prior to body, so that the intractableness of matter can no longer be the source of evil for him. In this Dialogue he seems to adopt, instead, the Zoroastrian hypothesis of two spirits or souls— one the author of good, the other of evil. *Vide* Jowett's *Plato*, v. pp. 467, 468.

far back in the history of creation. Satan appears in Scripture as the enemy of moral good, as an unbeliever in it, and as a tempter to moral evil. In Genesis the conception of an external tempter, in the mythological guise of a serpent, is employed to make more easily comprehensible the origin of sin, the doing of wrong by human beings previously free from transgression. In later Scriptures the same being, now called Satan, appears in the same capacity, endeavouring to seduce good men—David, Job, Jesus—to do evil actions contrary to their character.

Such is the function of Satan in the Bible. Waiving the ontological question of objective reality, what we have to ask is, Does the idea of a superhuman tempter really solve the problem as to the origin of evil in the first man or in any man? 'Who can understand his errors?' asks the Psalmist. Sometimes it is not easy; and in such cases we may employ the hypothesis of a transcendental tempter as a way of expressing the difficulty which impresses the imagination while it fails to satisfy the reason. This is all that it does, even in the case of Adam. 'Who,' we naturally inquire, 'can understand *his* error?' the error *ex hypothesi* of a previously errorless man. But do we understand it even with the aid of the tempting serpent, on any view of the primitive state? If it was a state of moral perfection in the strict sense, ought not the first man to have been temptation-proof, especially against such rudimentary forms of temptation as are mentioned in the story? If it was only a state of childish innocence, does not the introduction of supernatural agency invest with an aspect of mystery what is in itself a comparatively simple matter, the lapse of an utterly inexperienced person? The same remark applies to the case of David. In the pages of the Chronicler David appears as a saint, his moral shortcomings, faithfully recorded in the earlier history, being left out of the account; and Satan is represented as tempting him to number the people, as if to make conceivable how so good a man could do an action displeasing to God. But it is not difficult to imagine how even a godly king might be betrayed into a transaction of the kind specified by very ordinary motives. In the case of saints generally it may be remarked that their moral lapses would not appear so mysterious as they are sometimes thought to be, if the whole truth as to their spiritual state were known. The habit of referring these lapses, as otherwise incomprehensible events, to Satanic temptation is not free from danger. It tends to self-deception, and to the covering over of some hidden evil in the heart which urgently needs looking after.

Such abuses of the Biblical idea of a supernatural tempter are carefully to be guarded against. But the mischief they work is a trifle compared with the havoc produced by ascribing to Satanic agency the whole moral evil of mankind. That means that, but for Satanic interference, the page of human history would have been a stainless record of the lives of perfect men kept from falling by the gracious power of God. Such a view carries two fatal consequences. It convicts God of impotence, and it relieves men of responsibility. The one mighty being, and the one sinner in the world, is Satan. The story of our race is dark enough, but it is not so dark as that. It is the story of a race of free moral agents who are not the puppets of either Deity or devil. The sin of man is not a witness to a frustrated God, but to a God who would rather have sin in the world than have a world without sin because tenanted by beings physically incapacitated to commit it. The very transgression of a free responsible being is in God's sight of more value than the involuntary rectitude of beings who are forcibly protected from going wrong. If there is to be goodness in the world, it must be the personal achievement of the good. Not indeed of the good unaided. The Divine Being is more than an onlooker. He co-operates in every way compatible with due respect for our moral personality. 'Our Redeemer, from everlasting, is Thy name.' *That*, God has been from the first, and throughout the entire history of man. More—an absolute preventer of evil, *e.g.*—He cannot be, simply because He values morality. But a Redeemer He truly is, and His work as such cannot be frustrated by any number of

Satans, ancient or modern. If a Satan exists, it must be because it is always possible for a moral subject to make a perverted use of his endowments. If such a perverted being tempt man, his malign influence is simply a part of the untoward environment amid which they have to wrestle with evil. He cannot do more than make a subtle use of the evil elements in our own nature, with which alone we need concern ourselves. Let us watch our own hearts, and Satan will never have a chance. If he do gain an advantage over us, it may be for our ultimate benefit by showing where unsuspected weakness lies. Let us throw off the incubus of an omnipotent devil conjured up by modern dualism, and go on our way with good hope, and full faith that God is with us, and that He is stronger than all powers, visible or invisible, that may be arrayed against us.[1]

[1] That the diabolic element is held in check in human history take this in proof from Carlyle : 'It is remarkable how in almost all world-quarrels, when they came to extremity there have been Infernal Machines, Sicilian Vespers, Guido [Guy Fawkes] Powder-barrels, and such like called into action ; and worth noting how hitherto not one of them in this world has prospered. . . . In all cases I consider the Devil an unsafe sleeping-partner, to be rejected, not to be admitted at any premium ; by whose aid no cause yet was ever known to prosper.' *Historical Sketches*, p. 68 (1898).

LECTURE XI

MODERN DUALISM: RELIGIOUS AND SOCIAL ASPECTS

I ASK attention now to a type of dualism for which human reason is the antagonist of the Deity.

That human reason, in the exercise of its proper functions, might become the enemy of God, is the last thing that would occur to one who holds the view of man's place in the universe which I have made the foundation of my argument for a providential order of the world. On that view man is the crown of the creative process, the key to the meaning of the process, and also to the nature of its Divine Author. But reason is an essential ingredient in the distinctively human, therefore a part of the image of God, a ray of the divine. How unlikely that it should prove to be inherently inaccessible to the knowledge of God, and unserviceable to the great purpose for which He made the creature whom He endowed with so noble a faculty! Ought not reason rather to be a source of the knowledge of God, a revelation of God in part, and also of the world: man rational revealing a rational God, and unfolding the meaning of a world interpretable to reason? Ought not this same faculty to be a willing instrument in the hand of God for furthering the moral evolution of humanity, bringing to full fruition the latent possibilities of human nature?

This genial view of reason's promise and potency has not by any means found universal acceptance. On the contrary, there has ever been a tendency, especially among theologians, to the vilification of reason. Concisely formulated, the depreciatory theory of man's rational faculty is this: it cannot find God; it is unwilling to receive a revelation of God coming to it from without; it is reluctant to serve God so revealed as an instrument for advancing His glory and the higher interests of humanity. It is a very dismal and depressing theory. The dualism considered in last Lecture is sombre enough. It finds in the lower stages of evolution manifold traces of an antigod counter-working the beneficent purposes of the Creator. But it does not leave the Creator without a witness at any stage in the world-process; even its most pessimistic exponent, John Stuart Mill, being compelled to own that some faint evidence of divine benevolence is discoverable. But suppose it were otherwise, suppose the sub-human world were without a ray of divine light, unmitigated diabolic darkness brooding over all, what a comfort if, on arriving at the human, we found that we had emerged at last out of the kingdom of darkness into the kingdom of light with reason and conscience for our celestial luminaries! Another type of dualism, however, deprives us of this comfort, telling us in effect that with reason we are not yet in the kingdom of light, but still in a godless region; that reason in truth is simply a faculty enabling its possessor more cleverly and successfully to counterwork the moral purpose of the Creator. The Ahriman, the Satan, of this new form of dualism is a human endowment which we had fondly imagined to be a link in the chain of filial affinity connecting man with God. This view, if accepted, upsets our whole doctrine of a providential order based on man's place in the cosmos; therefore it is our imperative duty to subject it to careful scrutiny.

The first step in the vilification of reason is the assertion that it *cannot find God*. This position, in itself, does not necessarily involve a depreciatory estimate of reason's capacity. Inability to find may conceivably be due, not to any fault in the searcher, but to lack of clues to the thing sought. Such lack of clues to God in nature is asserted by many, *some* of whom at least have no wish to disparage reason. In our time men of different schools, theological and philosophical, agree in this position. Thus an English Nonconformist minister, an adherent of the Ritschlian school of theology, expounding its views, writes: 'If we will use words carefully, there is no revelation in nature.'[1] From the opposite extreme of the ecclesiastical horizon comes the peremptory voice of Cardinal Newman, telling us that from the surface of the world can be gleaned only 'some faint and fragmentary views of God,' and that the fact can mean only one of two things: 'either there is no Creator, or He has disowned His creatures.'[2] A Transatlantic philosopher, who describes his philosophical position as that of *radical empiricism*, in harmony with these utterances declares that natural religion has suffered definitive bankruptcy in the opinion of a circle of persons, among whom he includes himself, and that for such persons 'the physical order of nature, taken simply as science knows it, cannot be held to reveal any one harmonious spiritual intent.'[3]

These oracular verdicts on the nullity of natural theology are pronounced in different interests: the first in support of the thesis that Jesus Christ is the sole source of knowledge of God; the second with the view of making dependence on the Church for such knowledge as complete as possible;[4] the

[1] P. T. Forsyth on 'Revelation and the Person of Christ' in *Faith and Criticism*, p. 100.

[2] Newman's *Grammar of Assent*, p. 392.

[3] W. James, *The Will to Believe*, p. 52.

[4] In his *Apologia*, p. 198, Newman lays down the position that there is no medium in true philosophy between Atheism and Catholicity. On his whole doctrine concerning the impotence of reason in religion *vide* Principal Fairbairn's *Catholicism, Roman and Anglican*, pp. 116-140, and pp. 205-236.

third to inculcate the necessity of faith in an unseen supernatural order 'in which the riddles of the natural order may be found explained.'[1] The first-mentioned bias, that of the Ritschlians, possesses special interest and significance. It certainly means no disrespect to human reason. It denies not to reason an eye capable of discerning the light; it simply affirms that from the world, apart from Christ, no light is forthcoming. The Ritschlian is an Agnostic so far as natural theology is concerned, affirming that the course of nature supplies no sure traces of the being or the providence of God. Christ is for him 'the one luminous smile upon the dark face of the world.'[2] If reason, baffled in its quest after God, can recognise in that smile a light from heaven, her affinity for the divine is sufficiently vindicated.

It does not fall within the scope of this Lecture to criticise at length the Ritschlian programme: *Outside Christ nothing but agnosticism.* Suffice it, therefore, to remark that it seems to me to play into the hands of the absolute agnostic quite as effectually as the attitude of Cardinal Newman, whose watchword was: *No knowledge of God except through the Church.* To Newman the agnostic reply is this: Your position means that to follow reason lands in agnosticism as the only creed possible or rational for

---

[1] James, *The Will to Believe*, p. 51.
[2] Forsyth in *Faith and Criticism*, p. 100.

MODERN DUALISM

all outside the Catholic Church. Why, then, should we cease being agnostics and become Catholics? Those who maintain that no knowledge of God is possible save through Christ must be prepared for a similar response. 'Why,' it may be asked, 'must we become theists at the bidding of Jesus, if there be nothing in the universe witnessing to God's being and benignity? If Jesus be in possession of the truth, how is he so isolated? Is the isolation not a proof that he was mistaken in his doctrine of a Divine Father who cares for those who, like himself, devote their lives to the doing of good?'

If Christ's doctrine of God be true, there ought to be something in the world to verify it. There can hardly be a real Divine Father in the Gospels if there be no traces of that Father outside the Gospels, in the universe. If God can be known by any means, it is presumable that He can be known by many means. It is intrinsically probable that some knowledge of God can be reached by more than one road. Why should we be so slow to believe that the Divine can be known? The bankruptcy of natural theology is a gratuitous proposition. The Apostle Paul expresses only the judgment of good sense when he indicates that there is 'that which may be known of God' even by Pagans, and charges the heathen world, not with incapacity to know God, but with unwillingness to retain God in their knowledge.[1]

[1] Romans i. 19, 20, 28.

This is the reasonable view still for men who walk in the light of modern science. In view of man's place in the cosmos, it is *a priori* credible that there is a revelation of God in nature, and that man in the exercise of his cognitive faculties is capable of deciphering it. Man being rational, the presumption is that God is rational, and that Divine Reason is immanent in the world. Man being moral, the presumption is that God is moral, and that traces of a moral order of the world will discover themselves to a discerning eye. These two positions being conceded, it results that we men are God's sons, and that God is our Father. Christ's doctrine is confirmed. The new light is the true light. By intuition Jesus saw and said what modern science seals.

Thus far of reason's power to find God in nature. We have next to consider its capacity to receive what it cannot by its own unaided effort find. *Has reason an open eye for light coming from above?*

To simplify the question, let us suppose the celestial light to be the teaching of Jesus as reported in the Synoptical Gospels.

Now, even absolute agnostics can so far accept that light as to recognise its beauty and its worthiness to be true. If they are constrained to regard it as the poetic dream of an exquisitely endowed mind, they can frankly admit that the dream is very lovely, and that it would be well for the world if the fair vision corresponded to the outward fact. It is with regret, not with pleasure, they find themselves compelled by observation to arrive at the conclusion that such correspondence does not exist. Their reason hesitates to accept the idea of a Divine Father as objectively true, not for lack of liking but for lack of evidence.

Christian agnostics advance beyond this position. They accept the doctrine of Jesus as not only beautiful but objectively true, the one ray of divine light in an otherwise dark, godless universe. In doing so they do not consider themselves to be performing an ultra-rational act of transcendental faith. Christ's teaching in their view possesses a quality of 'sweet reasonableness' towards which receptivity is the only rational attitude. Christ's light, like that of the sun, appears to them self-evidencing, needing no supernatural attestation by miracles,[1] or enforcement by awful sanctions or compulsory imposition as a legal creed by ecclesiastical authority. The Christ of history can dispense with these aids of uncertain value, and stand upon His own merits, making His appeal directly from reason to reason, from soul to soul.

Not thus has the relation between reason and revelation been conceived by all. A hard anti-

[1] For the illustration of this attitude Mr. Matthew Arnold's *Literature and Dogma* may be consulted. Mr. Arnold, the agnostic, finds in Christ's doctrine a 'sweet reasonableness' which needs no miracle to win for it acceptance.

thesis has been set up between reason and faith, and men have been conceived as accepting revelation, so to speak, at the point of the bayonet, as if such acceptance could possibly have anything to do with either reason or faith. This has come about through two causes: an artificial view of the substance of revelation, and a disparaging view of human reason. As to the former, a notion long prevailed that revelation consists chiefly in a body of doctrines incomprehensible by reason, therefore unacceptable to reason, possessing no self-evidencing or self-commending power, needing therefore an elaborate apparatus of external evidences, chiefly miracles, to give them a chance of acceptance. This was the view generally adopted by the older apologists. One of its ablest and best-known exponents and advocates was Dean Mansel, who, in his Bampton Lectures on *The Limits of Religious Thought*, employed the Hamiltonian philosophy of the Conditioned for the defence of the Christian Faith. The position that philosophy led him to take up was something like this. Recognising that certain doctrines deduced by theologians from Scripture—such as the Trinity, the Incarnation, the Atonement, Eternal Punishment — were open to cavil from the point of view of reason, he interdicted criticism on the plea that the metaphysical and the moral nature of the absolute Being are both alike beyond human ken. The doctrines of atonement and eternal punishment, *e.g.*, might appear very liable to objection on ethical grounds; but we must remember that the absolute morality of God must be very different from the relative morality of men, and that therefore we may not presume to comprehend or judge divine action, but with the meekness of an uncomprehending faith accept what from reason's point of view appears revolting. It was not to be expected that this way of silencing objectors by the bugbear of the Absolute would pass unchallenged. Troublesome questions were sure to be asked. There is, it seems, an absolute morality whose nature we cannot know. If we cannot know the nature of such morality, how do we know that it exists? By revelation? But how can we be sure that it is revelation? If the morality ascribed to God in the Bible presents itself to our moral nature as immorality, can we help rejecting it as a false representation? And if we are asked to distinguish between the aspect under which God is presented to us in Scripture and the real truth of His Being, between what He is in Himself and what He would have us think of Him, can this properly be called revelation? How much better to give up pretending to know God either through reason or through revelation, and settle down in the conviction that the Being philosophers call the Infinite and the Absolute is altogether unknowable! So the agnostic apologetic of Mansel was likely to end. So it did end. The relative agnosticism of the disciple of Hamilton landed in the absolute agnosticism of Herbert Spencer and Leslie Stephen, who employed the weapons put into their hands by the theologian to undermine and subvert the foundations of all possible theology. The sooner this spurious apologetic was swept away the better, for we are worse off with it than with the modicum of knowledge concerning God allowed us by the philosophy of Kant. While denying access to God to the theoretic reason, Kant held a Divine Moral Governor to be a necessary postulate of the practical reason. This view implies that God's moral nature is essentially the same as man's; that God is interested in righteousness in the sense in which we understand it, and will use His power to promote its ascendency. Mansel, on the contrary, represents our ideas of God even on the moral side as anthropomorphic and unreal. God's righteousness, for anything we know, may be something very like what we should account unrighteousness. Kant's view is decidedly the more wholesome and acceptable. With such knowledge as he allows concerning God we could be content to remain in ignorance as to His metaphysical nature. It is on the moral side that knowledge of God is urgently needed, and, if I have reason to believe that on that side God is like man, I know where I am and what I have to expect. The belief that the human and the divine are essentially one in

MODERN DUALISM

the moral sphere is the very light of life. On the other hand, extend the shadow of the absolute into the moral world by proclaiming that morality is not the same thing in essence for God and for man, and you envelop human life in midnight darkness, and leave us without God and without hope. Faith in any so-called revealed truth which really implies the contrary is impossible. In such a case faith can only be feigning, make-believe.

The alleged antagonism between reason and faith is further based in part on *disparagement of reason*. The commonplaces here are : the pride of reason, its aversion to mystery, its reluctance to receive as truth whatever exceeds its comprehension. It is possible to quote with plausibility in support of such depreciatory reflections the Apostle Paul, as when he writes, 'The natural man receiveth not the things of the Spirit of God : for they are foolishness unto him : neither can he know them, because they are spiritually discerned.'[1] But the expression rendered the *natural* man does not mean the rational or reasonable man ; it signifies the *psychical* man, the man, *i.e.* who is under the dominion of the lower animal soul, instead of the higher reasonable soul, the spirit. The natural man is one who is in bondage to passion, instead of being under the free guidance of enlightened reason. The contrast suggested is analogous to that indicated in another

[1] 1 Corinthians ii. 14.

Pauline text: 'With the mind I serve the law of God, but with the flesh the law of sin.'[1] The mind that serves the law of God will not be shut to the truth of God. And this service to divine law, and this openness to divine truth, are in accordance with the true nature of man as a rational and moral being. The 'psychical' man is not man in his true normal nature. He is psychical because he is not man enough, because he is more of the brute than of the man. In so far as he is unspiritual, neither knowing nor valuing the things of the spirit, he is irrational. For, be it carefully noted, it is a purely arbitrary conception of reason which regards the ethical and the spiritual as lying wholly outside its sphere. Reason, morality, and religion are but different phases of the one essential nature of man—of that which constitutes the distinctively human. And these three are one; they imply each other and cannot exist separate from each other. 'Thought,' it has been well said, 'may for certain purposes abstract rational intelligence from moral character. But, in fact, there is no such thing in human experience as rational intelligence by itself; rational intelligence that is not the intelligence of a moral person; that has not, therefore, inseparably from its rational existence and activity, a moral character. Neither can there exist any moral which has not also a rational aspect and character. There

[1] Romans vii. 25.

is no such thing as a non-moral rational. There is no such thing as a non-rational moral.'[1] In the same way it may be maintained that spiritual insight and appreciation presuppose morality and rationality. It is the pure in heart that see God. And seeing means knowing, thinking true, wise, worthy thoughts of God—the highest function of the faculty of reason.

In the exercise of this function reason may become unduly elated. Divine philosophy may be lifted up with pride, and through pride fall into foolish presumption. But reason is not the only thing that is exposed to this danger. There is a pride of morality and a pride of spirituality as well as a pride of reason. The righteous man and the saint have need to be on their guard not less than the philosopher. Each, through pride, may be led into the devious paths of false judgment. The complacent righteous man despises his fellow-men; the 'saint,' in the proud consciousness of his spirituality, looks down with contempt on the world; the philosopher, in self-reliant arrogance, may be unduly agnostic, or unduly gnostic, either sceptically reducing that which may be known of God to zero, or presumptuously affirming that there is nothing which may not be known through and through, and that whatever cannot be so known has no reality. All mystery, or nothing mysterious: such are the two extremes.

Reason as such has no inherent inclination to

[1] R. C. Moberly, *Reason and Religion*, p. 17.

assume so presumptuous an attitude. On the contrary, it is thoroughly reasonable to recognise limits to the ken of reason. And in regard to that which presents an aspect of mystery to human thought, reason may be divided in its sympathies. By the metaphysical side of the mystery it may be repelled, by the moral side it may be attracted. Take the idea of incarnation as an illustration. That idea is not wholly repugnant to philosophic reason. On the metaphysical side it may appear to involve an impossibility—the finite taking into itself the infinite. But on the moral side it offers compensating attractions: God not dwelling apart in solitary majesty, enjoying his own felicity indifferent to man's destiny, but sharing in the sorrows of humanity, a hero in the strife. In virtue of its innate affinity with morality, reason can appreciate that conception. The reason of the Aryan race especially takes kindly to it. It loves to think of God as immanent rather than as transcendent. Its tendency, as Professor Tiele in his Gifford Lectures has pointed out,[1] is theanthropic, as distinct from that of the Semitic mind, which is theocratic; whence it comes that *apotheosis* and *incarnation* find frequent recognition and exemplification in Aryan religions.

In spite, however, of all that one may say in defence of reason against plausible but ill-founded charges, men will persist in ascribing to it, in refer-

[1] *Elements of the Science of Religion*, part i. pp. 156, 166.

ence to things divine, an intractableness analogous to that ascribed by ancient philosophers to matter. Reason on this view is one of the chief obstructives to the *work of God as the Maker of the spiritual world.* Its anti-divine bias is as inveterate as that of Satan. It cannot be converted; it can only be curbed and put in chains, so that its power for mischief may be as restricted as possible. And what are the chains by which it is to be bound? Miracles and fears of eternal loss have been tried, but the fetters most in fashion for the present are those of *authority*—the authority of the past or of custom, or the authority of the Church. There is a conspiracy on the part of many who underestimate reason's power to find God, and reduce to a minimum that which may be known of God independently of ecclesiastical illumination, to reinstate the Church in mediæval dominion in matters of faith and practice. In reference to this portentous reaction it has been well remarked: 'It is devout agnosticism that to-day is becoming the mother of a menacing institutionalism that is exerting itself to instal over the religious mind extreme high-churchism. Let it be understood that the movement originates and derives all its vigour from the acknowledged incompetency of the moral reason of man to fix the object of his worship, and Protestants will see the alternative that divides the field against them with Atheism.'[1]

[1] G. Gordon, *Immortality and the New Theodicy* (Boston, 1897), p. 69.

Now, with reference to the claims of authority under all aspects, traditional, social, or ecclesiastical, let it be at once frankly admitted that much that is true, useful, and wholesome can be said by way of asserting its legitimacy, necessity, and vast extent. But care should be taken that it be not said to the prejudice of reason. When we find reason and authority pitted against each other, and the praise of authority descanted on in a manner that sets reason by contrast in an unfavourable light, our suspicions are awakened, and we cannot help feeling that an attempt is being made, doubtless in all good faith, to give to authority in religion a place and power to which it is not entitled, and which, if conceded, would bear disastrous fruit. A tendency in this direction may be discovered in all statements to the effect that the influence of reason in the production of belief is trifling compared with the 'all-prevailing influence emanating from authority,' and that the fact is no cause for regret, inasmuch as reason 'is a force most apt to divide and disintegrate; and though division and disintegration may often be the necessary preliminaries of social development, still more necessary are the forces which bind and stiffen, without which there would be no society to develop.'[1]

Such language indicates heavy bias, and is very

[1] A. J. Balfour, *The Foundations of Belief*, pp. 228, 229.

provocative of criticism. Take, *e.g.*, the representation of the influence of reason, compared with that of authority, as insignificant. This is a very superficial judgment, all the more misleading that it wears an aspect of truth. It may with great plausibility be maintained that the great mass of our beliefs and actions rest on authority or custom. Yet, quite compatibly with the admission of this contention, it might be asserted that, after all, reason is the more important and even the mightier factor. Reason like the word or Logos of God, is 'quick and powerful,' as the tiny acorn out of which the great forest oak grows. The analogy of seed or of buds helps us to grasp the real significance of reason, as may be seen from the following sentences taken from a recent work by an American writer, entitled *Evolution and Religion*. 'Seeds have not much bulk, but the potentialities of the world are in them. The buds of a tree are but a small portion of its entire mass, yet they alone are the significant parts. All has been built up in due order by them. The thoughts of men, as swayed by reason and reconstructed under it, are the intellectually vital points in the spiritual world. Here it is that human life takes on new forms, new powers, new promise. Reason leaves behind it a great deal of authority—as the succulent bud deposits woody fibre—but no authority goes before it. Evolution is always directing our attention to the next significant change; and that is sure to be, in the spiritual world, the fresh product of thought.'[1]

The reference to evolution in the last sentence of this extract reminds us of the part played in the evolutionary process by the complementary forces of variation and heredity. Both of these are alike necessary to the process, and no scientist would think of indulging in a one-sided partiality for either of them as against the other. We do not find in any scientific book such statements as this: 'Variation is no doubt necessary, but much more necessary is heredity.' Why, then, should we find in works on the foundations of religious beliefs such biassed observations as this: 'Reason is doubtless needful, but still more indispensable is authority'? Why not put them on a level, viewing reason as the analogue of variation, and authority as the analogue of heredity? Why set up between them an invidious antagonism? Why not rather conceive them as counterbalancing forces serving the same purpose in the spiritual world as the centrifugal and centripetal forces in the planetary system?

It may indeed be deemed a sufficient justification of prejudice against reason that its tendency is to divide and disintegrate. That fresh prophetic thought does always act more or less in this manner is not to be denied. But what if it has more of this work to do than there is any need for, just because

[1] John Bascom, *Evolution and Religion*, pp. 100, 101.

of the prevalence in undue measure of an unreasoning partiality for authority and custom? 'Have any of the rulers or of the Pharisees believed on him?' No, and just on that account the rejected one came, in spite of himself, to send not peace but a sword. Do not throw all the blame on the prophetic thinker. Perhaps he is not to blame at all, but is simply the man who happens to see clearly the truth the time needs, and to have the sincerity and courage necessary for proclaiming it. In any case, do not lay the whole burden of blame on his shoulders; let him share it with the man who sets an overweening value on custom. It takes two to make a quarrel: the man who wishes the world to move on, and not less the man who wants the world to stand still.

It is when we look at the question at issue in the light of a great crisis like the birth of the Christian religion, that we see what a serious thing it may be to lean too heavily in our sympathies to the side of authority. If those who do this now, in our nineteenth century, possibly in lauded attempts to support the Christian faith as an established system of belief, had lived in the first, what would have been their attitude? Would they have been with Jesus or against Him? It might be invidious to offer a direct answer to this question; but something may be learned from the behaviour of the friends of authority among contemporary Jews. We may fail to see the moral, because Jesus is now for Christians the ultimate authority in religion. But Jesus did not, in His time, represent the principle of authority in the sense under discussion. He represented rather the principle of prophetic vision, of fresh religious intuition, of devout reason acting within the spiritual sphere. He spake *with* moral authority, not *by* authority of the legal, institutional, traditional type. He appealed from the schools to the human soul, and spake from the heart to the heart truth carrying its own credentials, and needing, as little as it enjoyed, backing from custom or Rabbinical opinion. The common people heard him gladly. Not so the supporters of authority. It is not their way to espouse any cause when it has nothing but reason, spiritual insight, and intrinsic truth on its side. They wait till the new has become old and customary, and the little flock a large influential community. Their patronage at that stage may in some ways be serviceable; but one cannot forget that, but for the existence of some who were open to other influences than those of authority, there never would have been any Christianity to patronise.

And what were these other influences? Does reason comprehend them all? Yes, if you take reason in a sufficiently, yet not unjustifiably, large sense. In the antithesis between reason and authority we are entitled to include under reason all that is usually found opposed to authority in critical periods, new eras, creative times, and gives to the prophet his opportunity of gaining disciples—healthy moral instincts, affinity for fundamental spiritual truth, openness to the inspirations of God. The antithesis, in short, is essentially identical with that taken by our Lord, in reference to Peter's faith, at Cæsarea Philippi, between 'flesh and blood' and the revelation of the Father in Heaven. It is therefore a hopelessly inadequate view of reason which reduces it to a faculty of reasoning having arguments as its sole instruments for producing conviction.[1] It is before all things a faculty of seeing with the spiritual eye of an enlightened understanding,[2] and of receiving truth seen with a pure heart. The Bible is the literary product and inestimable monument of this rare, precious gift. It is a divine protest against the domination of custom and authority in religion. Prophets and apostles were all in a state of revolt, in the interest of personal inspiration, against the brute force of a traditional belief at whose hands they all more or less suffered. Defences of Biblical religion by idolaters of authority are simply tombs built in honour of men whom kindred spirits in their lifetime persecuted and killed. If any one should be startled at the close affinity between human reason and divine inspiration implied in these statements, it may be well to remind him that the

[1] Mr. Balfour seems to take reason in this narrow sense. Vide *The Foundations of Belief*, p. 212.   [2] Ephesians i. 18.

common antithesis between reason and faith is unknown to Scripture.[1]

We pass now to the third charge against reason, that, viz., of being a rebel against God's will conceived as having for its aim the moral and social progress of mankind. It was reserved for the author of *Social Evolution* to bring this charge in the most explicit and uncompromising terms. Mr. Kidd leaves us in no doubt as to his meaning, though it is difficult on a first reading of his book, or even a second, to make up one's mind that his statements are to be taken in earnest. His position, in short, is that reason cares only for the present interest of the individual, not at all for the interest of society or of the remote future. The teaching of reason to the individual must always, he thinks, be 'that the present time and his own interests therein are all-important to him.'[2] In startlingly strong language he describes reason as 'the most profoundly individualistic, anti-social, and anti-evolutionary of all human qualities.'[3] Thus it results that man, in so far as he is merely rational, is a selfish animal, who uses his reason as an instrument enabling him more cleverly than other animals to gratify his desires. Fortunately for the interests of society and of human progress, man is not merely rational; he is also *religious*. Religion supplies the

---

[1] *Vide* Moberly, *Reason and Religion*, p. 85.
[2] *Social Evolution*, p. 78.   [3] *Ibid.*, p. 293.

antidote to the egoistic tendency of reason; it works for the good of society, making the religious man willing to sacrifice his own interest for the benefit of the community, in spite of reason's constant counsel to care solely for himself. It follows from this, of course, that religion and reason have nothing in common. They are necessarily antagonistic in nature as in tendency. Reason is irreligious, and religion is irrational. This also is plainly declared: 'A rational religion,' we are informed, 'is a scientific impossibility, representing from the nature of the case an inherent contradiction of terms.'[1] Religion has neither its source nor its sanction in reason; its doctrines are supernatural, and its sanctions ultra-rational. And these two powers are constantly at war with each other. The social organism is the scene of an incessant conflict between a disintegrating principle 'represented by the rational self-assertiveness of the individual units,' and an integrating principle 'represented by a religious belief providing a sanction for social conduct which is always of necessity ultra-rational, and the function of which is to secure in the stress of evolution the continual subordination of the interest of the individual units to the larger interests of the longer-lived social organism to which they belong.'[2]

What a revolting, incredible account of human nature and of human society! Mr. Kidd's view is not

[1] Vide *Social Evolution*, p. 101. [2] *Ibid.*, p. 102.

caricatured when it is graphically depicted in these terms: 'Reason a sort of more-than-animal cleverness, of purely selfish animal cunning; social morality, the demand upon individuals to sacrifice themselves and their reason for the sake of the community; and religion as a sort of non-rational bogey-policeman coming in to enforce the non-rational demand of society.'[1] One would be justified in stubbornly refusing to surrender to such a libellous misrepresentation, even though he found himself unable to refute in detail the subtle and plausible argumentation based on false assumptions; saying as he laid down the book, 'Very able, unanswerable at least by me for the moment, yet utterly unconvincing.'

This modern scheme of social evolution involves a veritable dualism—a double dualism indeed. There is first a *psychological* dualism, a constant deadly warfare in man between his reason and his religious instincts. This is a dualism unknown to Greek philosophers and Christian apostles, who knew of a conflict between flesh and spirit, but never dreamed of reason and religion being deadly foes. Plato and Paul would have said: the more rational the more religious, and the more religious the more rational. Then there is a latent *theological* dualism, an antagonism between the gods who are the objects of worship in the various religions and the reason of their worshippers. For the gods, at least the

[1] Moberly, *Reason and Religion*, p. 4.

gods of religions which happen to have a wholesome, humane, ethical ideal, desire the moral and social progress of mankind, and use religion to promote that end. And reason constantly and strenuously resists the divine goodwill—resists with such persistency and passion that religion must be provided with the awful sanctions of eternal penalties to give it a chance of keeping reason in a due state of subordination.

As is usually the case with theories of the unanswerable yet unconvincing type, the weakness of Mr. Kidd's position lies in his initial assumptions, which are that reason is inherently selfish, and religion inherently non-rational. Neither of these assertions is true. Reason is not inherently selfish. Reason may indeed be used for selfish purposes by men in whose nature animal passion predominates. But that is not the proper function of reason free to work according to its own nature; it is the abuse of its powers when in a state of degradation and bondage. Man, in so far as he is rational, is also social. Sociality is not a thing imposed on man from without and reluctantly submitted to by his reason. It is an essential element of human nature, without which a man would not be a man, and reason readily acknowledges its claims. It is rational to care for others, and for this generation to care for future generations, as parents care that it may be well with their children after their decease. We do not need to be religious, still less to be under the influence of ultra-rational religious sanctions, to perceive the reasonableness of altruism or the nobleness of self-sacrifice. Heroism, self-devotion, is latent in every man. It has been truly said that 'the service of society is not, as Mr. Kidd assumes, the sacrifice of the individual: it is his gratification and realisation. Though labour leaders and socialistic agitators usually appeal to selfishness, yet it is not the selfishness of the working men, it is their nobleness, their fidelity to what they believe to be a principle, their loyalty to their order or union, or class, which responds to these appeals, and gives to strikes and labour movements whatever strength they have. It is not individualism, but a new manifestation of the social spirit that is blindly struggling for expression in the labour movements of our day.'[1]

If reason as such is not selfish, as little is religion as such irrational. Only by taking Mediæval Christianity as the type can the contrary position be maintained with a show of plausibility. To form a sound judgment of the true relation of Christianity to reason, we must study it as it appears in the Gospels in the teaching of Jesus. Do we not all feel the 'sweet reasonableness' of that teaching—

[1] W. De Witt Hyde, *Outlines of Social Theology*, p. 47. On the social nature of reason, vide *Lectures and Essays on Natural Theology and Ethics*, by the late Professor Wallace, edited by the Master of Balliol College, Oxford (1899), p. 110.

in its doctrine of God and of man, and in its ethical ideal? Does it need ultra-rational sanctions in the shape of miracles or eternal fears to commend to our reason the Father in heaven, our filial relation to that Father, and our fraternal obligations arising out of our common privilege as the sons of God? Is it not when our reason is eclipsed, and the baser part of our nature is in the ascendant, that the self-evidencing, self-commending power of these truths becomes obscured and the need for appeals to our superstitious fears arises?

Mr. Kidd's conception of religion is doubtless in harmony with a widely prevalent religious mood, manifesting itself in the portentous combination of agnosticism with traditionalism previously spoken of. This consideration only makes it more incumbent on every man to be fully persuaded in his own mind, and to speak out his mind with all possible plainness. My own view is this: Mediævalism, Sacerdotalism, is opposed to reason, but not true religion, not genuine Christianity. Mediævalism is a caricature of Christianity, as much so as Rabbinism was a caricature of the religion of the prophets. The power of Christianity lies not in the fear of hell, or even in the hope of heaven, but in the intrinsic credibility of the truths it teaches; in the words of wisdom and of grace spoken by Jesus, which, with Paul, we feel to be credible sayings and worthy of all acceptation. I trust what is before us in the future is not a return to the Middle Ages, but a better acquaintance with, and a growing appreciation of, the Galilæan gospel. Therein lies, I believe, the true ground of hope for social progress.

It is certainly hard to see how such a hope can be based on an external power brought to bear on man's nature forcing it into a line of action with which it has no affinity. This conception of compulsory goodness has nothing in common with the Biblical view of man's relation to divine influence. The Bible presents a sombre picture of man's natural condition as vitiated by a depraving process from which human reason has not been exempted. But nowhere do we meet with the idea that, purely by the constraining force of religion appealing to their fears, men can be compelled to seek the good of their fellows contrary to their own permanent inclination. Scriptural theology saves itself from this crudity by its doctrine of *regeneration*, or of a moral renewal bringing with it a new heart delighting to do God's will and a clarified reason in sympathy with the true and the good. Modern philosophers may have their own ideas as to the possibility of such a change; but it will not be denied that if the alleged renewal be possible it provides within man something to which religion, duty, social obligation can appeal and on which they can work, something akin to the moral law and the divine purpose

—a mind approving the right, a heart loving to do it. The doctrine indeed implies that there is something of the kind even in irregenerate man, a germ of the divine, and of the humane, of what is now called altruism, dormant in the soul and capable of being quickened into active, vigorous life. And the very existence of the doctrine implies that, in the view of those who taught it, nothing can be made of man until his own rational and moral nature has been brought into a state of sympathy with the good, that he cannot be compelled into doing the right by threats or the most awful penal sanctions. This, indeed, as is well known, is the plain teaching of Scripture in both Testaments. It finds expression in Jeremiah's oracle of the New Covenant, with its great thought of the law written on the heart as distinct from the law written on stone tablets, and remaining a dead letter because written there alone. St. Paul caught up the prophetic idea and gave it a further development, teaching that the law without is worse than a dead letter, even an irritant to transgression, provoking into rebellious reaction, rather than restraining, the evil principle within.

Paradoxical as it may seem, the apostle's doctrine is no whimsical exaggeration but the statement of a fact. And if we put religion in the place of law the formula still holds. Religion with its penal sanctions, without, powerless to make men unselfish; rather, provocative of more violent manifestations of selfishness. Religion indeed, so conceived, is simply a law, as distinct from an inward spirit of life. Religion as it ought to be, as defined in the Bible, means: loving God with all the heart, and all the soul, and all the *mind*; in a word, with all that is within us. Religion, as the supposed driving-power of social evolution, is an outward commandment to be altruistic addressed to a stubbornly non-altruistic subject, with the whip of an 'ultra-rational sanction' held over his head to subdue his recalcitrant heart, soul, and mind into sullen submission. It is an affront to our common sense to ask us to see in such a slave-driving invention the sole and all-sufficient guarantee for social well-being. Its utmost achievement would be to induce moribund worldlings to bequeath part of their wealth for pious uses, in hope thereby to save their souls from perdition. It never could bind into a coherent social brotherhood a race of men devoid of a social nature. As Dr. Bascom puts it: 'An altruism induced, as an irrational habit, on a spiritual nature alien to it, could never become the ground of permanent order. The inner conflict uncorrected would fret against the restraints put upon it, and might at any moment break out afresh. The spiritual development, when it comes, must be supremely natural.'[1]

Perhaps, if the issue were thus clearly put before him, the author of *Social Evolution* would not care

[1] *Evolution and Religion*, pp. 116, 117.

MODERN DUALISM 377

to meet the position so clearly stated with a direct negative. For it has to be borne in mind, in justice to Mr. Kidd, that he does not credit every religion with the power, through its sanctions, to compel men into involuntary altruism, but only such a religion as Christianity, which happens to have a humane spirit and an eminently social ethical ideal. This is indicated in the following sentences: 'The Christian religion possessed from the outset two characteristics destined to render it an evolutionary force of the first magnitude. The first was the extraordinary strength of the ultra-rational sanction it provided. . . . The second was the nature of the ethical system associated with it.'[1] It is indeed an evil omen that he places the ultra-rational sanction first, as if his chief reliance were on its compulsory power. But one may hope that he would not deny to the second characteristic of Christianity, its humane ethical ideal, power to work on men after its own manner, that is, not as a mere outward commandment saying: this is the road along which you must go; but as an ideal, by its 'sweet reasonableness' commending itself to the human soul. Who can doubt that it has such power when he reflects whence that ideal came? It had its source in the mind or reason of Jesus. Altruism was not imposed on Him at least by ultra-rational sanctions. He was a friend of man by nature. His reason was not anti-social and individualist, but

[1] *Social Evolution*, p. 130.

emphatically the reverse. Are we to hold that in this respect He was utterly isolated, the only man in the world who in any measure cared for others? How much more credible that in His spiritual nature was revealed the normal constitution of human nature generally; that He was what all men ought to be, what all men in some degree are, what every man is in proportion as he is rational! If this be true, then the ethical ideal of Christianity can, by its intrinsic reasonableness, work independently of all supposed ultra-rational sanctions. And it is the first motive-power, not the second. The ideal takes precedence of the sanction, and can even dispense with its aid. Without the self-commending ethic, the sanction, however tremendous, is impotent; where the power of the ethic is felt the sanction is unnecessary. 'The law is not made for a righteous man.'

Our main reliance, then, for social progress must be on 'the law written on the heart,' the law of love accepted by reason and enforced by conscience. Religion can reinforce the power of the moral ideal, but it does this, not chiefly by offers of future rewards and threats of future punishments, but by setting before men, as the object of faith and worship, a God whose inmost nature is love. And because God is love, and because man is truest to his own rational and moral nature when he cares not only for his own things, but for the things of others, the form of modern dualism which turns human reason into the enemy of God and of the social wellbeing ordained under His benignant Providence, may be treated as a bugbear having no terrors for those who walk in the daylight of truth. The unwelcome conception may be dismissed from the mind as the theoretic exaggeration of a powerful intellect rejoicing in its logical acumen, and accepting fearlessly the most startling results of bold ratiocination, without having sufficiently considered the premises from which the ultimate conclusions are drawn. As a theorist Mr. Kidd is chargeable with great inconsistency. He has made it his chief business to exhibit human reason to all who desire social wellbeing as an object of deadly distrust, and in performing this ungenial task he has put unlimited confidence in his own individual reason and its powers of argumentation. It would have been well if he had had a little less faith in his own logic, and a little more faith in the social instincts of average humanity.

LECTURE XII

RETROSPECT AND PROSPECT

WE have come to the end of our pilgrimage through the ages in quest of wise, weighty, light-giving words concerning the moral order of the world and the Providence of God. It remains now to cast a farewell glance backward and a wistful anticipatory glance forwards, that we may sum up our gains and fortify our hopes.

Looking back, then, on the thought of the ancients, we see that the sages of various lands, in far-past ages, unite in the emphatic assertion of a *Moral Order* as the thing of supreme moment for the faith and life of man. This message, handed on from antiquity, the wisest of our own time earnestly re-affirm, saying to their contemporaries in effect: 'Believe this and thou shalt live.' The *consensus gentium* firmly supports this cardinal article in the religious creed of mankind.

The consensus in favour of a moral order is the more remarkable that it is associated with the most discrepant theological positions, having for their respective watchwords: no god (in the true sense of the word) as in Buddhism, two gods as in Zoroastrianism, many gods as in the religion of the Greeks, one God as in the religion of the Hebrews. In view of this theological diversity, the common faith in an eternal august moral order may be regarded as the fundamental certainty, the vital element in the religion of humanity.

The root of this basal faith is an intense moral consciousness. Men believe in a moral order in the cosmos, because they have found a commanding moral order in their own souls. The prophets of the moral order on the great scale — Buddha, Zoroaster, Æschylus, Zeno, Isaiah, Jesus — have all been conspicuous by the purity and intensity of their own moral nature. In the clear authoritative voice of conscience they have heard the voice of God, or of what stands for God. It is ever so. For no man has a moral order in the universe been a dread, awe-inspiring reality for whom the sense of duty has not been the dominant feeling within his own bosom. Only the pure in heart see God — whether He be called Karma, Ahura, Jove, Jehovah, the Father-in-heaven, or by any other name, or remain nameless. For all others the faith in a moral purpose pervading the world is but a hearsay, and all the elaborate theologies built on that faith which they profess to believe are of little account.

Yet the theological position, though secondary, is not indifferent. Because we see men of all conceivable attitudes towards the question of God's being concurring in a primary belief we are not to argue: 'It does not matter what we believe concerning the Gods, whether that there are none, or that they are two or many or one, so long as we believe that it goes well with the righteous and ill with the wicked, and join ourselves heart and soul to the company of the righteous.' It does matter. It is well to believe that there is a reward for the righteous, but it is also well to believe that there is a God who confers the reward. We need a theory of the universe congruous to our ethical faith. It would have been better for Buddha, and for the vast portion of the human race who confess his name, if he had found in the universe a Being who realised his own moral ideal. One who, like Euripides, admires self-sacrifice in noble-minded men and women needs faith in a God who shares his admiration and who is the fountain of all self-sacrificing love. Moral sentiment and theological theory act and react on each other. Our moral nature creates faith in God, and faith in God invigorates our moral nature. Therefore it is by no means a matter of indifference whether we affirm or deny the being of a God, or what kind of a God we believe in. 'No faith' means the individual heroically asserting his moral personality over against an unsympathetic universe. 'Unworthy faith' means a man divided against himself, his moral nature asserting one thing, his religious nature holding on to another, with fatal weakness in character and conduct for result.

We have seen that the common faith in a moral order has been associated, not only with diverse theological positions, but with conflicting judgments about human life. In India life appeared an unmixed evil, in Persia a mixture of good and evil, in Israel the prevailing tendency of religious thinkers was to a more or less decided optimism, which found much good in life and viewed the evil as capable of being transmuted into good. In each case the mood corresponded to the estimate. The pessimistic Buddhist was despairing, the dualistic Zoroastrian defiant, and the optimistic Israelite cheerfully trustful. The mood of the Greek also was buoyant and joyous, but his gaiety was eclipsed by the gloomy shadow of fate or destiny which turned trust in a wise, benignant Providence into a grim submission to the inevitable. It is helpful to have it thus conclusively shown that the faith in a moral order and the earnest moral temper congenial to it can maintain themselves alongside of all conceivable moods; that a Buddhist with his pessimism, and a Stoic with his apathy, can be as loyal to duty and as fully alive to the truth that the ethical interest is supreme, as the Zoroastrian with his severe sense of the radical distinction between good and evil, or the Hebrew with his unwavering faith in the unchallengeable sovereignty of a just God. Only we must beware here also of imagining that the mood does not matter so long as the ethical spirit remains. The mood affects the quality of the morality. The Buddhist at his best is as earnest as any one can desire. He is devoted to his moral ideal with a fervour which few adherents of other faiths can excel or even equal. But his ideal takes its shape from his pessimism, and under its influence becomes such as finds its proper home in a monastery. The ethical fervour of the Stoic likewise was above reproach, but his ideal also suffered under the influence of his characteristic mood. If the Buddhist errs on the side of passivity and gentleness, the Stoic erred on the side of inhuman sternness. Strong in the pride of his self-sufficiency, he had no sympathy with the weak who could not rise to the height of his doctrine that pain is no evil.

These remarks lead up to the observation that in all the types of ancient religious thought which have come under our consideration (leaving Christianity for the present out of account) strength and weakness are curiously combined. It may be worth while to note the strong points and the weak points, respectively, in each case.

The strength of Buddhism lies in its gentle virtues and in its firm faith in the imperious demands of

Karma for a retributive moral order under which moral actions shall receive their appropriate awards. Its weaknesses are numerous. There is, first of all, the lack of a religious ideal answering to its ethical ideal, what we may call its atheism. Then there is the extravagant form in which it applies the principle of retribution, viewing each good and evil act by itself and assigning to it its appropriate reward or penalty, instead of regarding the conduct or character of a moral agent as a whole. To these glaring defects must be added the pessimistic estimate of life characteristic of the system, the conception of the *summum bonum* as consisting in Nirvana or the extinction of desire, and the consequent conviction that the only way in which a wise man can worthily spend his days on earth is by the practice of asceticism within the walls of a monastery.

The strength of Zoroastrianism lay in its manly, militant, moral ideal, and in its devout belief in a Divine Good Spirit for whom moral distinctions are real and vital, and who is the Captain, the inspiring, strengthening Leader, of all who fight for good against evil, as soldiers in the great army of righteousness. Its weakness lay in its dualism, its faith in an antigod, and in its hard, abstract, unsympathetic antithesis between good and evil men. The second of these two defects was probably the true source of the first: the harsh Puritanic ethics the fountain of the crude theology. Had the Persian prophet been able to look on those whom he regarded as the children of Ahriman, even on the neighbouring Turanian nomads, as his brethren, to have thought of them as men and not mere devils, as weak and not absolutely wicked, as having in them, with all their pravity, some rudimentary possibilities of human goodness, and of himself and others like-minded, on the other hand, as far enough from spotless moral purity, it would have been possible for him to conceive of Ahura as the common Father of all men, and to dispense with an antigod in his theory of the universe.

The Greeks were not a whit behind the Asiatics in respect of faith in the reality of a moral order in the life of nations and of individual men. The assertion of this order was a leading didactic aim for the three great dramatists. Taken together, they taught a very full doctrine on the subject. Æschylus laid the foundation in a grand broad proclamation of the principle of *nemesis*, taking no note of exceptions, either because he was unaware of them, or because he was not in the mood to recognise them. Sophocles followed, saying: 'The foundation laid by my predecessor is unassailable, but there are exceptions, numerous, perplexing, mysterious, inexplicable.' Euripides came last, not gainsaying the law enunciated by Æschylus, still less disputing the fact of exceptions insisted on by Sophocles, but throwing light on the darkest cases in the list of exceptions—those presented in the sufferings of the eminently good—by exhibiting them as instances of self-sacrifice for the benefit of others. Yet each of the three was one-sided as a teacher of the common doctrine. Æschylus was, consciously or unconsciously, inobservant of instances in which the great law of Nemesis failed; Sophocles was too conscious of the exceptions; Euripides found in his heroes and heroines of self-sacrifice the one source of light and consolation in an otherwise dark, unintelligible world. And common to all three was this defect, that behind the moral order they saw the dark shadow of *necessity* (*ananke*), a blind force exercising a morally indifferent sway over gods and men alike. This was the tribute paid by the Tragic Drama of Greece to the principle of dualism embodied in the Persian doctrine of the Twin Spirits, and which in one form or another has so often made its appearance in the history of religious thought.

The Stoics were strong in their conception of man's sovereign place in the universe, and in their firm, cheerful faith in the rationality of the cosmos. They saw and said that in the world, after God, there is nothing so important as man, and in man nothing so important as reason; that, therefore, the true theology is that which offers to faith a rational divinity, and the true life that which consists in following the dictates of reason as active in the individual and immanent in the universe. But their errors were serious. They starved and blighted human nature by finding no place or function for passion, and worshipping as their ethical ideal apathetic wisdom. They shut their eyes to patent facts of experience by pretending to regard outward events as insignificant and pain as no evil. They silenced the voice of humanity in their hearts by indulging in merciless contempt for the weak and the foolish; that is to say, for the great mass of mankind who have not mastered the art of treating pain as a trifle, and gained complete victory over passionate impulse.

Passing from the Stoic philosophers to the Hebrew prophets, we find in them more to admire and less to censure. They do not, by extravagances like those of the Stoics, lay themselves open to ridicule. Their sound Hebrew sense keeps them from thinking that any part of human nature is there to be extirpated, or that any part of human experience can be valueless or meaningless. Passion has its place in their anthropology as well as reason, and prosperity in their view is worth having and adversity a thing by all legitimate means to be shunned. These are among their negative virtues. To their positive merits belong their inextinguishable passion for righteousness; their faith in a God who loves right and hates ill, and in one God over all, or, putting the two together, their great doctrine of *ethical monotheism*; and, finally, their firm belief that the present world is, if not the sole, at least a very real theatre wherein the moral government of God is exercised. But even they had the defects of their qualities. While doing full justice to the prophetic doctrine of the moral order as against the diviner's doctrine of a merely physical order of interpretable signs premonitory of the future, we were constrained to acknowledge three defects in their teaching. These were: (1) a tendency to assert in an extreme form the connection between the physical order and the moral order, between particular events in national or individual history, and particular actions of which they are supposed to be the reward and punishment; (2) a tendency to lay undue emphasis on the *vindictive* action of divine providence; and (3) the tendency to attach too much value to outward good and ill as the divinely appointed rewards and penalties of conduct. In the first of these defects, the prophetic doctrine bears a certain resemblance to the atomistic way of applying the principle of Karma characteristic of Buddhism, according to which each separate act finds in some future time its own appropriate recompense. It is, however, unnecessary to remark that of the extravagance wherewith Buddhism doles out the awards due to separate deeds there is no trace in prophetic literature. In the third of the defects above specified the Hebrew prophet presents, not a resemblance, but a contrast to the Greek Stoic. While the Stoic reckoned outward good and ill matters of indifference, the prophet, on the other hand, all but found in these things the chief good and the chief ill. At this point the Stoic position represents an advance in ethical thought; but both positions are one-sided: the truth lies between them.

One does not need to be a clergyman or a professed apologist, but only a candid student of comparative religion, to satisfy himself that the teaching of Christ combines the merits and avoids the defects specified in the foregoing review. On all subjects that teaching shuns absolute antitheses, onesidedness, the falsehood of extremes. In its moral ideal it unites the gentleness of Buddhism with the militant virtue of Zoroastrianism. Its doctrine of God satisfies all rational requirements. In contrast to Buddhism it teaches that there *is* a God, to Zoroastrianism that there is *one* God over all, Lord of heaven and earth; for the Jehovah of Hebrew prophecy, whose chief attribute is retributive justice, it substitutes a Divine Father in whose character the most conspicuous quality is benignity, mercy, gracious love. Its doctrine of man equally commends itself to the instructed reason and conscience as all that can be desired. With Stoicism it affirms the supreme, incomparable worth of man, but, unlike Stoicism, it does not nullify the significance of its affirmation by creating a great impassable gulf between wise men and fools, saints and sinners. Its assertion of the moral order reaches the highest degree of emphasis. In common with the sages of India, Persia, Greece, and Israel, Jesus found in the world clear traces of a Power making for righteousness and against unrighteousness; and, far from exempting His own people from the scope of its action, He saw in her approaching doom the most terrific exemplification of its destructive energy. But He interpreted the laws of the moral order with unique discrimination. He did not, like Buddha, and to a certain extent the Hebrew prophets also, assert the existence of a retributive bond between individual moral acts and particular experiences, but broadly recognised that there is a large sphere of human life in which good comes to men irrespective of character, and wherein not Divine Justice but Divine Benignity is revealed. With the Stoics He recognised the inner life of the soul as the region within which the rewards and punishments of conduct are chiefly to be sought; but He did not, like them, regard outward events as wholly without moral significance. With the Greek poet Euripides, and the author of the fifty-third chapter of Isaiah, He perceived that the doom of the best in this world is to suffer as the worst, but more clearly than either He saw that such sufferers need no pity, that to describe them as men of sorrow is to utter only a half-truth, that an exultant, irrepressibly glad temper is the concomitant and appointed guerdon of all heroic conduct.

Christ's doctrine of Providence possessed the same circumspect, balanced character. He taught that God's providence is over all His creatures—plants, animals, human beings; over all men, good or evil, wise or foolish, great or small. 'God cares for great things, neglects small,' said the Stoic. 'A sparrow shall not fall on the ground without your Father; the very hairs of your head are all numbered,' said Jesus. Yet this minutely particular Divine Care is not conceived of as working spasmodically and miraculously, but quietly, noiselessly, incessantly, through the course of nature. God adds a cubit and more to the stature of men, but not *per saltum*, rather through the slow unobserved process of growth from childhood to maturity. Growth is the law everywhere, even in the moral world, there trying to an uninstructed faith which expects consummation of desire in a day. The clear recognition of this law by Jesus shows that, if His habitual mood was optimistic, His optimism was not blind or shallow. He saw that the highest good in all spheres was to be attained only gradually, and He was content that it should be so. One other element in His doctrine of Providence remains to be specified. Providence, as He conceived it, is not only universal, and at the same time minutely particular, but likewise mindful of all human interests. It cares for the body as well as for the soul, for time as well as for eternity, for social as well as for spiritual well-being. Yet an order of importance is duly recognised. To the Kingdom of God is assigned the first place, to food and raiment and all they represent only the second. By this balanced view of providential action the teaching of Jesus steers a middle course between the opposite extremes of asceticism and secularism, between the morbid mood for which the temporal is nothing, and the worldly mind for which it is everything.

From all this it would seem to follow that the path of progress for the future must lie along the line of Christ's teaching; that the least thing men who seek the good of our race can do is to serve themselves heir to the thoughts of Jesus concerning God, man, the world, and their relations, and work these out under modern conditions. Reversion to the things behind is surely a mistake. No good can come of a return, with Schopenhauer, to the pessimistic despair of Buddhism, or, with other modern thinkers, to the dualism of Zoroaster, or, under the sturdy leadership of a Huxley, to the grim, defiant mood of Stoicism. Such movements are to be regarded as excusable but temporary reactions, and the Christian attitude is to be viewed as that which must gain more and more the upper hand. For men thus minded the summary of faith and practice will be: 'One supreme Will at the heart of the universe, good and ever working for good; man's chief end to serve this supreme will in filial freedom, and in loyal devotion to righteousness; life on earth on these terms worth living, full of joy if not without tribulation, to be spent in cheerfulness and without ascetic austerities; life beyond the tomb an object of rational hope, if not of undoubting certainty.'

It would, however, be too sanguine a forecast which would anticipate for this short Christian creed a speedy universal acceptance even within the bounds of Christendom. It is natural that we who stand on the margin between two centuries should wistfully inquire, What is before us? what is our prospect for the future? By way of answer to this question three competing programmes present themselves. One has for its watchword: 'No religion with a definite theological belief, however brief; at most, a purely ethical religion.' A second offers us a perennial ultra-rational religion, with awful sanctions steadily promoting social well-being. A third claims that for all the higher interests of life the best thing that could happen would be the revival of the simple Christianity of Christ and the working out of His great thoughts.

The first of these programmes indicates fairly well the position of those who have devoted their efforts to the promotion of what is known as the *ethical movement*. This movement, which originated in America and is spreading in Europe, is one of the significant spiritual phenomena of our time. Its avowed aim is to insist upon the supreme importance of the moral nature of man, apart altogether from theological dogmas and religious sanctions. Its promoters think that, without bringing a railing accusation against the Church, it may be affirmed with truth that organised Christianity does not provide for ethical interests in a manner so effectual, and in all respects so satisfactory, as to make a special effort outside the Churches by men having that one end in view superfluous. This opinion it is not necessary to contest. Churchmen have no occasion to be jealous of a new departure in the interest of morality, or to resent any criticism on the Church as an institute for the culture of morality offered by supporters of the movement in justification of their conduct. There need be no hesitation in recognising the value of the aim which the ethical movement sets before itself. It directs attention to what is undoubtedly the main interest of human life, the maintenance in strength and purity of the moral sentiments. If it can do this more impressively than the Church, which has many other interests to care for besides ethics—creed, ritual, government, finance—why, then, in God's name let it bestir itself in the good work. Let ethical societies spring up on every side, and do their utmost to impress on men's minds that conduct is the supremely important matter, the test of the worth of all religion and the fruit by which it is known what any religion is good for, and that this life and its affairs are the theatre in which right conduct is to be practised. If they succeed in this, a one-sided emphasis on ethics as man's exclusive concern, and as an interest much neglected by religious communities, will be very pardonable.

The representatives and literary interpreters of this new movement do not repudiate the Christian name. They accept in the main the ethical teaching of Jesus, and they value Christian civilisation. One of the most influential of their number, Mr. Bosanquet, advises the brotherhood to keep their minds alive to the grand tradition of their spiritual ancestry, 'the tradition that human or Christian life is the full and continuous realisation in mind and act of the better self of mankind.'[1] Neither he nor any other representative man connected with the movement would care to be described as irreligious, or would, with M. Guyau, adopt as his watchword 'Non-Religion,' as the goal towards which Society is moving. They seem rather inclined to claim for their cause a religious character, and to give Duty something like the place of Deity. Their tone, indeed, is not quite uniform. Mr. Leslie

[1] Bernard Bosanquet, *The Civilisation of Christendom*, p. 98.

Stephen, *e.g.* says: 'We, as members of ethical societies, have no claim to be, even in the humblest way, missionaries of a new religion; but are simply interested in doing what we can to discuss in a profitable way the truths which it ought to embody or reflect.'[1] But another of more devout temper, and not less intellectual competency, Mr. Sheldon, speaks in this wise: 'To me this movement is not a philosophy but a religion.'[2] Of the sense of duty he writes: 'It is to me what the word "God" has stood for; it represents to me what the phrase "for Christ's sake" has implied; it means to me what I once attributed to the unconditional authority of the Bible.'[3] Mr. Bosanquet expressly repudiates the designation 'agnostic' for this significant reason: 'Strictly, to be an agnostic is to be a heathen, and we are not heathens, for we are members of Christendom.'[4] His dislike of the title is so strong that he devotes a whole discourse to the discussion of the question, 'Are we Agnostics?' his answer being an emphatic negative: not, of course, because he has no sympathy with the agnostic's position, but because he does not care to be defined by a negative, or to spend his life in reiterating the barren thesis that God is unknowable, and would rather be occupied 'with the life and with the good that we know, and

---

[1] *Social Rights and Duties*, vol. i. p. 43.
[2] W. L. Sheldon, *An Ethical Movement*, p. 13.
[3] *Ibid.*, p. 63.
[4] *The Civilisation of Christendom*, p. 79.

with what can be made of them.'[1] This position one can understand and respect. At the same time, it cannot be said that great injustice is done by applying the epithet 'agnostic' to a system which recognises Mr. Leslie Stephen as one of its accredited teachers, and whose *raison d'être* is to exalt ethics as the supremely important interest, as the one indubitable certainty in the region of the spirit, and as able to stand alone without theistic and theological buttressing.

The importance, certainty, and independence of ethics no earnest man can have any zeal in calling in question. Least of all the first of these three affirmations. On the contrary, we must wish godspeed to all who make it their business to impress upon their fellow-men that duty is the supreme fact of human life, duty understood as 'the command of our highest self, bidding us, in scorn of transient consequences, to act as if we belonged not to ourselves, but to a universal system or order, and to render unconditional obedience to the highest law or highest measure of value that we know of.'[2] In spite of the variations in moral judgments, we admit with equal readiness the second proposition: the certainty of man's moral nature as a great fact. Whatever may pass away, the human soul remains. Theologies may come and go, but conscience abides.

---

[1] *The Civilisation of Christendom*, p. 35.
[2] Sheldon, *An Ethical Movement*, p. 57.

Mr. Leslie Stephen says: 'I believe in heat, and I believe in the conscience. I reject the atoms, and I reject the doctrine of the atonement.'[1] The meaning is that heat and conscience are ultimate undeniable facts, while atoms and the atonement are but theories about these facts. So be it; let the theories go for what they are worth, and let it be admitted that the facts do not depend on the theories, and that they would remain if the theories were demonstrated to be fallacious. This is tantamount to admitting the third contention also: the capacity of ethics to stand alone without theistic or theological buttresses. The admission is made willingly. The dilapidation of the buttresses would not, I acknowledge, involve the tumbling into ruin of the moral edifice. I do not believe that the decay of religious faith would necessarily lead to the withering of moral sentiment and the demoralisation of conduct. So far from thinking that religion creates conscience, I rather incline to the view that conscience creates religion.

But just on this account I am persuaded that the new ethical movement will not long remain merely ethical. If it has real vitality and fervour, it will blossom out into a religious creed of some kind. It will do so if it enlist in its service all the powers of the soul, the heart and the imagination as well as the conscience and the reason. It must do so if

[1] *Social Rights and Duties*, vol. ii. p. 218.

it is to escape from the aridity of prose into the fertility and beauty of poetry. It must do so, once more, if it is to pass from the lecture-hall into the market-place and become a great power in the community. Indications are not wanting that the apostles of the new movement are half-conscious that this is their inevitable destiny. Germs of a new creed indeed can be discovered in their writings. They do not care for the word 'God'; they sympathise with those who, like Goethe, Carlyle, and Arnold, have tried to invent new names for the Ineffable, but they acknowledge that there is Something in the universe calling for a name, a mystery, a unity, yea even a bias on the side of goodness. One writes: 'We fancy somehow that the nature of things "takes sides," as it were, in the struggle going on within itself—not, however, in reference to every form of conflict, but in the great battle between good and evil'—is, in short, 'on the side of those who devote themselves to the ideally Good.'[1] Hence the comforting assurance that 'a divine providence is taking our side in the conflict,' or, if you prefer to put it so, 'that we are taking sides with the divine providence.'[2] To the same effect another writes: 'I do not believe that ethical faith—faith in the reality of the good—is the spirit of a forlorn hope, though, if it were so, it would still be the only spirit

[1] Sheldon, *An Ethical Movement*, pp. 94, 95.
[2] *Ibid.*, p. 96.

RETROSPECT AND PROSPECT

possible for us.'[1] He means thereby to express faith in God, shorn of some useless or distracting accessories, that faith which still governs life under the new name of faith in the reality of the good.[2] The same author ascribes to the universe 'a reasonable tendency,'[3] and even 'grace,' manifesting itself through heredity and education, which confer on the individual unmerited good gifts,[4] and declares 'that man's goodness consists in being effectually inspired by divine ideas.'[5]

Here are germs of a new faith in a wise, righteous, benignant Providence. They are only germs, but all vital beginnings are significant and potent. They are very vague and colourless in expression. They are indeed but the shadowy ghosts of old Christian beliefs which were embodied in fuller, richer, more inspiring forms of language. The Father in heaven of Jesus has become the universe, or nature endowed with reasonable, righteous, and gracious tendencies, but denuded of personality and intelligence. The question forces itself upon us: What is gained by the change of nomenclature? At most, a temporary escape from religious phrases which had become threadbare, or debased by vulgar, unintelligent, insincere use. The dislike of cant in religion all earnest men feel, but, that allowed for,

---

[1] Bosanquet, *The Civilisation of Christendom*, p. 115.
[2] *Ibid.*, p. 115.   [3] *Ibid.*, p. 114.
[4] *Ibid.*, p. 121.   [5] *Ibid.*, p. 121.

it may reasonably be maintained that for permanent purposes the old dialect is better than the new. Better every way, even in point of intellectual consistency. Surely it is more philosophic to connect reasonable, righteous, gracious tendencies in the universe with personality and intelligence than to dissociate the two sets of qualities! As for impressiveness, there is no comparison between the two dialects. You could not go before a popular audience with such bloodless phrases as Mr. Bosanquet has coined. They would appear either unintelligible or ludicrous. But speak of a Father in heaven, then all people, learned and unlearned, know what you mean when you talk of the reason, justice and grace immanent in the universe. They not only understand you, but they are touched by what you say. They admire the felicitous fitness between name and thing; they are moved by the pathos of the name; they are stirred to religious affection—to faith in the goodwill of the Supreme, to cheerful confidence in His providence, to an inspiring, invigorating sense of dignity as His sons, and of the high responsibilities arising out of filial relations. The ethical movement aspires to be a new reformation. If it desires to realise the ambition implied in the name it will have to recognise more unreservedly the Mastership of Jesus.[1] The Ethical

---

[1] In harmony with this statement, Professor Tiele closes his second course of Gifford Lectures with the declaration 'that without preach-

Movement must become an Ethical *Theism*, with this for its message to men : 'We love virtue for its own sake and desire the prevalence of disinterested devotion to the good. But it is no easy thing in this world to live up to one's moral ideal. We need Divine inspiration and aid. And what we need we have. There is an Almighty One who sympathises with our aim, and who will help and guide us in our endeavour after its attainment.' Morality must be touched with emotion to become infectious, and emotion springs out of religious faith. The world belongs to the religious 'enthusiast, for enthusiasm is necessary to mankind ; it is the genius of the masses and the productive element in the genius of individuals.'[1]

2. Of the theory which offers non-rational religion as the great propelling power in social evolution, enough has already been said in the way of exposition and criticism. Only a few words need here be added regarding it as an alternative gospel of hope for the future.

It will be obvious in what radical antagonism this theory stands to the view which has just been considered. Morality independent of religion and capable of flourishing in vigour when religion has become a thing of the past—such is the watchword

ing, or special pleading, or apologetic argument,' the science of religion ' will help to bring home to the restless spirits of our time the truth that there is no rest for them unless they arise and go to their Father.'

[1] M. Guyau, *The Non-Religion of the Future*, p. 401.

of men like Guyau and Renan, and, less bluntly expressed, as becomes the gravity of English-speaking men, of the American aud British apostles of the ethical movement. Morality, in the sense of altruism, devoted self-sacrificing regard for the well-being of others, impossible without the compelling influence of non-rational religious beliefs, supported by sanctions which powerfully appeal to men's hopes and fears, and make it their interest to be disinterested—such is the watchword of the author of *Social Evolution* and of all who accept him as their spokesman. Positions more utterly opposed it is impossible to conceive. It is surprising and discouraging that at this time of day views so absolutely incompatible in their direct statements and in their whole implications can find advocates in a Christian community. Both positions are tainted with the falsehood of extremes. The motto, Morality without religion, divorces two things which nature has joined together as cause and effect, as reality and ideal. Given morality with the needful depth and intensity, and it will inevitably create a Deity and a religion congenial to itself wherein all the cherished ideals towards which it incessantly aspires and struggles find rest-giving realisation. The motto: Altruistic morality impossible, without religion furnished with compulsory sanctions, means, in the ultimate result: such morality impossible even with such a religion. For it implies that love, care for others, sociality, is foreign to human nature. That being so, how vain to think of driving men into love through fear! It can at most only produce a simulated love, an interested disinterestedness which may bear some fruit in socially beneficial acts, but has no part or lot in the spirit of self-devotion. That even so much good will be reaped is far from certain; for, as we saw in last Lecture, the law without to which nothing within responds is more likely to produce reaction against itself than to ensure even feigned submission to its behests. A loveless nature will either sweep away a religion which seeks to curb its individualistic impulses, or it will alter it to suit its taste. It will have no affection for a religion with a lofty, pure, humane, ethical ideal. It will eliminate the humanity and transform the religion in question, retaining the name, into a scheme of self-salvation for the next world, combined with a life dominated by covetousness in this world.

Neither of these extremes is to be accepted as a satisfactory programme, but of the two evils the first-named is the lesser. It gives at least one good thing—altruism, social instinct, as an inalienable element of human nature. This undoubtedly it is. There is more to be said of man in the average than that he is rational, and that he has religious instincts—even this, that he is essentially social. When you tell him that God is a Father, there is that in him which helps him in some measure to appreciate the moral significance of the name. Though there be much evil in him, yet he has the heart to give good gifts to his children.[1] Man had in his nature the rudiments of sociality from the day he began to belong to a *family*. Sociality in the form of family life is the primary datum, the foundation, of human civilisation, and its root and source was, not any religion furnished with awful sanctions, but the prolonged dependence of the human child upon the care of its parents. And there is still a real, valuable morality independent of religion, depending simply on 'the facts that men have certain emotions; that mothers love their children; that there are such things as pity, and sympathy, and public spirit, and that there are social instincts upon the growth of which depends the vitality of the race.'[2]

3. But there is a better way than either, even the acceptance of the teaching of Jesus concerning God and man and Providence as the wisest and most reasonable the world has yet known, and the surest guide to all who seek the higher good of humanity. On the religious side, those who adopt this position differ from both the parties previously described. They differ from the ethicists in attaching importance to the religious element, that is to say, to a

---

[1] Matthew vii. 11.
[2] Leslie Stephen, *Social Rights and Duties*, vol. ii. p. 219.

definite, earnest belief in a God who is best named Father, and in a benignant providence answering to the name. In this faith they find inspiration for endeavour, and hope for ultimate success, and in the correlate conception of man as son of God they find a strong support to that sense of the moral worth of human nature which is the fundamental postulate of Christian civilisation, but which many anti-social influences tend to weaken. On the other hand, while at one with the class of thinkers of whom Mr. Kidd is the spokesman in attaching high value to religion, they differ radically from them in their conception of the nature of the Christian religion and in their views as to the secret of its power. That religion appears to their minds intrinsically reasonable, credible, and acceptable, and in their judgment its power lies, not in mystery revealed either in dogma or in sacrament, nor in awe-inspiring vistas of a future existence, but in its capacity to satisfy the whole spiritual nature of man, including reason, conscience, and heart. Its great, grand thoughts of God, man, and duty are its best credentials and persuasives. These speak for themselves to the human soul; they awaken a response in manly natures utterly indifferent to eternal terrors; their very elevation is their charm, for lofty ideals appeal to the heroic in our nature, and so make way when low accommodating ideals are treated with contempt. '"Love ye one another; by this shall all men know that ye are My disciples, if ye have love one to another." In this admirable and eternal precept there is more of inexhaustible, practical power than in : Ye shall be cast into the fire; there shall be wailing and gnashing of teeth.'[1] The fact is so, because there is that in man which is able to respond to such teaching, and which gives its response with the greatest promptitude and earnestness when the doctrine is made to rest on its own intrinsic merits.

Men who profess to be disciples of Jesus cannot consistently ignore the hope of a life beyond the tomb, or refuse it a place among the motives to right conduct. But, if they be intelligent disciples, they will not allow the eternal to swallow up the temporal. They will recognise the substantial value of the present life, and see in social well-being the practical outcome of the Christian faith. In this respect leaders of thought, amid all variations of opinion, are happily agreed. Secularism, in a good sense, is a phase of the modern spirit. There is no reason in this fact for alienation from the Christianity of Christ. For Christ's doctrine of providence, as we saw, included all the good elements of secularism, asserting divine care for man's body as well as for his soul, for social as well as for spiritual health.

While that doctrine should commend itself to all men of goodwill, it contains little or nothing that can offend philosophers and men of science. For

[1] Guyau, *The Non-Religion of the Future*, p. 406.

Jesus taught a providence that works and achieves its ends through the processes of nature, and that reaches the accomplishment of its purpose *gradually*, not *per saltum*. In His conception of Divine Providence Jesus gave no undue prominence to the *unusual* and the *catastrophic*. His watchwords were: Nature God's instrument; and, Growth the law of the moral as of the physical world.

Men of all schools, therefore — moralists, religionists, philanthropists, philosophers, scientists — might reasonably be expected to march together under Christ's banner, and fight with one heart for the sacred cause of humanity in the name of God the Father, for men, His sons. Or, if it be too much to hope for general agreement as to the religious aspect of Christ's teaching, one may surely count on a cordial consensus as to the rational, wholesome, beneficent tendency of the ethical principles enunciated in His recorded sayings! Dissent, vehement contradiction, may indeed be encountered even here; but those who at present take up this attitude are not a numerous body, and it may be hoped that they will become fewer in the course of time. Intelligent, cordial acceptance of the Christian ethic will mean much, *e.g.*, a conservative view of *marriage*, the *family*, and the *state*, as institutions rooted in the nature of things, the subversion of which is not to be thought of, but at most only their improvement in the light of experience. Whether it should mean conservation of certain other things, *e.g.*, *private property*, is a question on which much wider divergence of opinion may be looked for. There are some so hostile to property, or 'capital,' that to destroy it they would be ready to destroy other things hitherto held sacred—Deity, government, wedlock. One can guess what such revolutionaries would have to say to the Founder of the Christian faith. They would offer Him the peremptory alternatives: 'Take our side, or we renounce you.'

What the bearing of Christ's teaching on the Socialistic movement of our day really is, is not a question that can be answered offhand. It is not, as religious conservatives may imagine, a matter of course that it is against that movement simply because the latter would amount to a social revolution; for the words of Jesus have acted, in certain instances, as a revolutionary force in the past, and they may do so again. As little is it a matter of course that it is on its side. As to the general tendency of Christ's doctrine, there is no room for doubt. It is emphatically *humane.* Jesus was on the side of the weak, of the little child and all that the little child represents. Therefore He was the friend of the poor; and were He living amongst us now He would regard with intense compassion the many whose lives are made wretched by the burden of abject, hopeless poverty. In not a few instances His keen eye might perceive that the poverty was the natural penalty of the poor man's folly. But in many others He would with equal clearness discern in poverty the undeserved result of social injustice, and therefore a wrong to be righted by a return to justice and mercy on the part of the wrong-doers.

What such a return would imply is the abstruse question. The humanity of the Gospel ultimately led to the abolition of slavery, because slavery was slowly discovered to be an inhuman thing. Must it likewise, sooner or later, lead to the abolition of property or capitalism and the introduction of a Collectivist millennium? That depends on the character of said millennium. Is it to be an economical one mainly, or is the ethical to be in the ascendant? For Christianity the ethical is the supreme category, and it judges all things by their bearing thereon. How, then, does it stand with Socialism? Does it place ethical interests first? does it even tend to promote the higher morality as a secondary interest? That it does is by no means so clear as one could desire. It is a significant fact that the thinkers of the day who have devoted themselves to ethical propagandism express grave doubts on the subject. Mr. Bosanquet is of opinion that Economic Socialism does not tend to Moral Socialism, or altruism, but rather to Moral Individualism, or selfishness.[1] Mr. Leslie Stephen contends for the moral value of competition, and hints that the Socialist ideal is a land

[1] *Civilisation of Christendom*, pp. 315 ff.

in which the chickens run about ready-roasted, and the curse of labour is finally removed from mankind.[1] M. Guyau bluntly describes the Socialist ideal as 'a life which is completely foreseen, ensured—with the element of fortune and of hope left out, with the heights and the depths of human life levelled away —an existence somewhat utilitarian and uniform, regularly plotted off like the squares on a checker board, incapable of satisfying the ambitious desires of the mass of mankind.'[2] Mr. Sheldon is more sympathetic in his tone. Taking his stand 'at a spiritual distance from all the scramble, the strikes and the lock-outs, the boycotts, the turmoil and the violence, the accusations and recriminations,'[3] he tries to see what the movement implies as a whole, what it means 'as a historic wave-movement.' He hopes that in spite of all the materialism, selfishness, petty rivalries and ambitions connected with it in the meantime, the trend is towards higher moral manhood, and that at the end of another century, when the ideal industrial system of Socialist expectations shall have been proved to be a dream, the prevailing enthusiasm will be for the ethical ideal.[4] Socialists will probably not thank him for his charitable forecast. It virtually makes their case analogous to that of the Jews, who looked for a

---

[1] *Social Rights and Duties*, vol. i. pp. 133-173.
[2] *The Non-Religion of the Future*, p. 369.
[3] *An Ethical Movement*, p. 288.
[4] *Ibid.*, p. 298.

political Messiah and an ideal national prosperity that never came, and got instead a spiritual Christ and a Kingdom of heaven which they did not appreciate.

But no estimate of Socialism emanating from the ethical school is so unfavourable as that formed by Mr. Kidd. It is to the following effect: The aim of Socialists is perfectly natural. It is simply a case of men who toil trying to better themselves by asserting what they believe to be the just claims of labour against capital. Nevertheless the carrying out of the Socialist programme would be ultimately ruinous. But on mere grounds of reason that is no sufficient answer to advocates of Socialist principles. They are entitled to reply: 'What do we care for the future of the country?—our sole concern is for our own present personal interest.' Against this quite rational yet ruinous movement the only barrier is the altruistic spirit which ultra-rational religion engenders. What graver indictment could be brought against any movement than this, which represents Socialism as destructive of public well-being sooner or later, indifferent to the ruin it will ultimately entail, and bound in self-defence against anti-socialistic altruism to assume an attitude of uncompromising antagonism towards religion?

Mr. Kidd is a biassed witness, as he is chiefly concerned to make out a case for the necessity of a religion mysterious in its doctrines and armed with supra-rational sanctions as the sole guarantee

of social progress. I should be sorry to think so ill
of any movement which has for its professed aim to
improve the economic condition of the industrial
part of the community. I have no right and no
intention to pronounce any opinion on the question
at issue. My general attitude is one of mingled
sympathy and apprehension. I care greatly more
for the million than for the millionaire. But I dread
leaps in the dark. It will be wise to move slowly,
lest too great haste in well-meant but ill-instructed
endeavour should have a disastrous issue. Evolution, not revolution, should be the motto. Of one
thing I am sure, viz., that no ultimate good will
come of movements which set economic above moral
interests. It is true that in the case of many the
pressure of poverty is so heavy as to make the higher
life all but impossible, and that there is need for
ameliorative measures that will bring goodness within
easier reach. But it must never be forgotten that
the chief end to be striven after is moral manhood—
character. The ethical must take precedence of the
economical in our thoughts and aspirations. First
righteousness, second food and raiment. If this
order be not observed, national character will
deteriorate, and with deteriorated character prosperity will wane. The wise of all ages, we have
seen, have believed in a moral order as real and
certain as the planetary system. If they are not
all mistaken, there is such an order as a matter of

fact, whatever theological phrase we employ to describe it. Call it a moral government of God, or a tendency in the universe: it is all one; there it is. And we have to reckon with it. It cannot be disregarded with impunity any more than the ship of Carlyle's parable could get round Cape Horn, with whatever unanimity of the crew, if they disregarded the conditions 'fixed with adamantine rigour by the ancient elemental powers, who are entirely careless how you vote.'[1] I trust that in the time to come an increasing number of men will be thorough believers in the moral order. Let all in their various spheres do their utmost to propagate this faith. The pulpit of the future will have to devote more attention to it, and strive to impress on men's minds that God is, and that He is the Rewarder of them that diligently seek Him. To do this with effect is not, I am aware, every preacher's gift. Special spiritual discipline is needed for the task. But it will be well for the community when, in every considerable centre of population, one man at least has the prophetic vocation and impulse to propagate the passion for righteousness, and the faith that this sacred passion burns in the heart of the Great Being who guides the destinies of the universe. The promoters of the Ethical Movement contemplate the ultimate disappearance of the Church, and the advent of a time when it will

[1] *Latter-Day Pamphlets*, p. 40.

become a practical question, What use can be made of ecclesiastical edifices no longer needed for their original purpose? If that ever happen, it will be the Church's own fault. If she forget the adage, 'By their fruits ye shall know them,' if she lose sight of the truth that morality is the ultimate test of the worth of religion, if she get out of sympathetic touch with the ethical spirit of Jesus, then she will be perilously near the awful doom of savourless salt. But there will be no risk of such a doom overtaking her so long as the ethical ideal of the Gospels has a sovereign place in her heart, and it is manifest to all the world that she cares more for righteousness than for anything else, and that her deepest desire is, that God's will may be done upon this earth as it is in heaven.

INDEX

A

Æschylus—
    attitude towards mythology, 68.
    belief in retributive justice of providence, 71.
    an innovator in moral thought, 75.
    Nemesis in individual experience, 76.
        is disciplinary as well as punitive, 78.
    theories as to his doctrine of Prometheus, 78.
    Prometheus a culture hero, 80.
    defects of the Prometheus legend, 81.
    Eumenides, doctrine of Nemesis in, 82-84.
Agnosticism—
    of Huxley, 314-15.
    of Ritschlian theology, 350.
    of Cardinal Newman, 350.
Ahriman—
    place in Gâthas, 39.
    an ethical being, 41.
    a mere negation of the good Spirit, 42.
    conception of, natural though crude, 46.
    used as a foil to Ahura, 56.
Ahura-mazda. *See* Ormuzd.
Amschaspands, doctrine of, 44.
Angra-mainyu. *See* Ahriman.
Arnold, Matthew, 'sweet reasonableness' of Christ's doctrine, 353.
Aurelius, Marcus—
    legitimacy of suicide, 135-6.
    on future life, 137.
    religious tone of his writings, 137-8.

B

Balfour, Arthur James—
    authority in belief, 362.
    narrow conception of reason, 367.
Bascom, John—
    reason and authority, 363-4.
    futility of 'ultra-rational' sanction, 376.

Baxter, Richard, no hard-and-fast line between good men and bad, 290.
Blackie, John Stuart—
    purpose of Greek tragic drama, 72.
    translation of Æschylus quoted, 76, 78, 80.
Bosanquet, Bernard—
    Stoical idea of worth of man, 139.
    does not repudiate Christianity, 396.
    is not agnostic, 397-8.
    necessity for ethical faith, 400-1.
    on Socialism, 411.
Browning, Robert—
    general character of his optimism, 282-3.
    his creed Christian, 284-5.
    his doctrine of God, 285-7.
    and of man, 287-9.
    good even *in* evil, 289.
    no hard-and-fast line between good men and bad, 290.
    value even in failures of the good, 291.
    mode of dealing with problem of evil, 292.
    his theory of moral evil:—
        (1) morality the highest good, 294.
        (2) progress by conflict necessary to morality, 295-6.
        (3) evil the foe to be fought, 297.
        (4) evil needed to make a struggle possible, 297-8.
        (5) ignorance of true nature of evil necessary to give reality to struggle, 299-301.
        (6) struggle will always have a happy issue, 301-2.
    problem finds its solution in world beyond the grave, 302-3.
    his optimism compared with Emerson's, 304.
Budde, Karl, on Book of Job, 212, 231, 235 (note), 238 (note).
Buddha—
    originator of Buddhism, 4.
    contrast between Buddhism, Vedic Indian and Brahman religions, 5.
    essence of his doctrine, 6-7.
    emphatic assertion of moral order, 8.
    theory of transmigration, 9-10.
    Buddhist Birth Stories, 11, 12.
    doctrine of Karma, 13-17.
    desire, the will to live, 17.
    doctrine of Nirvana, 18.
    theory of future rewards and punishments, 21.

Buddha—
    function of a Buddha, 22.
    plurality of Buddhas a necessity, 23.
        reason for this theory, 26.
    six great virtues necessary to a Bodishat, 25.
    knows no overruling Providence, 25.
    criticism of his doctrine, 27.
    relation to caste, 28.
    strength and weakness of his teaching, 29-32, 384-5.
    links with Zoroastrianism, 35-6.
Bunsen, Baron—
    on ameliorating influence of Buddhism, 33.
    on scepticism of Euripides, 91-2.
Burnouf, Eugene—
    Buddhist doctrine of transmigration, 12-13.
    the making of a Buddha, 22.
    Buddhism of the North, 24.
    Buddhism and Siva-worship, 33.
Butler, Bishop, continuance of life after death, 310.

C

Campbell, Dr. Lewis, estimate of Euripides, 92 (note).
Carlyle, Thomas, on diabolic element in life, 345 (note).
Caste, relation of Buddhism to, 28.
Cheyne, Professor T. K., on Book of Job, 231 (note).
Christ—
    comparison between His teaching and that of Hebrew Prophets, 243-5.
    His teaching in so far as peculiar *in re* external good and evil paradoxical, 245.
    His teaching may be summed up in three propositions :—
        (1) external good and evil common to all men, 246-8.
        (2) suffering inevitable for the righteous, 248-9.
        (3) those who suffer not to be pitied, 249-51.
        these propositions involve new idea of God, 251.
    His teaching as to God, 251-4.
    geniality of His doctrine, 254.
    His optimism, 255-61.
        takes account of adverse facts, 256-9.
    His teaching contrasted with Paganism, 262.
    His estimate of the value of the temporal, 263-4.

Christ—
   significance of His healing ministry, 265-6.
   the worth of man, 267-70.
   comprehensiveness of conception of providential order, 270.
   conception of Satan, 271-2.
   the stern side of His teaching, 273-5.
   methods of Providential working—election, solidarity, sacrifice—recognised, 275-7.
   His doctrines acceptable, 277-8.
   His teaching combines merits and avoids defects of all systems, 390-3.
   future progress must lie along line of His teaching, 393.
Cicero—
   criticism of Stoicism, 119.
   on Stoic doctrine of Providence, 128, 129, 132.
   on divination, 140, 142, 151, 157-8, 160, 161 (note), 163, 164, 168.
Conversion, Zoroastrian belief in, 50, 51.

D

Darmesteter, James—
   on origin of Zoroastrianism, 36.
   dualism latent in primitive Aryan religion, 39.
   Vedic dualism, 40.
   character of Ahriman, 42.
   doctrine of Amschaspands, 44.
Davids, Thomas William Rhys—
   Buddhist Birth Stories quoted, 12.
   on doctrine of Karma, 14.
   Buddha's theory of desire, 18.
   on Nirvana, 19.
Desire—
   the will to live, 17.
   its place in Brahmanism and Buddhism, 17.
Divination—
   attitude of Stoicism to, 140-1.
   belief in, common to all ancient ethnic religion, 142.
   a primitive form of revelation, 143-4.
   compared with prophecy, 145-6.
   media of revelation—the *fortuitous*, the *unusual*, and the *marvellous*, 148.
   augury, 149.

INDEX

Divination—
    haruspicy, 150-1.
    astrology, 152-4.
    the Greek Oracles, 154-5.
    decline of Oracles, 156-7.
    a reality or a delusion? 157-60.
    objections to, 162-3.
    its moral tendency, 164-6.
    Epictetus on, 166-8.
    modern attitude to, 168-9.
    effects of its abolition on doctrines of Providence and prayer, 170-1.
    a barrier to moral and religious progress, 172-3.
    relation to Hebrew prophecy, 174.

Dualism—
    Zoroastrian, 39, 49.
    is characteristic of all primitive religions, 39.
    fact-basis of Persian, 46.
    defects of   do.,   57.
    influence of   do.   on Hebrew and Manichæan religions, 61-2.

Dualism, Modern—
    two types, 3.
    distinct from pessimism, 312.
    agnostic type, 314-15.
    John Stuart Mill's, 316-19.
    of author of *Evil and Evolution*, 320-28.
        his theory of Satan, 323-28.
        criticism of his theory, 328-37.
    cure for dualistic mood, 337-39.
    human reason as antagonist of the Deity, 346.
    tendency to vilify reason, 347.
    assertion that reason cannot find God, 348-9.
    in Ritschlian theology, 350.
    denies revelation of God in nature, 351-2.
    capacity of reason to appreciate revelation, 352-3.
    causes of antithesis between reason and faith:—
        (1) artificial view of substance of revelation, 354-7.
        (2) disparagement of reason, 357.
    reason, morality, and religion inseparable, 358.
    authority of the Church, 361-3.
    criticism of theory that influence of reason as compared with authority insignificant, 363.

Dualism, Modern—
    antagonism between reason and authority non-scientific, 364.
    evils of trusting too much to authority, 365-6.
    Kidd's theory that reason anti-social, 368-9.
        criticism of this theory, 371-9.
Duhm, B., on Hebrew prophets, 191, 192 (note).

E

Emerson, Ralph Waldo—
    his optimism, 281-2, 288, 338.
        compared with Browning's, 303-4.
Epictetus—
    on things indifferent, 111.
    benefits derivable from external evil, 117-18, 122-3.
    doctrine of God, 134-5.
    legitimacy of suicide, 136.
    on divination, 166-7-8.
Epicureans, conception of chief good, 107.
Ethical movement, the—
    its origin and aim, 395-99.
    its value, 398.
    cannot long remain merely ethical, 399-403.
Euripides—
    attitude towards mythology, 68.
    doctrine of Nemesis, 71.
    his alleged scepticism, 92.
    proofs of his religious convictions, 93-4.
    theory of self-sacrifice, 95-100.
        compared with that of Æschylus, 96.
        importance of this theory, 100.
    his dualism, 102.
    on divination, 146, 150.
Evil and Evolution—
    the author's dualism, 320-8.
    his theory of Satan, 323-8.
    criticism of the theory, 328-37.
Evolution in future life, 309-11.

F

Forsyth, Peter Taylor, on revelation in nature, 348-9-50.
Froude, James Anthony, on the Book of Job, 207, 208.

G

Gordon, Dr. George—
    his views on immortality, 305-7.
        identical with Browning's, 307.
    estimate of his views, 307-9.
    on Huxley's pessimism, 339.
    on the authority of the Church, 361.

Grant, Sir Alexander—
    on the origin of Stoicism, 104.
    translation of Cleanthes quoted, 138.

Greek mythology, 66.

Greek Tragedians—
    their religious creed, 67.
    combination of mythology and religion, 67.
    their themes, 73.
    their strength and weakness, 386-7.

Guyau, M.—
    necessity for divine inspiration, 403.
    practical power of Christ's teaching, 407-8.
    on socialism, 412.

H

Hagio-theism, 45.

Haigh, Arthur Elam—
    attitude of Greek Tragedians towards myth, 70.
    on Æschylus quoted, 75-76.

Hardy, R. Spence, on Buddhist doctrine of Karma, 15.

Harnack, Adolf, on Persian dualism, 57 (note).

Haug, Martin, on origin of Zoroastrianism, 36.

Hebrew Prophets—
    their relation to divination, 174.
    contrast between prophet and diviner, 175-6.
    substitutes for diviners, 177.
    their characteristics, 177-9.
    their belief in creed of Moses, 178-9.
    their ideas as to connection between lot and conduct, 181, 186.
    their religious thought, its profoundly ethical character, 182.
    their passion for righteousness, 185.
    views of earlier and later prophets compared, 187-93.
    Isaiah, oracle of the *Suffering Servant of God*, 191-5.
    Jeremiah, oracle of the *New Covenant*, 197-8.

Hebrew Prophets—
    their defects:—
        (1) exaggerated idea of connection between physical and moral order, 199-202.
        (2) one-sided emphasis on punitive action of divine providence, 202-3.
        (3) outward good and ill overestimated, 203-4.
    the service they rendered to higher interests of humanity, 205-6.
    their strength and weakness, 388-90.
Hegel, G. W. F., on Persian dualism, 57 (note).
Hippolytus, on diviners, 164.
Huxley—
    analogy between *Karma* and heredity, 14.
    Nirvana and *apatheia* of Stoics compared, 109-10.
    an exponent of agnostic dualism, 314-15.
Hyde, W. De Witt, on Kidd's views, 372.

I

Immortality—
    Browning's belief in, 303.
    Dr. George Gordon on, 305-7.
    reasonableness of idea of, 307-8.

J

James, W., on revelation in nature, 349-50.
Job, Book of—
    its *raison d'être*, 208.
    its date, 209-10.
    relation of author to opening and closing sections, 211-12.
    analysis of, 212-28.
    progress in Job's theology, 228-31.
    didactic significance of, 233-36.
    rationale of the suffering of the good, 237.
    attitude of author to the views expressed, 238-42.
    traces of doctrine of vicarious suffering, 242.
Jones, Professor Henry—
    on Emerson's optimism, 281.
    on Browning's optimism, 298.

K

Kalpa, definition of, 20.
Kant, Immanuel—
    Karma equivalent to his Deity, 17.
    on the Divine Moral Governor, 356.
Karma—
    what it is, 13.
    an isolated entity, 16.
    endowed by the Buddhist with power of physical causation, 16.
    equivalent to Kant's Deity, 17.
    creates succession of worlds, 20.
Kautzsch, Emil, on Book of Job, 238 (note).
Kidd, Benjamin—
    reason anti-social, 368.
    statement of his views, 368-9.
    criticism of his position, 371-9.
    on Socialism, 413-14.
Koeppen, Carl Friedrich, on Buddhism, 7, 10, 17.
Kunala, story of, 12.

L

Lang, Andrew—
    dualism in primitive religion, 39, 40.
    distinction between mythical and religious elements in belief, 66.
    on the Prometheus myth, 82.
Leclercq, A. Bouché—
    on divination quoted, 142-3, 170.
Lightfoot, Bishop—
    on origin of Stoicism, 104-5.
    contradictions of Stoicism, 106.

M

Manichæism, its relation to Zoroastrianism, 61.
Mansel, Dean, on revelation, 354-5.
Mill, John Stuart—
    his dualism, 316-19.
    a modified dualism, 335-6, 337.
Mills, L. H.—
    on date of the Gâthas, 34.
    separation of Buddhism and Zoroastrianism, 36.
    estimate of value of Gâthas, 55.

Moberly, R. C.—
   reason and morality inseparable, 358-9.
   antithesis between reason and morality unknown to Scripture, 367-8.
   on Kidd's views, 370.
Modern thought, optimistic or dualistic, 3.
Mommsen, Christian Matthias Theodor, on Cato quoted, 129.
Moral Order—
   consensus gentium for, 380-1.
   root of faith in, 381.
   theological position not indifferent, 382.
   faith in, associated with conflicting judgments about human life, 383.
   Buddhist belief in, its strength and weakness, 384-5.
   Zoroastrian do.,   do.   do.,   385-6.
   Greek   do.,   do.   do.,   386-7.
   Stoic   do.,   do.   do.,   387-8.
   Hebrew   do.,   do.   do.,   388-90.
   Christ's doctrine summarised, 390-93.
   progress for future must lie along line of Christ's teaching, 393.
   three new programmes :—
      (1) the ethical movement, 395-99.
      (2) non-rational religion, 403-6.
      (3) acceptance of Christianity of Christ, 406-10.
   bearing of Christ's teaching on Socialism, 410-11.
   modern estimates of Socialism, 411-13.
Muir, John (D.C.L.), translation from Rig-Veda quoted, 17.

N

Nägelsbach, Karl Friedrich—
   Æschylus an original moral thinker, 74 (note).
   on augury, 149.
   on haruspicy, 152.
Nemesis—
   in Greek Tragedians, 66.
   Æschylean doctrine, 71 ; in individual experience, 76, 81, 82-84.
   doctrine of Sophocles, 71, 86.
   doctrine of Euripides, 71.
Newman, Cardinal, on revelation in nature, 349.
Nirvana—
   doctrine of, 18.
   compared with Stoic *apatheia*, 109-110.

INDEX

O

Ogereau, F., materialism of Stoics, 113-4.
Optimism—
    Christ's, 255-61.
    modern, compared with Christ's, 279.
    tone and tendency of modern, 281-2.
Ormuzd—
    place in Gâthas, 38.
    Ethical Deity, 41.
    character of, 43.
    originator of cosmic and moral order, 46.
    his power over evil, 53.

P

Parker, Theodore, his optimism, 281.
Paul, his dualism, 339-40.
Plato, his dualism, 313, 339, 341 (note).
Plumptre, Edward Hayes—
    translation of Æschylus quoted, 76, 77.
    translation of Sophocles quoted, 86, 87, 88, 90, 91.
Plutarch, on cessation of oracles, 156-7.
Prometheus, *cp*. Æschylus.

R

Reason—
    capacity of, to appreciate revelation, 352-3.
    causes of antithesis between reason and faith :—
        (1) artificial view of substance of revelation, 354-7.
        (2) disparagement of reason, 357.
    reason, morality, and religion inseparable, 358.
    authority of the Church, 361-3.
    criticism of theory that influence of reason as compared with authority insignificant, 363.
    antagonism between reason and authority non-scientific, 364.
    evils of trusting too much to authority, 365-6.
    Kidd's theory that reason anti-social, 368-9.
        criticism of this theory, 371-9.

Renan, Ernest—
    on Satan, 63.
    the genius of the Book of Job, 233.
Rendall, Gerald Henry, attitude of Stoics to outward good or evil, 110.

S

Satan—
    Hebrew doctrine of, 62, 341-2.
    how far Hebrew doctrine derived from Persia, 62-5.
    in the Gospel narratives, 271-2.
    theory of author of *Evil and Evolution*, 323-8.
        criticism of theory, 328-37.
    Paul's belief in, 339-40.
    havoc produced by assigning whole moral evil to, 344.
Seneca—
    on the chief good, 107.
    on things indifferent, 121.
    on moral uses of adversity, 123-4.
    the wise man, 126.
    evil bias in human nature, 133.
    legitimacy of grief, 133-4.
    legitimacy of suicide, 136.
Sheldon, W. L.—
    duty the supreme fact of human life, 397-8.
    the bias on the side of goodness, 400.
    on Socialism, 412.
Socialism—
    bearing of Christ's teaching on, 410-11.
    modern estimates of, 411-13.
Sophocles—
    attitude towards mythology, 68.
    doctrine of Nemesis, 71, 86.
    changefulness of life, 87-8.
    suggestions of an evil order in the world, 89.
    traces of idea of vicarious atonement, 91.
    on diviners, 146.
Spencer, Herbert, his agnosticism, 356.
Stephen, Leslie—
    his agnosticism, 356.
    a morality independent of religion, 397, 406.
    on facts and theories in morals, 399.
    on Socialism, 411-12.

INDEX

Stobæus, Joannes—
    Eclogæ of, quoted on views of early Stoics, 109, 147.
Stoicism—
    its moral distinction, 103.
    its origin, 104.
    at once ethical and individualistic, 105.
    on the chief good, 107.
    place of pleasure in, 108.
    doctrine of *apatheia*, 109.
        compared with Nirvana, 110.
    its theology, 111-12.
    its materialism, 113.
    relation of theology to ethics, 114-16.
    its contribution to doctrine of Providence, 116-18.
    criticism of, 118-22.
    later views on ethics of suffering, 122-4.
    its ideal Wise Man, 126-7.
    its moral ideal criticised, 129-30.
    modifications of original system, 131.
    influence of Roman thought on, 132-4.
    defects of the Roman type of, 135-6.
    on the future life, 136.
    appreciation of, 137-9.
    its attitude towards divination, 140-1.
    its strength and its weakness, 387-8.
Suicide. *See* under Marcus Aurelius, Epictetus, Seneca.
Symonds, John Addington—
    progression in art in Greek poets, 68-70.
    comparison of Æschylus, Sophocles, and Euripides, 70.
    on *Prometheus Bound* quoted, 79.
    on Erinnyes quoted, 83 (note).
    translation of Sophocles quoted, 89, 95.
    on the 'pluck' of Greek men and women, 100.

T

Tacitus, on diviners, 164.
Thompson, D'Arcy—
    translation of Sophocles quoted, 86, 88, 89.
    translation of Euripides quoted, 93, 102.

Tiele, Professor C. P.—
    tendency of the reason of the Aryan race, 360.
    on the necessity of Theism, 402 (note).
Transmigration—
    its place in Buddhism, 9.
    explanation of its origin, 9-10.
    its analogy to heredity, 14.
    not identical with heredity, 15.
Tylor, Edward Burnet—
    on transmigration, 10, 11.
    on dualism in primitive religion, 39.

U

Ur-Buddha, a postulated divine head of all Buddhas, 24.

V

Vedic Indians—
    their religion, 4.
    dualism of, physical not ethical, 40.
Verrall, Arthur Woolgar—
    attitude of Greek Tragedians towards mythology, 70.
    Euripides' view of legend of Alcestis, 99.

W

Wallace, Professor William, on social nature of reason, 372 (note).
Watson, Professor John—
    Euripides' doctrine of self-sacrifice, 101.
    on Christ's teaching on Providence, 245.
Way, Arthur S., translation of Euripides quoted, 94, 99, 102.
Whitman, Walt, his optimistic audacity, 282.
Wodhull, Michael, translation of Euripides quoted, 99.

Z

Zeller, Eduard, Stoics' attitude to outward goods, 109.
Zoroaster—
    date of, 34.
    links with Buddha, 35.

Zoroaster—
    theories of separation from Buddhism, 35.
    relation to Vedic worship, 36.
    Ormuzd, controller of natural and moral order, 38.
    dualism of, 39.
    his dualism ethical, 40.
    importance of his ethical conceptions, 41.
    his belief in conversion, 50-1.
    merits of his religion, 54.
    purity of his theology, 55.
    criticism of his dualism, 56-9.
    historic influence of his religion, 60.
    strength and weakness of his religion, 385-6.

www.ingramcontent.com/pod-product-compliance
Lightning Source LLC
Chambersburg PA
CBHW071223230426
43668CB00011B/1278